THE SELF
BETWEEN

From Freud to the
New Social Psychology
of France

The Self Between

*From Freud
to the New
Social Psychology
of France*

EUGENE WEBB

UNIVERSITY OF WASHINGTON PRESS

Seattle and London

To DOUGLAS COLLINS,

amicus in veritate

E'l mio conforto: "Perché pur diffidi?"
a dir mi cominciò tutto rivolto;
"non credi tu me teco e ch'io ti guidi?"

Library of Congress Cataloging-in-Publication Data
Webb, Eugene, 1938–
    The self between : from Freud to the new social psychology of France / Eugene Webb.
        p. cm.
    Includes bibliographical references and index.
    ISBN 0-295-97226-2 (alk. paper)
    1. Psychoanalysis—France—History. 2. Psychoanalysis—Social aspects—France—History. 3. Girard, René, 1923–   —Influence. 4. Freud, Sigmund, 1856–1939—Influence. 5. France—Intellectual life—20th century. I. Title.
BF175.W36   1993
150'.944'0904—dc20   92-46472
                                                              CIP

The paper used in this publication meets the minimum requirements of American National Standard for Information Sciences—Permanence of Paper for Printed Library Materials, ANSI Z39.48-1984.

Contents

v

CONTENTS

Preface

THIS book offers a sketch of some important developments in recent French thought—principally, though not exclusively, psychological thought. It is a characteristic of French thought generally that it tends, more than that in the English-speaking world, to stretch across the boundaries of the intellectual disciplines. One of the features of the Baconian conception of the scientific enterprise that has been so influential in English and North American intellectual life is that it encourages focusing on what can be known with a relatively high degree of objective precision through the application of particular methods of inquiry. This has produced impressive results in many domains. But as Michael Polanyi, himself a distinguished scientist, pointed out in his later philosophical works, such as *Personal Knowledge* and *The Study of Man,* it has also had the effect of fostering a certain narrowness of focus that makes it difficult to explore the specifically human in all its dimensions. In many respects, French intellectual life has developed in a manner sufficiently different from our own that to see certain problems explored in a French perspective can help considerably to counteract the limitations of focus that arise from an exclusive preoccupation with our normal disciplinary procedures. Just as it is always helpful in getting to know any subject to read several works by different investigators representing different approaches, so it can be helpful to consider from the point of view of more than one culture some of the broad issues that interest all of us as human beings.

That is at least one contribution I hope this study of recent French psychological and social thought will be able to make. Another is to present to the English-speaking public some developments in that area that have taken place in the last decade or so but have gone largely unnoticed abroad. How comparatively unknown they are was brought home to me rather dramatically when I presented a paper on some aspects of this material at a conference in November 1988 and one of the other speakers told me that the topic was especially interesting to her because although she was herself a specialist in modern British and American psychoanalytic thought and was teaching about it in Paris, she knew relatively little about recent French developments—not even much about Jacques Lacan, who really represents an earlier generation—let alone the more recent figures I mentioned in the paper. This book should therefore help to fill a significant void, especially since, although some of the material discussed here has begun to appear in English translation, there have been virtually no efforts to consider it as a whole and to place it in perspective.

Naturally this perspective will have limitations imposed by the nature of its own focus. I have not tried to encompass everything taking place in psychology and related areas in France in recent years but have made a selection of items that seem to me interesting both in themselves and in relation to one another. What emerges is a definite theme, which is indicated in the title: the theme of the self as constituted dynamically and continuously by the relationships it finds itself involved in. This is a theme that gives expression to a particularly French sense of the psychological field as one in which individuals can never be adequately understood in isolation because their sociality is of their very essence. It is characteristic, I think, that one of the figures discussed here, Jean-Michel Oughourlian, speaks of psychology and sociology as "two sciences that are artificially separated, but that in reality make up a single science" (*The Puppet of Desire*, p. 7).

The others to be discussed would probably also share that view, and some would even insist that it is not just these two sciences that have tended to be artificially separated. The same has been true of all areas of inquiry pertaining to human affairs, including politics, economics, and religion. This is another reason why the present study, although focusing primarily on psychology, will reach into these other domains as well, even if it will not attempt to do more than sketch them briefly with an interest in their connection to developments in psychology.

The selection of figures to discuss has been due in part to my own particular interests. I have written previously about René Girard and Oughourlian in another book, *Philosophers of Consciousness: Polanyi, Lonergan, Voegelin, Ricoeur, Girard, Kierkegaard,* in which I placed them in relation not to psychology as such but to certain currents in modern philosophical thought. In that work I focused on philosophical issues, but I brought Girard and Oughourlian into the discussion because I thought its emphasis on primarily rational consciousness needed to be balanced by some consideration of nonrational factors that also play a role in human thinking, and sometimes extensively subvert it, and that can be very effective at disguising themselves as the supposedly logical implications of conceptualities. Girard proved particularly pertinent to that discussion because his thought extends into just about every area of the human sciences and because his concept of "metaphysical desire" (to be discussed at some length in chapter three) was especially germane to the ongoing debate between the thinkers I was talking about on the relative merits of metaphysical as compared with existential thinking in philosophy.

Here, too, Girard and the school of thought that has formed around him will be central. But this is not only the accidental result of my prior interest in his work; it is also a function of the importance his work has gained in France. In fact the book that remains the most extensive systematic presentation of Girard's thought in the realms of philosophical anthropology, religion, and psychology, *Things Hidden since the Foundation of the World,* which he wrote in collaboration with the psychiatrists Jean-Michel Oughourlian and Guy Lefort, became a best-seller in France when it was published in 1978, and major news magazines, such as *L'Express,* have done cover stories on him. His school of thought is one approach among others, but it seems to me the only new one that might eventually acquire a weight somewhat like that of the Lacanian school, which remains the dominant one in the field of analytical psychology in France.

In case it is not sufficiently clear from what I have said so far, I should state explicitly that what I intend to offer in this book is not a general survey of all that has been happening in French psychological thought or even psychoanalytic thought in recent decades. Rather I wish to identify and describe what seems to me an important emerging trend within that universe of thought—the trend that my title refers to as "the new social psychology of France." This is not, as will become clear, a specifically psychoanalytic movement, although some of those who are discussed are definitely psychoanalytic thinkers, but it has developed against a psychoanalytic background. I will therefore begin by explaining the special way in which that tradition developed in France. The first chapter sets the scene for our understanding of recent developments by sketching the history and cultural milieu of the reception of Freudian thought in France, with respect to which Lacan played a leading role. Since Lacan's thought itself has been extensively written about in English, and also since it represents an earlier generation of thought than the approach described here, I do not go into it in extensive detail. But because its distinctive features are also important for understanding French Freudianism generally, I discuss it sufficiently to provide a basic orientation. The second chapter presents three important recent critiques, growing principally out of the Lacanian school, of Freud in particular, but also, directly or indirectly, to some extent of Lacan as well. The next three chapters consider the basic ideas of René Girard and some of the other principal figures associated with his thought whom I refer to collectively as "the Girardian school": Jean-Michel Oughourlian, Jean-Pierre Dupuy, Paul Dumouchel, André Orléan, and Michel Aglietta. The sixth chapter is about the ways both Girard and Marie Balmary, one of those discussed for her critique of Freud in the second chapter, have been pushing their exploration of psychological matters toward its limits—that is, toward the point at which psychology issues into philosophical and religious questions as it attempts to make sense of human experience in its fullness and to consider the ultimate range of possibility toward which human psychological and spiritual development seem to lead. The concluding chapter presents my own effort to assess the significance of the ideas discussed in the preceding chapters and to situate them in that larger context of questioning—in the hope of clarifying further what seems to me to be the ultimate, if neither fully articulated nor even perhaps fully developed, thrust of the searching thought they give expression to.

Regarding translations, I have used published translations whenever possible, but in the case of works that were not translated at the time of this writing, all translations are my own.

I would like, finally, to express my appreciation to all those who have given me help, advice, and encouragement in various proportions while I was working on this project. These include Marie Balmary, Mikkel Borch-Jacobsen, René Girard, Jean-Michel Oughourlian, and Rusty Palmer, and especially Douglas Collins, without whose broad-ranging and discerning guidance through the labyrinth of contemporary French intellectual life I would never have had the temerity to undertake an exploration such as this. I hope he will accept in return the small tribute of my dedicating this volume to him as a memento of many enriching conversations over the past ten years. Neither he nor any of the others to whom I offer my heartfelt thanks should be held responsible, however, for my interpretations of their work or that of any of the others here discussed.

Seattle, April 1992

THE SELF
BETWEEN

From Freud to the
New Social Psychology
of France

CHAPTER I

The Cultural Situation of Psychoanalytic Thought in France

A N Y O N E looking at the French intellectual scene in the 1970s and 1980s would have to be impressed by the pervasiveness of Sigmund Freud's influence. Psychoanalytic thought, even if not psychoanalytic activity itself, had acquired the kind of centrality in French intellectual life once associated with existentialism and Marxism and later with structuralism—a centrality it probably never really possessed in the United States, even at the peak of its popularity. As one of the people interviewed in Paris in the late 1970s by the sociologist Sherry Turkle put it in describing the cultural status of psychoanalysts, "After all, they're the only visible intellectuals around—the existentialists' cafés have given way to the psychoanalysts' couches."[1]

It took a long time, however, for the Freudian thought to attain that eminence in France, and it met with a great deal of resistance along the way.[2] Freud's acceptance in France had to wait, moreover, on an adaptation that would make him assimilable to French ways of thinking. This purpose was eventually served by his filtration through the thought of Jacques Lacan, who drew from Freud what could be effectively recast in the mold of French linguistic, literary, and social interests. The intellectual historian H. Stuart Hughes has remarked that the French resisted psychoanalysis until they had produced in Jacques Lacan an "indigenous heretic" whose interpretation of Freud by way of structuralism and linguistics gave him a

---

1. Turkle, *Psychoanalytic Politics: Freud's French Revolution* (1978), p. 217.

2. For a concise account in English of how Freud's acceptance in France came about, see the book by Sherry Turkle just referred to; for a more detailed account in French that brings the history up to 1985, see the two-volume work by Elisabeth Roudinesco, *La Bataille de cent ans: Histoire de la psychanalyse en France* (1986).

Gallic flavor that made him palatable.[3] Although Freud had been of interest to a small number of important thinkers as early as the 1920s and 1930s, most notably André Breton and Jacques Lacan, it was not until the publication of Lacan's *Ecrits* in 1966 that psychoanalytic thought became a topic of wide and serious discussion among French intellectuals, and it did not become widely accepted by the French public until after 1968, in the aftermath of the student uprisings. The disillusionment that soon set in when the upheaval of May 1968 did not produce the utopian changes the protesters had hoped for resulted in a multiple disappointment with previously prevailing schools of thought and led people to look seriously at Freudianism, in its Lacanian transformation, for a new way of understanding human relations and the relation between human beings and society.[4] Since that time, the quantity of literature published in France on psychoanalysis has multiplied explosively, as have discussions of psychoanalytic themes and theories on television talk shows and among the general public.[5]

The picture of a Freudian hegemony in French thought that these facts might foster should not, however, be taken at face value. France has remained France, and the French Freud is a Freud considerably altered. He won acceptance in France over the resistance of a long and deeply rooted tradition of indigenous French thought on questions of human psychology, and his thought is already being reexamined in ways that penetrate to its foundations and challenge it radically. It is this French movement of reassessment and rethink-

---

3. Hughes, *Between Commitment and Disillusion: The Obstructed Path and The Sea Change, 1930–1965* (1987), p. 290.

4. This disillusionment had many aspects, but especially important was the obvious failure of Marxian analysis to explain the uprising. According to Marx, the masses would revolt when they were starving, but in this case the uprising came not from a starving proletariat but from mostly middle-class students, who were seeking not basic material necessities but the possibility of a life with greater opportunities for a variety of nonmaterial satisfactions. Cf. Vincent Descombes, *Modern French Philosophy* (1980), pp. 171–72.

5. For example, there is currently a regular program on evening television in France consisting of videotapes of psychoanalytic sessions.

ing, as yet almost unknown to the American public, that is the subject of this book.

This is also to a certain extent the story of a return of French psychological thought to French roots in the thought of such thinkers of the late nineteenth and early twentieth centuries as Gabriel Tarde, Gustave Le Bon, Pierre Janet, and Emile Durkheim, among whom psychology tended to be much closer to sociology than it has generally been for the Freudian tradition. One important difference between Lacan and the more recent thinkers to be studied here was that even when he was thinking in ways that were quite original, Lacan represented his thought as aiming at a return to Freud.[6] The later thinkers are, in varying degrees, explicitly critical of the fundamental premises of Freudian thought and offer radical alternatives to it. As will be explained in the chapters that follow, these new currents differ from Freudian thought in a variety of ways, not the least of which is that they tend to seek the source not only of mental disturbances but of normal psychology and the personality as such in interpersonal relations.

Certainly Freud, with his central Oedipal triangle and his teaching that the ego is not master in its own house, undercut any belief in the autonomy of the individual as a subject. Still, the psychological schema he eventually worked out (ego, id, and superego), even as it dethroned the ego, provided a new basis for belief in the individual self. The difference was that it was a larger and more complex self made up of both conscious and unconscious components, with the result that even those forces beyond the individual's conscious control could be conceived of as within him—in his "unconscious." Marie Balmary, an analyst in Lacan's tradition who has rendered explicit and further developed some of the extensive critique of Freud that remained implicit in Lacan, has argued, as will

---

6. However, Mikkel Borch-Jacobsen, *Lacan: The Absolute Master*, pp. 124–27, suggests that Lacan's famous "return to Freud" was more strategic than real; it was designed to preempt for himself the legitimacy of his more standardly Freudian opponents in the French psychoanalytic community and to legitimate his own ideas by claiming that they were the truth Freud was really searching for.

be discussed in more detail in the next chapter, that Freud's theory that symptoms are the fulfillments of libidinal drives, places the essential dynamic within the individual and reduces the importance of the interpersonal.[7]

One major mark of the difference between the traditional Freudian orientation in this respect and that of some of the newer thinkers to be studied in this volume is the term coined by René Girard, Jean-Michel Oughourlian, and Guy Lefort, in their highly influential *Things Hidden since the Foundation of the World*,[8] to designate the distinctive approach to psychology they were proposing there: "*la psychologie interdividuelle*" or "interdividual psychology." The purpose of the term "interdividual," as Oughourlian subsequently explained it in *The Puppet of Desire*,[9] was to emphasize the radically social character of human psychology—so radically social that the self as such had to be conceived of not as individual but as a function of all the relationships in which the person (or "holon" as Oughourlian termed him, following a coinage by Arthur Koestler) is involved. (The term "holon" was coined by Koestler to refer to something that can be thought of as a whole considered in relation to the parts it comprises and also as a part considered in relation to a more comprehensive system.)[10]

Oughourlian describes his conception of the "interdividual self" in the following manner (*Puppet of Desire,* pp. 11–12):

> I have always thought that what one customarily calls the *I* or *self* in psychology is an unstable, constantly changing, and ultimately evanescent structure. I think . . . that only *desire* brings this self into existence. Because desire is the only psychological motion, it alone, it seems to me, is capable of producing the self and breathing life into it.

7. Balmary, *Psychoanalyzing Psychoanalysis*, p. 128.

8. Originally published in French as *Des choses cachées depuis la fondation du monde* (1978).

9. Originally published in French as *Un Mime nommé désir* (1982).

10. Koestler introduced the term in his *Ghost in the Machine* (1968). In a later work, *Janus* (1978), p. 33, he explained it in etymological terms, saying that he took it "from the Greek *holos*=whole, with the suffix *on*, which, as in proton or neutron, suggests a particle or part."

The first hypothesis that I would like to formulate in this regard is this: *desire gives rise to the self and, by its movement, animates it*. The second hypothesis . . . is that *desire is mimetic*. This postulate, which was advanced by René Girard as early as 1961, seems to be capable of serving as the foundation for a new, pure psychology—that is, one unencumbered by any sort of biologism. We have chosen to call this *interdividual psychology*.

As this passage indicates, at the heart of the currents of thought we shall be examining is a particular anlaysis of human psychology that is centered on relationships, and especially on relationships that have to do with patterns of desire that are communicated, usually without either party being explicitly aware of it, from one person to another. In the process, they shape the personalities of those involved and are reshaped in turn.

As Oughourlian interprets it, the causality of the relationship can be formulated either in terms of what is called "influence" or in terms of imitation, or "mimesis." The holon and the other, as he terms them, are linked in a field of force: looked at from one side it can be read as suggestion or influence worked upon the passive holon by the other, and looked at from the other side it can be read as the active reaching out in mimesis by the holon toward the other as a possible model (see, for example, *Puppet*, pp. 28–29, 97–98). As René Girard has put it, with regard to the latter perspective: "Man is the creature who does not know what to desire, and he turns to others in order to make up his mind. We desire what others desire because we imitate their desires."[11] The belief that we are the originators and full owners of our desires, "the intimate conviction that our desires are really our own, that they are truly original and spontaneous," is, says Girard, "the dearest of all our illusions," and he goes on to add: "Far from combatting such an illusion, Freud flattered it."[12]

11. Girard, "Generative Scapegoating," in Robert G. Hammerton-Kelly, ed., *Violent Origins: Walter Burkert, René Girard, and Jonathan Z. Smith on Ritual Killing and Cultural Formation*, p. 122.

12. Girard, *"To Double Business Bound": Essays on Literature, Mimesis, and Anthropology*, p. ix.

On the other hand, the idea that desire is mimetic means two things that undercut the foundations of most traditional thinking on the subject and that could hardly be less flattering to our pretensions. One is that our desires are not validated by some inherent property of the objects that we find desirable: we do not reach out toward objects because of an intrinsic desirability in them that elicits (and justifies) our movements of desire; rather, prompted by a vaguely felt sense of insufficiency or incompleteness, we seek out *something to desire,* some object that may give us the feeling that if only we possessed it, we might find satisfaction in it and come to rest. The other is that far from being autonomous in relation to other people, we are acutely dependent on them. Even when we defy the world in the pursuit of our desires, it is the world that pulls our puppet strings.

The implications for an understanding of human motivation, it should be apparent, could hardly be more radical, even when one bears in mind that the position of interdividual psychology involves a qualifying distinction between "appetites and needs," which can have specific objects and offer genuine satisfactions—as when one is hungry or thirsty and seeks food or drink—and "desires" in the sense in which Girard and Oughourlian use the terms, which are inherently artificial and lead to no real satisfaction but only to further craving.[13]

Certainly it has been the assumption of all previous schools of psychological thought, as of commonsense thinking generally, that desire is elicited by objects. This has been a particularly important assumption for Freudianism, which emphasizes the fundamentally biological character of all desire. For Freud, as is well known, there was one fundamental desire that underlay and set the pattern for all others: the sexual drive, and especially the desire for the first sexual objects to arouse it, such as the infant's mother or whatever

---

13. See *Things Hidden,* p. 283, and "*To Double Business Bound,*" p. 90. This important distinction is discussed further in later chapters, especially chapters three, four, and seven; it is my contention that it is of more fundamental importance than its authors realize, and has not yet been fully developed.

"*pflegende Weib*" ("nurturing woman"), may have played a similarly central role in his early life.[14] As Girard phrased the issue, "For
modern students of desire, the main question has been: what is the
true object of human desire? To Freud, for instance, our 'true' object is always our mother. From the mimetic standpoint, this makes
no sense. Desire can be defined neither by its object nor by some
disposition of the subject."[15]

What this implies amounts to a Copernican revolution in psychology. Perhaps an even better analogue would be the shift to Einsteinian relativity, since in this view there is no longer an absolute
point of reference either in the object of desire or in its subject, as
there had been for earlier thinking. As Oughourlian stated the issue
with reference to his two hypotheses referred to above (that desire
gives rise to the self and, by its movement, brings it into existence;
and that desire is mimetic): "These two hypotheses make it necessary to revise earlier psychologies, since these are psychologies either of the subject or of the object. They demand that one renounce
the mythical claim to a self that would be a permanent structure in a
monadic subject" (*Puppet*, p. 12).

This shift of paradigm was prepared, of course, by earlier developments. It was anticipated in part by the Lacanian revision of Freud,
which put more emphasis on the relativity of both personal identity
and desire than did Freud himself, even though it tended, as the
various schools of psychoanalysis usually have, to attribute the
source of its own original contributions to Freud's "true intent."
Lacan was perhaps even more inclined than most founders of Freudian schools to interpret his own ideas as a rediscovery of the true
meaning of Freud, but in many respects the meaning he found there
led clearly in the direction of the quite non-Freudian, or even anti-
Freudian, lines of thought currently pursued by Girard, Oughourlian, Balmary, and the others to be considered here.

Lacan introduced the main body of his 1936 essay, "Beyond the

14. Freud, *Gesammelte Werke*, 10:154, quoted by Girard in *Things Hidden*, p.
353.
15. Girard, "Generative Scapegoating," p. 122.

Reality Principle," for example, with the statement, set entirely in capital letters: "ALTHOUGH LIMITED TO FACTS ABOUT DESIRE, PSYCHOLOGY BECAME A SCIENCE WHEN FREUD ESTABLISHED THE RELATIVITY OF ITS OBJECT."[16] Here he was paying homage to the leadership of Freud, but he was already pointing beyond Freud's thought in his emphasis on the extent to which a human being was to be understood as entirely a function of relationships: "It is in the specific reality of *inter-human relations* that psychology can locate its proper object and its method of investigation. The concepts implied by this object and this method are not subjective, but *relativistic*" (p. 88, Lacan's italics).

As he eventually formulated his own mature position, Lacan came to see himself as preserving a truth in Freudian thought that he claimed Freud himself had lost sight of or betrayed in his later works, such as *Group Psychology and the Analysis of the Ego,* where he presented his influential idea of the tripartite structure of the human psyche—as composed of ego, id, and superego—and proposed a therapeutic emphasis that would aim at strengthening the ego as opposed to the other two forces. This emphasis in Freud's thought was subsequently reinforced by his daughter Anna and became the predominant pattern of thinking among later Freudians and neo-Freudians. As such, it has come to be known as "ego psychology" and was trenchantly criticized by Lacan in terms that also point toward the Girardian critique of desire, since not only did Lacan deny that the ego could be a reliable source of psychological strength but he also asserted its dependence on desires that infiltrated it from its social field. Rather than being worthy of trust as an ally, the ego deserves to be profoundly mistrusted because it is unable to discriminate the subject's own desires from the desires of others and tends to lose itself in the objects (people and images) with which it identifies in the course of life.

The first of these objects of identification, according to Lacan, is the objectified image of a self that forms in what he termed "the mirror stage" of developement—called such because the identifica-

16. Lacan, *Ecrits* (French), p. 73.

tion often takes place on the occasion of the infant's first seeing his image in a mirror:

> This event can take place ... from the age of six months, and its repetition has often made me reflect upon the startling spectacle of the infant in front of the mirror. Unable as yet to walk, or even to stand up, and held tightly as he is by some support, human or artificial ..., he nevertheless overcomes, in a flutter of jubilant activity, the obstructions of his support and, fixing his attitude in a slightly leaning-forward position, in order to hold it in his gaze, brings back an instantaneous aspect of the image.... We have only to understand the mirror stage *as an identification,* in the full sense that analysis gives to the term: namely, the transformation that takes place in the subject when he assumes an image....[17]

"This jubilant assumption of his specular image by the child at the *infans* stage" (p. 2), as Lacan calls it, is a fundamental and fateful error. The subject is not that object or any other, but it *would like to be,* and its pursuit of its own status as an ideal object becomes the driving force of its life, just as the mirror stage itself becomes the foundation for all the subsequent errors that will entangle it, "the *méconnaissances,*" as Lacan terms them—those misconceptions and refusals to recognize reality "that constitute the ego" (p. 6).[18]

Out of this captivation of the incipient person by his or her own objectified image evolves what Lacan called *l'imaginaire,* the "imaginary" dimension of one's life, which is carried forward into all later development as a fundamentally narcissistic fascination that tends to draw all relationships into an unrealistic and futile striving for identification with the ideal "other," whether this is one's own self-image, or the mother, or any other object. In the resulting process of identification, the individual not only loses a clear sense of his or

17. *Ecrits: A Selection,* pp. 1–2.
18. Borch-Jacobsen, *Lacan,* pp. 46–47, says that although Lacan claimed to have "invented" the idea of the "mirror stage," it had already been developed in detail and presented in 1931–32 by Henri Wallon.

her difference from the other but also confuses his and the other's desires—in a way that is both motivated by and reinforces the individual's egoism. Groping for a way to believe in itself as an object, the ego seeks to see itself as the object of the other's desire and by imaginative identification with that other, to desire itself with that same desire.[19]

The "imaginary" is the home ground of the ego, for Lacan, and *méconnaissance* is both its root and its main function. This, therefore, is why he believed that "ego psychology" was a mistake. A therapy aimed at strengthening the ego would amount to an effort to reinforce the very problem it sought to cure. As he pointed out in his essay on "Aggressivity in Psychoanalysis" (1948), when Freud "asks himself where the ego obtains the energy it puts at the service of the 'reality principle,' " the answer must be that it derives from "narcissistic passion."[20] The attempt to draw on that passion to find a cure from ills that derive from a narcissistic falsification of personal and social reality was, he believed, the source of the aporias of Freud's later thought:

> The theoretical difficulties encountered by Freud seem to me in fact to derive from the mirage of objectification, inherited from classical psychology, constituted by the idea of the *perception/consciousness* system, in which Freud seems suddenly to fail to recognize the existence of everything that the ego neglects, scotomizes, misconstrues in the sensations that make it react to reality, everything that it ignores, exhausts, and binds in the significations that it receives from language: a surprising *méconnaissance* on the part of the man who succeeded by the power of his dialectic in forcing back the limits of the unconscious (P. 22)

Despite Lacan's frequent references to him, Freud was ultimately less important to the formation of his thought than is generally recognized. A much more important influence, and one that has been fundamental not only to Lacan's thought but to that of most

19. Cf. *Ecrits: A Selection*, pp. 197–98.
20. Ibid., p. 21.

French thinkers of his generation and the next, was that of Hegel as interpreted by Alexandre Kojève. Mikkel Borch-Jacobsen, in his book on Lacan, says, for example, that Kojève was the only person Lacan ever described as his "teacher" ("*maître*").[21] This combination of Freud with Kojève's Hegel was probably one of the bases for Lacan's special appeal to his audience, since, as Stephen W. Melville observed in his *Philosophy Beside Itself*, "A central element in the French reception of Freud is its coincidence with the reception of Hegel"; Melville also suggests that in his combining of Hegel and Freud, Lacan was entering "a tacit claim for the adequacy of a science of mind to the task and place of philosophy," another major point of appeal.[22]

Kojève presented his ideas in lectures at the École des Hautes Études from 1933 to 1939, where his audience included not only Lacan but also Georges Bataille, Maurice Merleau-Ponty, and Raymond Queneau, the last of whom later edited and published this material under the title *Introduction to the Reading of Hegel* (1947). One of the main points in Kojève's treatment of this theme is that he considered the dialectic of master and slave an inherent, inescapable feature of the human condition. His argument, stated simply (that is, what he conceived Hegel's argument to be), is that human self-consciousness is necessarily tied up with desire, and in particular with desire for recognition (animal desire for material or biological satisfaction producing only animal consciousness), and that the desire for recognition both requires the presence of "others" who can confer that recognition and leads inevitably to a "fight to the death" to win it from them. Thus each person is driven by necessity of human nature to try to become a master and to reduce others to slaves—the essential quality of a master being that he can force recognition from the other, and that of a slave being that he is constrained to give it to the other without receiving it in return. This results in a situation that Kojève thought also carries the ironic

21. Borch-Jacobsen, *Lacan*, p. 16.
22. Stephen W. Melville, *Philosophy Beside Itself: On Deconstruction and Modernism* (1986), pp. 61, 86.

implication that the master is therefore dependent on the slave for the recognition that enables him to gain and keep his status as a master. A further irony is that it is ultimately better to be a slave than a master, since the master, as Kojève says, "is always enslaved by the world of which he is the master," while the slave alone, through rebellion, is capable of transcending and transforming the world in which he is enslaved.[23]

According to Lacan, this dialectic of master and slave is the special dynamic of "the imaginary," in which the "other" to whom one addresses oneself is always drawn into a struggle for recognition and dominance that can ultimately end only in death (the "absolute master"), unless some strategy can be found to avoid this. Because, in Lacan's version of this dialectic, the relation to the "other" always involves a drive toward identification with the specular image projected into the other—a drive that can take on the proportions of "fusional cannibalism"[24]—every relation with an "other" is threatened by absorption into narcissism and practical solipsism. The major challenge faced by each person in the course of development is to learn to relate to the other as genuinely other. This is what has to be accomplished in the analytic process by working through the "transference": "The subject . . . begins the analysis by speaking about himself without speaking to you, or by speaking to you without speaking about himself. When he can speak to you about himself, the analysis will be finished."[25]

What makes this transition to relatively peaceful coexistence possible, according to Lacan's further theorization, is an adequate accommodation with what Lacan calls the "symbolic" order, the realm of language and social and cultural symbolism that constitutes the actual world in which we all finally have to find a way to live as mature, responsible persons. As Lacan put it in his Rome discourse, "The Function and Field of Speech and Language in Psychoanalysis" (1953): "The psychoanalytic experience has redis-

23. Kojève, *Introduction to the Reading of Hegel*, p. 29.
24. Lacan, *Les Complexes familiaux dans la formation de l'individu*, p. 29.
25. Lacan, *Ecrits* (French), p. 373.

covered in man the imperative of the Word as the law that has formed him in its image. It manipulates the poetic function of language to give to his desire its symbolic mediation. May that experience enable you to understand at last that it is in the gift of speech that all the reality of its effects resides; for it is by way of this gift that all reality has come to man and it is by his continued act that he maintains it" (*Ecrits: A Selection*, p. 106). Lacan was a friend of Claude Lévi-Strauss, and his conception of "the symbolic" is closely associated with the latter's structural linguistics as a realm of differential signs marking and protecting the boundaries between—along with other elements of the social world—the "self" and the "other" and enabling the two to live together without attempting to annul and devour each other.

Lacan and Freud will both be discussed further in the chapters that follow as background for the more recent developments that will be our primary focus, but from this brief anticipation one can see that Freud's probings of the complexity of human motivations have proved for French thought to be a springboard to profound and original reflections. It says something about the French approach to psychology that Freud would be criticized as we saw above even by his most effective advocate in France, but it is also significant that even to those who depart from him more radically than Lacan, he has remained a figure to advocate or wrestle with in a way that he no longer seems to be in North America.

In the United States, Freud was first adopted in a medicalizing manner that, if it did not altogether falsify him, at least emphasized the positivistic and pragmatic side of his thought at the expense of the cultural and hermeneutic.[26] Then he came to be revered and dogmatized as one who had created a comprehensive natural science of the human mind. Subsequently he was eclecticized and reduced to generalities, to the point that much of the strongly biological specificity of his thought dropped away, leaving little more to Freudian theory than the idea that "repressed ideas never disappear but reemerge in harmful distorted form," with the consequent ther-

26. Cf. Bruno Bettleheim, *Freud and Man's Soul*, pp. 43–44.

apy consisting of "uncovering that which has been repressed so that it can be dealt with in more conscious, rational ways."[27] Finally, in recent years, his particular theories and methods have largely been left behind with the emergence of a vast variety of alternative schools of psychotherapy, so that Freud himself now remains of interest primarily to intellectual and cultural historians rather than to active therapists.

In France, on the other hand, Freud has become a truly central figure. I would like to suggest that one important, though not at all obvious, reason for this is that Freud has played an essential role in the French effort to deal with unresolved tensions in its own heritage—specifically between the characteristically French awareness of the sociality of personhood and its tradition of belief in the Cartesian autonomous self. In this respect, Freud has led French thought through a detour that, paradoxical as it may sound, has helped it to become more clearly and reflectively itself.

In the early years of his influence in France, Freud was looked upon with distrust as alien to the French spirit—and with good reason. Despite the emphasis some have placed on the Jewish element in Freud's thought, he was initially perceived by the French as a Germanic thinker, a characterization that makes a great deal of sense when one compares some of the fundamental tendencies of French and German thought generally. Freud's ideal of psychoanalysis as a rigorous science was formed in the German mold, for example, and from the start French thinkers generally tended to feel that this ideal was unsuited to its specifically human subject matter, especially to the protean symbolism of dreams.

This is one reason Freud needed mediation by Lacan to win an audience in France. Lacan had been closely associated with the surrealists during the 1920s and 1930s and had published poetry and literary essays in their periodicals, and his psychoanalytic writings as well tended to draw on a poetic mode of language. As Turkle put it, "Lacan's style, which is closer to Mallarmé's than to Freud's,

---

27. Robert Jay Lifton, *The Life of the Self: Toward a New Psychology*, p. 127.

satisfies the French taste for a poetic psychology," while Lacan's integration of Freudianism with structural linguistics and his famous dictum that the unconscious is structured like a language made psychoanalysis seem a new version of the type of literary *explication de texte* with which the French felt at home.[28]

Also in the Germanic vein was Freud's tendency to cast both himself as a person and the ego as a psychological entity in the imaginative mold of a lone hero battling implacable enemies.[29] Turkle speaks, for example, of how for Freud "the ego seemed almost a psychic hero as it battled off id and superego at the same time that it tried to cope with the world of the everyday" (p. 52). And Frank J. Sulloway, in his discussion of Freud's cultivation of his own "legend" and that of the birth of psychoanalysis, shows how extensively, and effectively, Freud falsified and obscured the history of his career and the origins of his movement in order to present himself to the world as a heroic figure battling alone against uncomprehending colleagues in the early days in Vienna, although in reality the early responses of the Viennese psychiatric establishment were not at all hostile and his subsequent period of isolation was self-imposed rather than imposed on him.[30] It might seem surprising to think of Freud as identifying imaginatively with such figures as Siegmund the Walsung or Siegfried, but as recent biographical studies have indicated, his imagination was organized from the time of his childhood around the idea of himself as a hero marked by fate

28. Turkle, *Psychoanalytic Politics,* pp. 49–50. Cf. Bice Benvenuto and Roger Kennedy, *The Works of Jacques Lacan: An Introduction:* ". . . Lacan evolved a style of writing whose aim was to avoid being over-systematized and reductive, and to reflect the workings of the unconscious. Lacan's prose thus often obeys the laws of the unconscious as they were formalized by Freud—it is full of puns, jokes, metaphors, irony and contradictions, and there are many similarities in its form to that of psychotic writing" (p. 12).

29. This imagery of the hero was shared by Freud with a number of his early psychoanalytic colleagues, such as Carl Jung, Otto Rank, and Alfred Adler.

30. See the chapter on "The Myth of the Hero in the Psychoanalytic Movement" in Sulloway's *Freud, Biologist of the Mind: Beyond the Psychoanalytic Legend,* pp. 445–95, esp. pp. 448–53.

for great works.[31] The image of the hero as lone warrior in a hostile world was not just a Wagnerian invention of the nineteenth century but, as Franz Borkenau has explained, a pervasive metaphor of the Germanic imagination from the time of the early Middle Ages, a lens through which the northern peoples tended to see human life as such.[32]

Historically, the French have, on the whole, inclined more toward the Roman and Latin tradition of cultural identity, with its emphasis on the group and on the individual in society rather than on the heroic exploits of the individual in isolation. An illustration of this can be seen, as Borkenau points out, in comparing the various versions of the Northern heroic saga with their closest analogue in French literature, the *Chanson de Roland*. In the latter, Roland chooses, against the counsel of his second in command, Olivier, not to summon the readily available help of Charlemagne's retreating army when the Saracens attack his position. His desire to seek individual glory without help results in both his own destruction and his army's annihilation. The moral is that such heroics have no place in the new Roman order of Charlemagne. As Olivier says when Roland finally wants to wind his horn for help after it is too late to do any good:

> Vassalage comes by sense and not folly;
> Prudence more worth is than stupidity.
> Here are Franks dead for all your trickery;
> No more service to Carlun may we yield. . . .
> In your prowess, Rollanz, no good we've seen! . . .
> Here must you die, and France in shame be steeped;
> Here perishes our loyal company.[33]

31. As will be discussed at greater length in the next chapter, Mikkel Borch-Jacobsen, in *The Freudian Subject,* p. 47, traces Freud's "undying thirst for greatness" to two prophecies of a heroic future made about him in his childhood.

32. See, for example, Borkenau, *End and Beginning: On the Generations of Cultures and the Origins of the West,* pp. 212–13, 256.

33. Quoted in Borkenau, *End and Beginning,* p. 426.

If one were to look in nineteenth-century French literature for a solitary hero fighting like Wagner's Walsung against a world of enemies, perhaps the nearest equivalent would be Stendhal's Julien Sorel in *The Red and the Black,* but the difference between the two is significant. Siegmund really *is* a lone wolf hounded by enemy hordes and an implacable fate; Julien, on the other hand, tries to become a lone hero but is in fact finally brought down precisely by the continuing force of his own passionate social entanglements.

Another point of contrast between the French and German cultural traditions is that the German has been deeply marked by Kantian reflection on universal ethical principles whereas the French passed directly from the materialism of eighteenth-century enlightenment thought to the socialism and sociology of the positivist movement in the late nineteenth century without ever having felt deeply the force of the type of question Kant brought to the attention of the Germans regarding the nature of self-transcending ethical commitments.[34] As a result, the French have tended to base judgments regarding questions of right or wrong on the interests of the groups they identify with: the family, the proletariat, the revolution, and so on. They characteristically think of themselves as individualistic, but their individualism tends to be mainly a chafing against the restraints of their group identities; it is rarely a matter of a solitary individual struggling to make a correct decision in fidelity to universal principles of justice that might require transcendence of both individual and group interests. The conflicts to which the heroes of the dramas of Corneille and Racine, for example, are subject do not involve abstract ethical principles so much as the demands of station in society, of family loyalty, and so on. Actual individuals living within the tradition of Germanic culture may fall short of such transcendence of self-interest as often as anyone else, but the ethical imperative for it is a cultural theme that gives it a weight for the conscience that it rarely has had among the French. Freudian ego psychology took shape in this context, and the famous Freudian principle "Wo

34. I owe this insight to a lecture by the historian Tony Judt, October 22, 1986.

Es war, soll Ich werden" ("Where id was, there shall ego be")[35] suggests, along with its overtones of heroism, a struggle for moral transcendence in relation to the purely self-interested appetitiveness of the id.

What this aspect of Freud's influence in France may eventually lead to remains to be seen. But it is clear that Freudian thought, or something like it, was needed to help the French reflect on and temper the Cartesian tendency to believe that the thinking self is both rational by nature and self-transparent with regard to its motives and therefore capable of radically autonomous decision. The social psychology of Tarde, Le Bon, and Durkheim at the end of the last century had placed more emphasis on the way the individual's thinking took shape in relations with others and with groups, but the individualistic thrust of Cartesian thought remained a powerful current that produced a major expression again in the existentialist movement of the period during and immediately after the Second World War. Aware as they were of the element of arbitrariness and even perversity that could characterize the "bad faith" of those who might make of their lives a hell with "no exit," the existentialists were not naïve about the complexity of human psychology. Still, their emphasis on the relative isolation of the individual in extreme situations, and on the way his actions incarnated fundamental commitments, gave expression to the experience of the war years and the Resistance better than it did to the world of class struggle and party identifications that became the matrix of French experience and of the powerful Marxist movement that was such a major part of French intellectual life in the decades following the war.

The intellectual career of Jean-Paul Sartre offers a particularly clear illustration of the pattern of French thinking during the years between the war and the time that Freudian thought became prominent. In *Being and Nothingness* (1943), Sartre adapted the thought of Heidegger and Hegel (by way of Kojève) to French purposes,

35. Freud, *Gesammelte Werke*, 15:86; *The Standard Edition of the Complete Psychological Works of Sigmund Freud*, 22:80. In subsequent references, the latter will be referred to as *S.E.*

infusing it with a strong Cartesian element in his insistence on total transparency of consciousness, at least as an ideal to strive for. To the extent that he took an interest in psychoanalysis, it was as an instrument for the analysis of the decisions by which an individual consciously determines the direction of his life and either rises to good faith or falls away from it. His comments on Freudian themes, for example in his *Baudelaire* (1947), were dismissive, especially of the idea of "the unconscious"; all existential decisions were conscious, and to the extent that a person could be said to be neurotic, his neurosis was a self-chosen commitment.

As time went on, however, Sartre was increasingly drawn to the communist movement, and in the process he became convinced of the Marxian theory that thought is determined unwittingly by material and class interests. By the 1960s, after he had published his *Critique of Dialectical Reason,* he had come to identify with Marxism to the point both of repudiating his earlier work and of insisting that the criterion of ethical goodness was loyalty to the communist party. Many of his compatriots had backed away from such unquestioning loyalty at the time of the Hungarian uprising and its violent suppression by Soviet troops, but Sartre maintained an uncompromising, and apparently uncritical, commitment. It is as if in his intellectual and political extremism, Sartre was acting out the dialectic of French thought for his generation: having carried Cartesian individualism to its ultimate expression and then having come to feel its deficiency, he subsequently felt the need to correct his earlier extremism by a radical swing in the opposite direction, trying to escape his own French bourgeois mentality by merging himself with the international proletariat.

The events of the 1960s—the loss of Algeria, the Soviet invasion of Czechoslovakia, and the American war in the former French colony of Indo-China—effectively precluded any hope that might have been placed in the possibility that some grand movement of history led by some trustworthy agent or chosen people within it would result in a new and more promising world. The uprising of 1968 was the last desperate outburst of utopian expectations, and it ushered in a new introspectiveness that looked to psychoanalysis for explanations that philosophy and politics no longer seemed able to give.

To understand what this meant for the French, however, it is important to realize what it means to say that they looked to psychoanalysis for explanations: psychoanalysis, especially as interpreted by Lacan, became for the French not a medical technique, as it did in the United States, but an extension of philosophy. They looked to it not for cure of specific symptoms but for an understanding of the human condition and general guidance in dealing with human relations. They sought in it not so much a science as a path of wisdom. Freud's theory of the unconscious and of irrational human motivation helped them to define and think about problems that had been left unarticulated by the rationalism of their tradition, and the French appropriation of Freud has consequently tended to emphasize either the contrast between Freud and Descartes or else the continuity between the two.

This is not a familiar focus in the reading of Freud in the English-speaking world, but there is a good historical basis for it. Lancelot Law Whyte pointed out, in *The Unconscious before Freud,* that the idea of an unconscious mind originated as a reaction to Descartes's theory of man as made up of two sharply contrasting elements, the opaque body and the thoroughly luminous mind: "Until an attempt had been made . . . to choose *awareness* as the defining characteristic of an independent mode of being called mind, there was no occasion to invent the idea of *unconscious* mind as a provisional correction of that choice. It is only after Descartes that we find, first the idea and then the term, 'unconscious mind' entering European thought"—entering it, that is, mainly among the Germans in the age of Goethe and only later, around the 1850s, being imported into France. Whyte says that although the word "unconscious" had already become familiar in both nominative and adjectival senses in German and English, *inconscient* was probably not used at all in French until the 1850s "and then mainly in translating the German terms." The importance of the idea of the unconscious was that it served to counterbalance the identification of the mind as such with consciousness. "Self-conscious man thinks he thinks," says Whyte, but this is an oversimplification: "The conscious person is one component only, a series of transitory aspects, of the thinking person."[36]

One of the most important implications of the French appropriation of Freud, as will become evident in later chapters, is that it has done away with any remaining traces of the Cartesian belief in a simple monadic self. Of course this belief had not stood alone in French culture without the challenge of countervailing conceptions of psychic life, such as that presented in Proust's *A la recherche du temps perdu,* which, as will be discussed in chapter three, was an important source for René Girard's theory of the mimetic organization of the personality, and perhaps also for Girard's own ability to read and critique Freud in the way he did. Still, the Cartesian idea of the self as a *res cogitans,* a "thinking thing," supposedly proven by Descartes's "Cogito ergo sum" ("I think, therefore I am"), has continued to be a force in French thought, and their reading of Freud has served French philosophers as an important vantage point for criticizing it.

Paul Ricoeur, for example, introduced his own work on Freud with the observation that "the positing of the self is the first truth for the philosopher placed within that broad tradition of modern philosophy that begins with Descartes . . . ," but he then went on to point out that the self thus posited is merely an idea: "The first truth—*I am, I think*—remains as abstract and empty as it is invincible. . . ." Ricoeur's own claim is that genuine self-discovery cannot be accomplished through a Cartesian apperception of thinking but requires a more suspicious hermeneutic: "Consciousness . . . is a task, but it is a task because it is not a given," and Freud is, with Marx and Nietzsche, one of the three "masters of suspicion" in the modern world.[37]

Another contemporary French philosopher, Michel Henry, on the other hand, has recently suggested that Freud was not suspicious enough, at least of the Cartesian roots of his thinking. Whereas Jacques Lacan had said in a 1949 lecture that "the formation of the

36. Whyte, *The Unconscious Before Freud* (1960), pp. 27–28, 67, 59.
37. Ricoeur, *Freud and Philosophy* (1965), pp. 43, 44, 33.

I as we experience it in psychoanalysis . . . is an experience that leads us to oppose any philosophy directly issuing from the *Cogito,*"[38] Henry claims that Freud is actually a late heir of Descartes's in that he accepts what Henry believes is Descartes's erroneous identification of consciousness as such with representation, with its implication that the "I think" of the "Cogito ergo sum" must mean "I represent myself to myself."[39] The function of the idea of the unconscious within the framework of thought thus established was, suggests Henry, to give a name of its own to what in actuality is only the rest of consciousness: the affective dimension of human life, which far from being unconscious is the matrix of all our experience. In reality, says Henry, "the unconscious does not exist" (p. 384) but is rather a name for that which I can only feel without representing it (p. 10). Freud appeals to us, therefore, because of the very features of his thought that put psychoanalysis at odds with itself; the reason for the immense resonance psychoanalysis has met with in the contemporary world "despite the inadequacy of its conceptual framework," Henry says, is that the idea of the unconscious "protects for man his most intimate sense of being; the unconscious is a name for life" (p. 348). It reminds us, that is, that despite the assumptions of Cartesian consciousness, which would reduce all mental life to intentionality and all that can be experienced to intentional objects, our actual life is not an object. Caught as he was himself in the Cartesian web, however, Freud was forced to interpret the unconscious as the blind consciousness of feeling—blind, that is, because it is nonrepresentational.

The French will probably continue to wrestle with both Freud and their Cartesian heritage for many years to come. The most recent developments in their dealing with Freud, however, have tended increasingly toward the most radical criticism. The difference between Ricoeur's highly respectful approach to Freud in the 1960s and the more sharply critical approach of Henry in the 1980s

38. Lacan, "The Mirror Stage as Formative of the Function of the I as Revealed in Psychoanalytic Experience," *Ecrits: A Selection,* p. 1.
39. Henry, *Généalogie de la psychanalyse* (1985), p. 8.

is one small indication of a change that has been taking place on a large scale. Girard and Oughourlian, as we shall see, have developed a completely new approach to psychoanalytic problems that dispenses completely with the Freudian conceptuality. Before proceeding to a detailed exposition of their scheme of "interdividual psychology," however, it will be helpful to consider in the next chapter some other critical approaches that make clear why many French thinkers have felt that a new beginning was needed.

CHAPTER 2

French Critiques of Freud

I F we were to try to identify one pervasive element as a sort of hallmark of French thought in all fields of humanistic inquiry in the last fifteen to twenty years, a good candidate would be the theme of the self-reflexive subject. French philosophy, literary criticism, psychology, and history have all come to share this as a common ground of thinking and often as a theoretical point of focus. The philosophies of Jacques Derrida, Michel Foucault, and Jacques Lacan, for example, are all founded explicity on this theme. What preoccupation with avoiding existential "bad faith" had been for the generation of Sartre, Camus, and de Beauvoir, had become by the 1970s a pervasive anxiety lest thinking slip into naïve belief by falling away from the self-reflexivity that keeps it continually aware of the constructed character of both personality and theory. The place occupied by man's longing for the impossible condition of existing as a mere "in itself" (*en soi*) instead of a conscious, reflective, and free "for itself" (*pour soi*) in the thought of Sartre had come to be occupied in the thought of Jacques Derrida by man's longing for an impossible direct cognition of reality through a "metaphysics of presence."

It had also come to be occupied in the thought of Jacques Lacan by the willed, or at least semi-willed, *méconnaissance* that underlies all the gestures of psychic life, from the child's narcissistic confusion of itself with its specular image in the mirror stage to its subsequent impossible quest in the Oedipal stage for the *objet a*, the universal symbol of ultimate lack that continues to haunt and lure the imagination. Just as for Sartre existential authenticity had required us to recognize and accept that we are both "condemned to be free" and driven perpetually by a "futile passion" to flee from existence into

mere being, so for Lacan we are torn all our lives between a narcissistic longing for fusion or identification with our mothers, with our
own idealized specular self-image, or with the phallus as the symbol
of an elusive sufficiency, on the one hand, and on the other, the
exigency to accept the fundamental facts of alterity in the differenti-
ated and divided existence imposed on us by the symbolic order of
language that we enter through our punning identification with *le
nom* (the name) and *le non* (the "no") of the father.[1] It is in its
demand that we face up to this fundamental dilemma of our being
and bear this fate with courage and resoluteness that Lacan's psychology is an extension of philosophy, as I suggested in the preceding
chapter, and specifically of the two versions of philosophy in addition to Marxism that dominated the postwar decades in France, first
existentialism and then linguistic structuralism.

All of Freud's concepts were assimilated in Lacan's thinking to
this basic pattern, as one can see from what he said about the
central psychoanalytic relationship of transference in the concluding session, "In You More Than You," of his 1964 siminar on *The
Four Fundamental Concepts of Psycho-Analysis:*

> It is not enough that the analyst should support the function of
> Tiresias. He must also, as Apollinaire tells us, have breasts. I mean
> that the operation and manipulation of the transference are to be
> regulated in a way that maintains a distance between the point at
> which the subject sees himself as lovable—and that other point where
> the subject sees himself caused as a lack by *a*, and where *a* fills the gap
> constituted by the inaugural division of the subject.
>
> The *petit a* never crosses this gap. Recollect what we learned about
> the gaze, the most characteristic term for apprehending the proper
> function of the *objet a*. This *a* is presented precisely in the field of the

---

1. It should be noted that there is a clear continuity here between the Sartrean
theme of "bad faith" and the Lacanian theme of "identification": the longing to
merge the "for itself" with the "in itself" that constitutes bad faith's attempt to evade
the human condition for Sartre parallels what for Lacan is identification's attempt to
evade the demands of the "symbolic order" by flight into the "imaginary."

mirage of the narcissistic function of desire, as the object that cannot be swallowed, as it were, which remains stuck in the gullet of the signifier. It is at this point of lack that the subject has to recognize himself. (P. 270)

As in Freud, in other words, the transference is a necessary instrument by which the patient is to be led through a sort of controlled regression and paranoia to project onto the analyst a composite image of the problematic features of the relationships that have formed him or her, and specifically a composite image of all the impossible demands and strivings that prevent him from adequately bearing his lonely fate as an individual among others. The goal of analysis is that by passing through this initiatory ordeal the patient should emerge with an adequate appreciation of the human condition and a willingness to accept and live it.

The critiques of Freud, as well as of Lacan, that are now being undertaken in French thought may all be seen as starting from precisely this point—as attempts to carry out more adequately than either Freud or Lacan succeeded in doing the demand Lacan believed he found in Freud for the radical authenticity of a self-reflexive subject that can avoid being taken in by its own inevitably self-generating fictions. We shall here consider three of these: first, François Roustang's critique of Freud and Lacan with reference to their failure to meet Lacan's demands for the management of the transference; second, Marie Balmary's critique of Freud as a compulsive self-fictionalizer who deceived not only his followers but himself as well; and finally a philosophical critique by Mikkel Borch-Jacobsen of problems in Freudian theory that suggest the comparative advantages of a theory of mimesis somewhat like—but also interestingly different from—that offered by the interdividual psychology of René Girard and Jean-Michel Oughourlian that will be discussed in the next two chapters.

François Roustang

Three books by François Roustang—*Dire Mastery: Discipleship from Freud to Lacan* (1976), *Psychoanalysis Never Lets Go* (1980), and *Lacan: De l'équivoque à l'impasse* (1986)[2]—have all been concerned with the problems that grow out of what he believes is an inherent conflict in psychoanalysis between its demands for critical reflection on the one hand and for uncritical subjection to the analyst and to psychoanalytic theory on the other. There have been both theoretical and practical sides to this conflict, as he sees it.

Both types of problem have grown out of the central place of "transference" in the theory and practice of psychoanalysis. Roustang says in *Dire Mastery*, "Psychoanalysis emerged from the theorization of a specific experience, the transference phenomenon" (p. 55)—the relationship in which the patient develops infantile feelings of dependency toward the analyst and generally attributes to the analyst qualities he saw, or thought he saw, in his parents or others who were important to him in his life.[3] The therapeutic necessity for transference according to psychoanalytic theory is that only through such a projection of infantile attitudes into the relation with the analyst does it become possible for the patient to become reflectively conscious of those attitudes and to learn to deal with them in a mature manner. One practical problem concerned with transference, on the other hand, is that although it is supposed to function as a kind of controlled dose of the source of psychological trouble, it can be as addictive in its own way as the original neurosis. In his essay "The Dynamics of Transference," Freud stated that the termination of transference and "the final independence of the patient" are the goal of analysis (*S.E.*, 12:104–5); in

2. *Dire Mastery* and *Psychoanalysis Never Lets Go* were published in translations by Ned Lukacher in 1982 and 1983, respectively; *Lacan* was not translated at the time of this writing. Roustang has also written *The Quadrille of Gender: Casanova's Memoirs*, published in translation in 1988.

3. J. Laplanche and J.-B. Pontalis have said that it is difficult to propose a definition of transference because "for many authors the notion has taken on a very broad extension, even coming to connote all the phenomena which constitute the patient's relationship with the psycho-analyst." They define it themselves as "a process of actualisation of unconscious wishes" in which "infantile prototypes re-emerge and are experienced with a strong sensation of immediacy." *The Language of Psychoanalysis*, pp. 455–56.

practice, however, Freud and subsequent analysts have found that the patient often has difficulty letting go.

This aspect of the problem of transference has often been noted. Another aspect of it that Roustang thinks is at least as important and has hardly been considered comes from the side of the analyst: analysts themselves, including Freud and Lacan, have to some extent deliberately and to some extent unwittingly encouraged continuing dependency and "discipleship" as a fundamental pattern within the community of psychoanalysts themselves as well as in their relations with patients. The first chapter of *Lacan: De l'équivoque à l'impasse* has as its title, "Pourquoi l'avons nous suivi si longtemps?" ("Why did we follow him so long?") The question refers specifically to the cult of Lacan in France, but Roustang sees the problem as going back to Freud himself.

"Although he denied it," says Roustang in *Dire Mastery*, "Freud was possessed by an uncontrollable need to have disciples and to surround himself with completely devoted followers" (p. 15). The decisive criterion, in Freud's eyes, for membership in the psychoanalytic movement was "the dependence or independence of his disciples in relation to himself, not to his ideas" (p. 6), despite the claims he often made to the contrary. Regarding the affair of the expulsion of Carl Jung from the psychoanalytic movement, for example, Roustang says that Jung's main offense was really insubordination in relation to Freud as a person, rather than any theoretical challenge he represented: ". . . it is precisely because Jung touched the imago of the uncontested master that he must perish, and perish at the hands of all the faithful. For there is nothing better than a crime perpetrated by one and all to ensure the cohesion of the horde" (p. 3). This theme, as we shall see, is developed more extensively in the thought of René Girard. Regarding the tangles of "insincerity" and "shabby morals" that the plot to expel Jung drew Freud into as he marshaled what he called his "gang" of "lions" and whipped up in each "the impulse to kill, so that the others have to restrain him" (p. 4),[4] Roustang says,

4. Roustang is quoting from Sigmund Freud and Karl Abraham, *A Psychoanalytic Dialogue: The Letters of Sigmund Freud and Karl Abraham, 1907–1926*, p. 168.

"His knowledge of the transference should have warned him; but he himself was so caught up in the relationship with his disciples, which he scarcely analyzed at all, and in a style that weighed heavily on the entire history of the psychoanalytic movement" (p. 5).

It has weighed on it because it was the very nature of psychoanalytic movement as created and defined by Freud to be, in Freud's own words, "a savage horde" (*Wilden Heer*), the phrase he also used in *Totem and Taboo* to refer to the sons that unite in retrospective devotion to the father they had themselves killed in the primordial murder that founds both society and religion. Freud used the same phrase again in 1917 in telling George Groddeck that unlike Jung and Adler he would always belong to the movement: ". . . I have to claim you, I have to assert to you that you are a splendid analyst who has understood for ever the essential aspects of the matter. The discovery that transference and resistance are the most important aspects of treatment turns a person irretrievably into a member of the savage horde."[5]

In creating his International Psychoanalytic Association (IPA) in 1910, Freud adopted the pattern of authority characteristic of the kind of traditional society represented most prominently by a religious order or the Catholic Church itself, with "a chief (*ein Oberhaupt*) who, on the death of the founder (*der Führer*), would be his successor, his *Ersatz*" (p. 12). "Without even noticing it," says Roustang, "in laying the rules for his association, he does nothing other than take up the norms of even the most obvious societies, the 'artificial crowds' (the Church, the army) whose unconscious structures he was to analyze in *Group Psychology and the Analysis of the Ego* (1921). It appears, however, that Freud never compared the association, which he himself founded, to the groups whose libidinal mechanisms he took apart piece by piece" (p. 13).

Roustang also goes on to make a point central to his own conception of the problem: "psychoanalysis . . . could not fit into such an institution." Psychoanalysis, that is, born as it was of reflection

5. George Groddeck, *The Meaning of Illness: Selected Psychoanalytic Writings*, p. 36, quoted in *Dire Mastery*, p. 7.

upon the phenomenon of transference, could not be bound forever in the unresolved transference its founder was trying to impose upon it. From Roustang's point of view: "There is a complete contradiction between the aim of psychoanalysis, which along with its rules, must remain an artifact, and the constitution of a society around an irreplaceable leader, whose thinking is adopted and who is acknowledged as the master. Here the contradiction is even more violent since, in order to be constituted, the society uses processes such as the transference, which properly belong to the analytic cure" (p. 13). "The group around Freud," he goes on to say, "was constituted through the transference onto him—which can be seen in the statutes of the association. This involved very real things like the use of power and the circulation of money. The surreptitious shift of the analytic transference into the realm of real social relations creates the ambiguity and even the untenability, by definition, of the psychoanalytic society" (p. 14).

If this was true of Freud's foundation of his society, it was all the more the case with Jacques Lacan, who not only joined other disaffected French analysts in founding a rival psychoanalytic society in 1953, the Société Française de Psychanalyse, for which he was himself expelled from the International Psychoanalytic Association, but who also broke with the 1953 society in turn to found his own École Freudienne de Paris in 1964 and then dissolved that organization as well in 1981 to create still another, La Cause Freudienne.[6] In each case a central feature of the organizations he created was a personality cult unlike anything yet seen in the psychoanalytic community, even in connection with Freud himself. And with each dissolution and reformation, this was intensified. Turkle, doing her research in the mid-1970s, before the last episode, found in her discussions with hundreds of French psychoana-

6. Lacan's expulsion from the IPA took place after ten years of debate in 1963, ostensibly because of his well-known practice of the "short session," rather than the standard fifty-minute session, but in reality probably for factionalism. Benvenuto and Kennedy, *Works of Jacques Lacan*, point out that Lacan "was using the short session, with official knowledge and approval, long before the French analytic society split into different factions" (p. 208).

lysts that almost all of them brought up their personal relations with Lacan or their feelings about him, mostly with reference to the still unhealed wounds of the 1964 upheaval.

Lacan was a characteristically French figure, both in his person and in the nature of his authority, which was highly personal. In the Germanic tradition, authority has usually taken a more institutional form; Germans and Austrians have tended historically to trust institutions and to respect the authority of those who wear their uniforms or bear the titles of their offices. In this cultural context, Freud's organization of the IPA was a logical device with which to maintain control of his movement, and the organization itself proved both stable and effective. Freud, one might say, founded a psychoanalytic bureaucracy in order to protect his own authority and that of his dogma; Lacan, on the other hand, set up rival bureaucracies in order to destroy them, and he delighted in theoretical paradox and the undermining of dogmas. The effect was to focus loyalty all the more exclusively on his person. "If the Lacanians can read Freud as a text-to-be-analyzed and not as the text of truth," says Roustang, "it is because Lacan has done the work for them. When they distance themselves in relation to Freud or even when they resolve, so to speak, their transference onto Freud, they are protected by an unanalyzed transference onto Lacan, who plays the role of guarantor and interpreter of truth. In advance and for the future, they put their trust in Lacan" (*Dire Mastery*, p. 21).

The French on the whole have tended to distrust institutions and to feel more comfortable with the kind of institutional anarchy Lacan generated than with stable hierarchies. This does not mean, however, that they are any less attracted to authority. Rather, in France authority tends to be charismatic, the authority of a "maître" or "grand homme"; it tends, to use Max Weber's phrasing, to be personal rather than official. French intellectual life consequently inclines perhaps more than any other to take shape around the following of leaders, who are expected to act the part.

Lacan acted his with panache. As a figure he was as much a walking and talking psychoanalytic exhibit as he was a theorist, dressing and acting flamboyantly and making a display of his own symptoms for the enormous audiences he drew to his seminars. He had been, as was mentioned in the preceding chapter, closely associated with the surrealists in his youth, and he made himself into something like a surrealist object for an eager public. Elisabeth Roudinesco's history describes the effect this had:

> In 1966, fawned upon by numerous disciples, he founded a school over which he reigned like an enlightened despot. They taught his doctrine there. Even more, they committed the irreparable error of reading the works of Freud in the light of Lacanian teaching, as if the former had no history of its own and could receive its importance only through confrontation with the latter. They sacralized the texts of Lacan, they imitated his person, they treated him as the sole founder of the psychoanalytic movement. Subjugated to him, an army of barons spoke like Lacan, smoked the cigars of Lacan. . . . If this army could have done so, they would have carried their heads tilted to the left like Lacan and stretched the cartilage of their ears so that they would have stuck out like his.[7]

There can be advantages sometimes to carrying things to an extreme. Just as it has been suggested in the French press that the Socialist victory in 1981 and the resulting abortive attempt finally to implement the utopian social and economic policies the left had been dreaming about for decades had the longer-range result of instilling in the French populace as a whole a new sense of economic reality and its inevitable constraints,[8] so Lacan seems to have served as an object lesson to some observers, such as Roustang, regarding the way in which psychoanalysis itself plays with rather dangerous medicine when it cultivates transference, which Roustang describes in *Psychoanalysis Never Lets Go* as "not only the place where the

---

7. Roudinesco, *La Bataille de cent ans: Histoire de la psychanalyse en France*, 2:118.
8. See, for example, Albert du Roy, "Nos Révolutions," *L'Expansion* (October 21–November 3, 1988), p. 46.

most archaic sado-masochism emerges but also the occasion for its reproduction" (p. 108).

This is a point to which French thought generally, as was explained in the preceding chapter, has been particularly sensitized by Alexandre Kojève's commentaries on Hegel, especially his analysis of Hegel's discussion of the complex psychology of the master-slave relation in the *Phenomenology of Spirit,* a theme which in the next chapter we will see also proved important for René Girard's discussion of sadism and masochism. Roustang does not especially mention Kojève in connection with Lacan's and Freud's, as well as every other analyst's, attempt to make himself the perpetual master of both his patients and any disciples he may have, but to any French thinker of his generation this pattern of analysis would come as naturally as a fundamental paradigm, although not all would draw upon it in Roustang's specific way.

The cult of Lacan, as seen in this light, underscored for Roustang the practical dilemma in the propagation and institutionalization of the psychoanalytic movement that he describes as "in danger of becoming a religion" (*Dire Mastery,* p. 24). One might say that Roustang has made himself, more than any other figure in French psychoanalytic thought, the voice of the slave's (that is, the client's) rebellion against the inherent tendency of the analytic situation to cultivate a relationship of dominance.

Roustang's reflection on this aspect of the problem of transference also made him acutely aware of a theoretical problem that he thinks the psychoanalytic community has been sweeping under the carpet since the beginning: the problem of establishing a substantial difference between psychoanalysis on the one hand and suggestion and hypnosis on the other. In his preface to the English-language edition of *Psychoanalysis Never Lets Go* he asks the question, "Why do analysts or those who have been analyzed have so little inclination to ask themselves what they are doing and what is at work in the treatment?" and he answers, "To put it as plainly as I can, it is because *psychoanalysis, through its intermediary the transference, has not really disengaged itself from hypnosis and sugges-*

tion. The result of this is that the treatment, without being noticed, risks leading to a more or less latent form of blindness" (p. viii, emphasis in the original). Subsequently, in the body of his text, he says: "All of Freud's work, during several decades, is marked by an effort to establish a radical difference between psychoanalysis and suggestion, but it is also marked by the difficulty of making this difference convincing" (p. 70).

Freud had opened his *Group Psychology and the Analysis of the Ego* with a discussion of the theme of suggestion as studied by such thinkers as Gustave Le Bon, William McDougall, Gabriel Tarde, and Hippolyte Bernheim, a theme that he indicates had been on the back burner of his own thinking for a long time: "Now that I once more approach the riddle of suggestion after having kept away from it for some thirty years. . . ." (*S.E.*, 18:89). He acknowledges: "There is no doubt that something exists in us which, when we become aware of signs of an emotion in someone else, tends to make us fall into the same emotion." But he concludes that an explanation in such terms for the tendency of people to think alike in crowds will not suffice and, in keeping with his own theoretical orientation, states his preference for an explanation in terms of sexual appetite, or "libido": "Instead of this, I shall make an attempt at using the concept of *libido* for the purpose of throwing light upon group psychology, a concept which has done us such good service in the study of psychoneuroses" (p. 90).

A passage from section four of this work will be worth quoting at length; not only does it illustrate what Roustang says about Freud's felt need to distance himself from theories of suggestion, but it also demarcates an area of inquiry that we shall later see opened up once again by Mikkel Borch-Jacobsen and Jean-Michel Oughourlian, with explicit reference to the thought of Le Bon, Tarde, and Bernheim.

> It is clear that rational factors . . . do not cover the observable phenomena. Beyond this, what we are offered as an explanation by authorities upon sociology and group psychology is always the same, even though it is given various names, and that is—the magic word

suggestion. Tarde calls it "imitation". . . . Le Bon traces back all the puzzling features of social phenomena to two factors: the mutual suggestion of individuals and the prestige of leaders. But prestige again is only recognizable by its capacity for evoking suggestion. Mc-Dougall for a moment gives us an impression that his principle of "primitive induction of emotion" might enable us to do without the assumption of suggestion. But on further consideration we are forced to perceive that this principle says no more than the familiar assertions about "imitation" or "contagion," except for a stress upon the emotional factor. . . . We shall therefore be prepared for the statement that suggestion (or more correctly suggestibility) is actually an irreducible, primitive phenomenon, a fundamental fact in the life of man. Such, too, was the opinion of Bernheim, of whose astonishing arts I was a witness in the year 1889. But I can remember even then feeling a muffled hostility to this tyranny of suggestion. When a patient who showed himself unamenable was met with the shout: "What are you doing? *Vous vous contresuggestionez!*" I said to myself that this was an evident injustice and an act of violence. For the man certainly had a right to counter-suggestions if they were trying to subdue him with suggestions. Later on, my resistance took the direction of protesting against the view that suggestion, which explained everything, was itself to be preserved from explanation. (*S.E.,* 18:89)

There are several items here that point in directions needing exploration. To begin with, Freud says that "rational factors . . . do not cover the observable phenomena." Roustang points out that Freud continued throughout his career to suspect that there was more to the phenomena of suggestion and hypnosis than could be explained in terms of rational thought or even in terms of his libido theory. We shall come back to that presently, but to continue for the moment in anticipation of further questions we shall see arising among recent French thinkers from issues embedded in this quite rich passage, Freud brings up, in order to dismiss it, the question of whether "suggestion . . . is actually an irreducible, primitive phenomenon, a fundamental fact in the life of man" that could itself "be preserved from explanation." His own preference is for object-oriented libido as an explanatory principle, but he does not seem to realize that this too would constitute a similarly "irreducible, primitive phenomenon" and "fundamental fact" and that his own choice of an object-oriented explanation is not only itself unexplained, but is not even noticed as an issue.

Oughourlian, as we shall see in the fourth chapter, not only adopts suggestion as a principle of explanation but also offers an explanation for it in turn by way of his and Girard's more comprehensive theory of "universal mimesis" as a fundamental tendency of human psychology. In Oughourlian's use, the concept of "mimesis" encompasses and explains both Tarde's "imitation" and Le Bon's and Bernheim's "suggestion."9 Depending on which is interpreted as active or passive in the relationship, the imitator or the model, he says, the relation may be called by either name. When the imitator is thought of as active, he or she is said to "imitate" the model. When it is the model who is thought of as active, then he is said to "influence" or to "suggest" something to the imitator. As Oughourlian explains it, the human tendency toward mimesis is not drawn by objects but reaches toward the subjectivity of the other, with the implication that imitation is really more fundamental than suggestion: the imitator is always unwittingly seeking out something in the subjectivity of the other to model himself on. Suggestion, therefore, does not need to be thought of as a mysterious sort of *actio in distans* or telepathic influence but can be quite easily explained as

9. According to Sulloway, Bernheim took the theory of suggestion as an explanation for hypnosis from Auguste Ambroise Liébault's *Du sommeil et des états analogues, considérés surtout au point de vue de l'action du moral sur le physique* (1866). See, *Freud, Biologist of the Mind*, pp. 46–47, 48, 50. Sulloway suggests (p. 47) that Freud began opposing the suggestion theory years earlier in a quite different theoretical context because it threatened his own position in his early work on hysteria: in 1888 Freud wrote a preface to his German translation of Bernheim's *De la suggestion et de ses applications à la thérapeutique* in which he argued on behalf of Charcot's physiological theory of hypnosis in opposition to Bernheim because, in Sulloway's words, "If hypnotism were purely the effect of suggestion, then the 'type' of *grande* (hysterical) *hypnotisme*, which Charcot had described as being characterized by contractures, neuromuscular spasms, and other symptoms of *grande hystérie*, was simply not genuine." Thus doubt would have been cast not only on Charcot's attempts to interpret hysteria but on Freud's at that time as well.

the result of inward action on the part of the one who undergoes the influence.

The important question from the point of view of psychological theory is not so much whether either principle, suggestion or libido, is fundamental or irreducible but whether an explanation in terms of it is able to account adequately for the phenomena. Oughourlian believes an approach in terms of subjective mimesis offers a clearer and simpler explanation for the phenomena of group psychology than does the Freudian theory of desire for a libidinal object—an approach so clumsy that Freud is led in his last pages to try to buttress it still more clumsily with the supposition of biologically inherited memories of the fascination of the primal horde for the father they had killed. This latter hypothesis Freud cast in terms of Lamarckian evolutionism, the belief in the inheritance of acquired characteristics, which had already been abandoned by the general scientific community at the time Freud wrote his essay but which Sulloway says Freud held to throughout his life—so that the effect was to attempt to support the questionable with the more questionable.[10] It is at least an important point in its favor that the theory of mimesis we shall see developed by Oughourlian offers an explanation that is both simple and comprehensive for what Freud described as "the riddle of hypnosis, about which so many points have yet to be cleared up" (*S.E.*, 18:117) and that he fell into such awkwardness in his attempt to deal with, acknowledging: "There is a great deal in it which we must recognize as unexplained and mystical" (*S.E.*, 18:116).

Freud was also long preoccupied, as Roustang points out, with the equally mysterious phenomena of "subconscious thought-transference," engaging in experiments in this with his daughter Anna and with Sandor Ferenczi and fearing that the telepathic intuitions of his thoughts by others might rob him of his right to claim

10. Sulloway, *Freud, Biologist of the Mind*, pp. 274–75. For further material on Freud's use of the ideas of Jean-Baptiste Lamarck (1744–1829) in other important aspects of his thought, such as the concept of the superego, see also pp. 91–94, 96, 375, 390, 392.

priority for his discoveries.[11] He also wrote on the theme in numerous places that indicate he took quite seriously the possibility of psychical processes leaping from one person to another "through what we call telepathy—in such a way that one possesses the knowledge, feelings, and experience of the other."[12] In his essay "Dreams and Occultism," for example, he discussed what he believed was an instance of thought-transference he had encountered in his work and then commented: "It is a familiar fact that we do not know how the collective will comes about in the great insect communities: possibly it is done by means of direct psychical transference of this kind. One is led to suppose that this is the original archaic method of communication between individuals and that in the course of phylogenetic evolution it has been replaced by a better method, that of communication by signs which are picked up by the sense organs. But the earlier method could have persisted in the background and still be able to put itself in effect under certain conditions, for example in passionately excited mobs."[13] It may well be that the difficulty Freud had in explaining such mimetic phenomena in terms of his libido theory left him especially susceptible to the appeal of occult or parapsychological explanations.

That, however, is not the issue that Roustang considers most important. Rather he believes that Freud's effort to distinguish between "thought-transference" (*Gedankenübertragung*) of this sort and the kind of "transference" (*Übertragung*) involved in psychoanalysis blinded him to another form of thought-transference: the unconscious influence of the analyst on the patient. "All of this," Roustang says, "suggests to him no questions about analytic work and what goes on there," and when Freud does talk about the connections "between thought-transference and transference proper . . . it is to prevent the question of thought-transference from penetrating like a red-hot poker into the very heart of analysis" (p. 55). "By this distant

11. Roustang, *Psychoanalysis Never Lets Go*, pp. 50–51.
12. "The Uncanny" (*S.E.*, 17:234); quoted in Roustang, pp. 50–51.
13. *S.E.*, 22:55–56; quoted in Roustang, p. 58.

interest in telepathy," he goes on to say, "Freud wants to repudiate a most formidable enemy, and that enemy is suggestion, which he has long practiced with hypnosis."

Freud, of course, had explicitly renounced hypnosis as a psychotherapeutic technique when he invented psychoanalysis. Marie Balmary, who is much more critical of Freud in most respects than Roustang is, admired him for this, especially since in doing so Freud was giving up, as she says, "the most widely used psychotherapy of his time, and one, moreover, that was not without apparent effectiveness."[14] She characterizes this as an instance of *sacrifice interdit* (the rejection of sacrifice that her own title alludes to): Freud forbade himself to govern in another and refused to accept that gift of power over them that his patients were so ready to sacrifice to him; he refused to treat them without awakening them or to cure them without allowing them to grow.

Roustang, however, thinks Freud only *thought* he was giving it up, but had brought back its essence in the transference relation. He suggests that this becomes obvious when one compares, as Freud himself never did, what he said about the similarity between transference and being in love in his "Observations on Transference-Love" (1915) and what he says about hypnosis and romantic love in chapter eight of *Group Psychology and the Analysis of the Ego;* both are described as corresponding to the state of being in love, but with sexual satisfaction excluded. Roustang also suggests that if one replaces the word "hypnosis" with "transference" in the following quotation from *Group Psychology,* it can serve "to unveil certain decisive aspects of the transference":

> From being in love to hypnosis is evidently only a short step. The respects in which the two agree are obvious. There is the same humble submission, docility, absence of criticism, toward the hypnotist as toward the loved object, the same absorption of the subject's own initiatives; no one can doubt that the hypnotist is in the place of the ego ideal. It is only that all the connections in hypnosis are clearer and

14. Balmary, *Le Sacrifice interdit: Freud et la Bible,* p. 284.

more intense, so that it would be more appropriate to explain being in love through hypnosis than the other way around. The hypnotist is the sole object, and no one else is considered in comparison to him. That the ego experiences as a dream whatever the hypnotist requests and asserts reminds us that we have neglected to mention among the functions of the ego ideal the business of testing reality. No wonder that the ego takes a perception for real if its reality is vouched for by the physical agency ordinarily charged with the task. The complete absence of impulses that are uninhibited in their sexual aims contributes further to the extreme purity of the phenomena. The hypnotic relation is the unlimited devotion of someone in love, but to the exclusion of sexual satisfaction; whereas in the actual case of being in love this satisfaction is only temporarily held back, and remains in the background as a possible aim at a later time.[15]

If Oughourlian were to comment on this passage, he would probably point out the awkwardness of trying to explain hypnosis as an erotic relation without the erotic element, and he would suggest that it would be more illuminating with regard to both hypnosis and being in love to approach each on its own terms and then try to understand how each can be explained as an effect of mimetic tendencies. We shall consider that problem further in chapter four. Roustang's concern, on the other hand, is not with any theoretical inadequacy in Freud's interpretation of hypnosis but rather with the fact that Freud failed to notice that transference is virtually identical in its essentials with hypnosis in that both involve intense relationships of dependency and both also involve "suggestions" or influence passing from a dominant figure to a subordinate one.

Freud avoided even thinking about the possibility "that thought-transference is at the very heart of analytic experience," says Roustang (p. 55), and that psychoanalytic transference might therefore involve an influence of the analyst's unconscious on the patient. Yet such influence, he suggests, is always involved in the actual relationship. Freud had said that in psychoanalysis "science

---

15. S.E., 18:114–15; quoted in Roustang, *Psychoanalysis Never Lets Go*, p. 85.

sets about restoring to words a part of their former magical power" but uses them to lead to "the patient's independence."[16] Roustang says, however, that "precisely because they do have a magical power, they cannot avoid having, on the one hand, the inverse effect of linking the patient more closely to the analyst (who wanted to free him from his shackles) and, on the other hand, side effects that bring on problems in the patient which the analyst cannot master, because in receiving the analyst's words, the patient also assimilates all that those words unconsciously carried" (p. 59). Even if the analyst then tries to avoid this effect by remaining silent, Roustang goes on to say: "Every silence has an intensity and a coloration that is perceptible to the patient."

The danger Roustang sees in this is one that could be expected to seem especially sinister to a psychoanalyst whose thinking was formed, like his, in the Lacanian tradition. This is the danger that one may be tempted to slip unwittingly from the symbolic order of language and society, with its demands for differentiation and individual responsibility, into flight toward a state of infantile fusion or of imaginative identification.[17] "What analytic treatment sets up and what the analyst reinforces," says Roustang, "whether through his speech or through his silence, is an immediate relationship of an archaic, infantile, erotic sort, the aim of which is the negation of all alterity" (p. 59).[18] Transference by its very structure, by its "logic," as Roustang terms it, tends "to produce both indistinctness and identity" so that "far from accentuating individuation . . . , the

16. *S.E.*, 7:283; quoted in Roustang, p. 59.

17. In Lacan's system, it may helpful to remember, infantile "fusion," which is prerepresentational and pre-"imaginary," is replaced at the mirror stage with "identification." Whereas in the infantile stage of development there is no distinction between self and other, at the mirror stage that distinction emerges as a factor in consciousness; but, dominated by the "imaginary," the newly emerging individual is tempted to slip away from it again through identification with the other.

18. Cf. Descombes, *Modern French Philosophy*, p. 22, on "the problem of the other" as a principal theme of French phenomenology; Descombes links this with the problem of solipsism for idealist philosophy in general and Cartesian "philosophy of consciousness" in particular (that is, in the French context, philosophy centered on the Cartesian cogito).

transference risk[s] dissolving individuation" (p. 124). Transference tends always, but especially when one is naïve about its character, toward an extreme to which Roustang gives the name "infinite transference": ". . . at first it is infinite in duration, in the sense of indefinitely postponed, because analysis can only undo a small part of it and because it repeatedly reinstates it, then infinite in intensity, from which it acquires uncanny forms of veneration . . ." (p. 60).

According to Roustang, a threat to differentiation, individuation, and alterity, all of which depend on one another, is built into the very process by which psychoanalysis seeks to foster them. The problem is not Freud's in particular, but that of psychoanalysis as such. In fact, despite his criticism of Freud for not considering this issue adequately, Roustang, like Balmary, thinks Freud made an honest, or at least fairly honest, effort to avoid imposing his thought and the force of his personality on his patients. In this respect he contrasts Freud with Lacan, who he thinks attempted to maintain the transference relation with everyone, both his patients and his students (and through his bureaucracies, with the students of his students), and ultimately to extend it universally by drawing the entire French intellectual world into the orbit of psychoanalysis.[19] Besides the "intellectual terrorism" by which he and his disciples sought to "shut the mouths" of anyone who said he did not understand some point of the master's doctrine or who had the daring not to adhere to everything Lacan said or did (p. 12), Lacan also made use of a particularly effective feature of the transference relation: the concealment of his own subjectivity that gives the analyst such preeminence over the patient:

> During the cure, and only for that time, my psychoanalyst becomes for me incomparable and unique. But that relation can be maintained only to the extent that the analyst refrains from showing too openly his own particularities of personality. Lacan succeeded in the *tour de force* of never appearing either in public or in private except as an analyst, or, to consider the matter more subtly, of acting in such a way

19. Roustang, *Lacan: De l'équivoque à l'impasse*, pp. 12–15.

44

that all the personal traits he allowed us to see became hidden the moment the figure of the analyst was constituted for us. While Freud disclosed himself by way of his dreams, his correspondence, or his case histories, Lacan consistently avoided letting slip any trace of his own subjectivity. He pushed this effacement to the limit in order to preserve with everyone the mysterious position of the analyst. (Pp. 13–14)

Roustang, however, overlooks the ways in which Freud himself played a similar role before his own early audience, even using similar stratagems. Frank Sulloway discusses this in connection with the theme of the subtitle of his book, *Freud, Biologist of the Mind: Beyond the Psychoanalytic Legend*. According to Sulloway, psychoanalysis has borne from the start a "myth of the hero" that Freud fostered and in which most of his biographers have wittingly or unwittingly cooperated. This legend includes a large number of distortions and even falsifications about Freud's life and the origins of the psychoanalytic movement—many of them deliberate on Freud's part.[20] Freud also, according to Sulloway, deliberately tried "to cultivate the 'unknowable' about himself and thereby to set himself apart from the more transparent nonheroes of humanity"; in 1885 and 1907, for example, he destroyed his personal papers so that no one would be able to trace his actual history and thereby to view him as a figure on the ordinary human scale: "As he revealed to his fiancé on the first of these occasions—in which letters, notebooks, private diaries, and manuscripts all perished—the holocaust was necessary so that the hero's past could be properly shrouded in

20. For a concise twenty-six point schematic summary of the main elements of this myth, see Sulloway, *Freud, Biologist of the Mind*, pp. 489–95. One finds in it many of the well-known supposed "facts" of Freud's biography, such as that Freud's ideas on male hysteria "were 'rudely rejected,'" thus marking the beginning of his 'isolation' from Viennese scientific life"; that Breuer broke with Freud over Freud's theory of the sexual etiology of neurosis; that Freudian theories met with a strongly hostile reception from about 1894 to 1906 and were not carefully considered by his colleagues, thus he was scientifically isolated at the time; that Freud discovered infantile sexuality and the unconscious; and that Freud's sexual theories grew out of his self-analysis.

mystery" (p. 497). The legend and the air of mystery worked together to give Freud's movement an effective force in the eyes of the intellectual public that greater honesty would probably have undercut. "This interlocking web of legend has been absolutely essential," says Sulloway, "to the strategy of revolution employed by Freud and his loyal followers. Indeed, their efforts would have been sorely deficient without a keen eye to Freud's potential value as a mythological being. And precisely because he and his followers were so personally caught up by the mythical history they sought to invent for themselves, they actually lived this history as subjective reality . . ." (pp. 488–89).

It may be true, as Roustang suggests, that Freud disclosed more of himself "by way of his dreams, his correspondence, or his case histories" than Lacan did, but even Freud may not have known how much he was also concealing, and he certainly knew that he was concealing a great deal. For the most part those who have written on Freud have generally credited him with much more honesty than Sulloway's study of his "legend" suggests he really deserves, but Sulloway too credits him with an unusually high degree of perspicacity in his self-analysis and discovery of the Oedipus complex. Few of those who have studied Freud have ever dared to suggest that he may have been so tangled in a web of deceptions that the very foundations of traditional Freudian psychoanalysis are unsound. The first person in France to have explored this last possibility was Marie Balmary in her *L'Homme aux statues: Freud et la faute cachée du père* (1979), translated as *Psychoanalyzing Psychoanalysis: Freud and the Hidden Fault of the Father*.

Marie Balmary

That web, suggests Balmary, was not of Freud's own weaving, but he was caught in it nonetheless. Some recently discovered information about his family and his early life show that his parents were engaged in a lifelong effort to cover up some facts about their past and Freud's own birth that would have cast his father, and perhaps his mother as well, in a light quite different from that in which he habitually viewed them—that is, as models of uprightness. One of

Balmary's own principal theoretical hypotheses is that what is re-pressed in one generation is likely to give rise to symptoms among the members of later generations until it is consciously faced and dealt with—or in a more general formulation: "The dominated carries out the repressed . . . of the dominant " (p. 35). Parents play a dominant role in the lives of most children, as did Freud's in his. They also like to be admired and thought of as good models, and they consequently tend to shield some aspects of their lives from view. This may or may not lead to problems for the child, but when the concealment involves elaborate falsifications, it is all the more likely to do so—particularly when the claim to respect for the parents, and especially the father, is as great as it was in Freud's family.

Balmary's own concern is not to judge Freud's parents but to consider the implications of their deception. What was important, she suggests, was the concealment as such, which indicates that Freud's parents themselves felt the hidden facts to be shameful. Another important element in the situation is that Freud, who never seems consciously to have suspected anything, nevertheless seems to have been exposed to enough signs that there was a secret in the household that he must have experienced some desire to get behind the facade. Freud himself, she points out, "always insisted that human beings can hide nothing. . . . We can therefore hypothesize an 'unconscious' Freud, in search of a truth that has been denied him" (p. 42).

Such an impulse to bring truth to light can be dealt with in two ways. One is to track it down; the other is to cooperate, consciously or unconsciouly, in the effort to keep it covered up. Balmary's inter-pretation is that Freud unconsciously took the latter course and that this had fateful consequences for his efforts as a psychological theo-rist, because it led him to follow paths that skirted the kind of truth hidden in his own background as well as to shy away from such truth when he came too near it. It also led him finally to develop a theory, that of the Oedipus complex, that served to bury the danger-ous truth still deeper.

The parental deception was, on the whole, remarkably successful: it took in all of Freud's followers and his biographers until 1968, when Josef Sajner discovered that Freud's father, Jakob, had been married not twice, as Freud's parents had claimed, but three times. Freud's mother, Amalie, contrary to his lifelong belief, was not the second wife of his father but the third.[21] This might not seem so important in itself, apart from the fact that it evidently seemed important enough to someone to be worth concealing, but it seems much more so in light of another detail that was also falsified: according to the birth register in the town hall at Freud's birthplace (Freiberg), Freud was born not on the date he himself and his early biographers had always thought but two months earlier.[22] Freud's official biographer, Ernest Jones, opens the first volume of *The Life and Work of Sigmund Freud* (1953) with the statement, "Sigmund Freud was born at 6:30 p.m. on the sixth of May, 1856."[23] The birth register, on the other hand, says he was born on the sixth of March, an entry that cannot easily be dismissed as a clerical error because, according to Wladimir Granoff, the shift in date appears "not just in one place but in everything that concerned the child in question, that is to say concerning not only his birth but also his circumcision."[24]

This, in turn, might not seem so significant if it were not for some other facts. One is that Freud's mother and father were married July 29, 1855—over nine months before his supposed birth, but only seven months and a week before his actual birth. Another is the cloudiness surrounding the second wife, whose name was Rebecca. It is clear neither when she entered Jakob's life nor when she died. It is known that Jakob and his first wife, Sally, were married in 1831 and that they had two sons, Emmanuel (1832) and Philipp (1836).

21. Sajner, "Sigmund Freuds Beziehungen zu seinem Geburtsort Freiberg (Pribor) und zu Mähren," *Clio Medica* 3 (1968): 167–80.

22. Balmary refers to works by Didier Anzieu, Wladimir Granoff, and Max Schur as sources, and expresses special indebtedness to Granoff for ideas that enabled her to develop her own interpretation.

23. Jones, *Life and Work of Sigmund Freud*, 1:1–2; cited in Balmary, *Psychoanalyzing*, p. 35.

24. Granoff, *Filiation: L'Avenir du complexe d'Oedipe*, quoted in Balmary, p. 36.

Jones says that Sally died in 1852, but neither Schur nor Granoff found any record of her death or even of her existence in the Freiberg registers, where Jakob had lived with his sons since 1840. Granoff did, however, find the family listed in 1852 as "Jakob Freud, thirty-eight years old, his wife Rebecca, thirty-two years old," Jakob's sons, Emmanuel and Philipp (who would then have been twenty and sixteen, respectively), and the wife of Emmanuel, all of whom would consequently have known about Rebecca and would have had to cooperate in keeping silent in order for Sigmund to grow up never having heard of her. By 1854, she is no longer listed in the register, but there is no reference anywhere to what became of her. The most likely possibilities are that she died or that she and Jakob divorced, but there is no evidence to confirm either. Balmary has her own guess as to what may have happened to Rebecca Freud, but for the moment we will pass on to another mysterious figure from the time in Freiberg whom Freud did know about and who had enough continuing importance to him that he mentioned her several times in letters and even dreamed about her.

This was his nursemaid, Monika Zajic. Jones describes her as "a nannie, old and ugly," whom Freud referred to as "a prehistoric old woman," of whom he said he was fond and that he used "to give her all his pennies," though he also speculated that the latter might be a "screen memory" connected with "her dismissal for theft later on when he was two and a half years old."[25] (It should be noted, however, that Freud did not himself remember the last item, the accusation of theft, but simply took his mother's word for that many years later.) In the *Interpretation of Dreams,* Freud says that his mother told him the nurse was "old and ugly, but very sharp and efficient."[26] In one of his letters to Wilhelm Fliess in October 1897, Freud describes her as "an ugly, elderly but clever woman who told me a great deal about God and hell, and gave me a high opinion of my own capacities"; he credits her with being the "primary originator" of his personal neurosis, though he does not explain in what

25. Jones, *Life and Work,* 1:5–6; quoted in Balmary, p. 134.
26. *S.E.,* 4:247–48; quoted in Balmary, p. 134.

way.[27] He also expresses gratitude to her for having "provided me at such an early age with the means for living and surviving," evidently through the self-confidence she helped instill in him.[28] In his letter of October 15, the letter in which the Oedipus hypothesis is mentioned for the first time, Freud gives a longer account of what his mother told him: "I asked my mother whether she remembered my nurse. 'Of course,' she said, 'an elderly woman, very shrewd indeed. She was always taking you to all the churches [*in alle Kirchen*]. When you came home you used to preach, and tell us all about how God conducted His affairs. . . . She turned out to be a thief, and all the shiny Kreuzers and Zehners and toys that had been given you were found among her things. Your brother Philipp went himself to get the policeman, and she got ten months.' "[29] He adds that until his mother told him the story in this conversation of 1897, he had been completely unaware of his nurse's having been a thief.

There are several things about this account that clearly invite closer scrutiny. (Balmary notes the irony that Freud, the master of suspicion, seems never to have doubted anything his parents told him.) That Monika Zajic was ancient at the time Freud was in her care has been found to be false, or at least a great exaggeration; according to Anzieu she was in her forties.[30] The nurse's age is of little importance in itself, of course, but that Freud's mother so emphasized her age and ugliness when she was not even old suggests a note of hostility in an account that clearly says much about how Amalie felt toward the nurse but perhaps less about the woman herself. She also said the nurse took the child "to all the churches"; in fact, there was only one church in the town. The

---

27. Perhaps it is relevant that, as was mentioned in the preceding chapter, Freud said the source of the Oedipus complex was the infant's desire for his mother or whatever "*pflegende Weib*," such as a nursemaid, may have played a similarly central role in his early life. It should be noted that this letter was dated just twelve days before his first mention of the Oedipus complex.

28. Freud, *The Origins of Psychoanalysis: Letters to Wilhelm Fliess*, Letter 70, October 3, 1897, p. 219; quoted in Balmary, p. 135.

29. Letter 71, ibid., pp. 221–22; quoted in Balmary, pp. 137–38.

30. Anzieu, *L'Auto-analyse de Freud*, 1:38; quoted in Balmary, p. 138.

exaggeration suggests that the trips to the church and the effect it produced—the "preaching"—probably irritated Amalie acutely. Since the family was of another faith, that would not in itself be surprising, but Balmary thinks there may be more to the matter, as I will explain in a moment.

The most important element in the mother's description is that the nurse was accused by the family of being a thief. What seems odd about this is that the theft she was accused of was so petty. For a mature woman who was supposed to have been intelligent and efficient to have risked jail for so little would seem surprising. Something else that is now known about their life in Freiberg that makes it seem even more surprising is that the Freud family lived in a single rented room on the second floor of a house belonging to Monika's family. "Is it credible," asks Balmary, "that this relative of the landlord, this shrewd and hard-working middle-aged woman . . . stole the pennies and the toys that this poor child was able to collect? . . . It hardly seems plausible" (p. 138).[31]

Briefly stated, Balmary's own hypothesis about all this, based on the facts already listed and on her reading of some of Freud's dreams about the nurse, is as follows: Monika Zajic was a native of Freiberg, and, since the town was not large—only about five thou-

31. It should be noted that although the identification of Freud's nursemaid as Monika Zajic is widely accepted, Paul C. Vitz has recently argued, in his *Sigmund Freud's Christian Unconscious* (1988), that it is incorrect. His argument is based on a hotel registration by the Freud family at the spa Roznau on June 5, 1857, giving their nanny's name as Resi Wittek (p. 5). Thus he doubts that she was a member of the landlord's family (p. 224, note 16). He also doubts that, whoever the nursemaid may have been, she was jailed for theft (pp. 16–17). He does, however, accept the story that she took the young Freud to church. His own book argues generally that this influence marked Freud for life with a "Christian unconscious"; he also thinks she may have secretly baptized him and that this may be the source for his dream about being washed by her in bloody water—not in menstrual fluid, that is, but "in the blood of the lamb" (see pp. 17–22). His own speculation regarding her dismissal from the family's employment is that Amalie Freud was having an affair with her stepson—Freud's half-brother, Philipp—and that she was afraid the nanny knew about it and might reveal it (p. 45). It was also, of course, an "incestuous" situation that Vitz thinks Freud, even as a child, could hardly have failed to be aware of and that may well have led to his later preoccupation with the Oedipus theme.

sand inhabitants—it is likely she knew a fair amount about the Freud family, including information about the fate of Rebecca. That she took the child to church and talked to him about divine judgment would seem to indicate that she took an interest in morality. It may be that she was trying by her "pious or magical practices," such as having him cross himself with holy water from the font (Balmary thinks the dreams indicate memories of this), "to protect him from the consequences of some tragic and reprehensible facts" (p. 139). The hostility toward the nurse and accusations against her could have been connected with fear of what she might disclose to the child about matters the parents would prefer to keep hidden. None of this can be proved, but it is in keeping with Balmary's hypothesis that the Freud family left Freiberg shortly after making the accusation, less time than the official biography indicates, and perhaps also for reasons other than those indicated. The reasons later advanced were anti-Semitism in the town and economic catastrophe in the textile business, in which Jakob was employed, but Freud himself later spoke of another Jewish family who stayed in Freiberg and became wealthy there in textiles. Balmary's guess is that a more likely reason for the family's departure is that it was easier to bury the past in forgetfulness by leaving the town in which there would be people around whose memories and tongues could not be controlled.

She also makes her own guess about what it was they wanted to hide. This is that Amalie, a very young woman at the time (nineteen or twenty), became pregnant by Jakob while he was still married to Rebecca and that Rebecca committed suicide, perhaps in some manner that was connected with a train (pp. 73–74, 98, 101).[32] Freud,

---

32. Vitz's hypothesis about the sudden departure is that it was connected with the end of the affair between Amalie and Philipp Freud; he notes in this connection that there was a subsequent estrangement between Philipp and Jakob. *Sigmund Freud's Christian Unconscious,* p. 45. This alternative speculation about Freud's early family background is obviously quite different from Balmary's and those of the investigators she relies on, but the difference is less significant for Balmary's interpretation of Freud's own psychological makeup than it might appear. For Balmary the essential thing is not the question of what the family secret was but rather that there was such

who himself had a phobia about train travel, seems to have felt that something sinister was being left behind in Freiberg and that it was associated in some way with the railroad; he said in another of the letters to Fliess: "At the age of three I passed through the station when we moved from Freiberg to Leipzig, and the gas jets, which were the first I had seen, reminded me of souls burning in hell."[33]

All of this, of course, is rather speculative. What Balmary thinks important, however, is not whether the Freud family secret had exactly this shape or some other, but that something powerfully charged in the imaginations of Freud's parents and in his own was hidden from Freud as a child and indeed throughout his life and that a good deal of evidence, such as the false date given for his birth, suggests that this secret had to do with what, in the eyes of the world he grew up in and those of the members of the family themselves, would have been viewed as a fault on the part of his parents. Even if the question of the fate of Rebecca were to be set aside, so that the only thing that would need covering up would be a premarital pregnancy, that alone could have sufficed to produce some disturbing effects of repression, especially since Freud was taught to believe, and evidently did believe wholeheartedly, at least as far as he had any consciousness of it, that his parents represented the highest standards of honesty and morality.

Balmary's hypothesis of "an 'unconscious' Freud, in search of a truth that has been denied him" (p. 42), was mentioned above. She also thinks that a fundamental element in human psychology is an interest in questions of ethical value. Speaking of the unsuccessful effort of his patient "The Ratman" to make Freud understand "that the unconscious was a question of good and evil," she adds, "And Lacan was also right when he dared to teach that the status of the unconscious was ethical" (p. 86). Engaged as they inevitably are

---

a secret at all, whatever it may have been, and that the attempt to keep it hidden left permanent marks on Freud and carried over into his own attempts to maintain the image of his parents as immune to reproach.

33. Letter 77 (December 3, 1897), *Origins of Psychoanalysis*, p. 237; quoted in Balmary, *Psychoanalyzing*, p. 80.

with what Lacan called the symbolic order, human beings seek, consciously or unconsciously, to understand both the reality of their world and how it makes sense, a matter that includes the moral structure of the social world and how one relates to it. Following Lacan, Balmary considers this not so much a question of what in particular is taken to be morally right or wrong as that something inevitably will be so interpreted and that the resulting value system will be taught to children, who will then feel the need to understand the moral order thus defined and to situate themselves and those who are important to them properly within it. When faults are committed, they will therefore seem all the more wrong when they are committed by people who represent the standards that are violated. In Balmary's words, "the origin of neurosis is not sexual desire alone nor even sexual trauma alone, but all the faults committed by the very people who present the law to the child, either directly or indirectly—faults that have not been recognized" (p. 164).

Freud's theory that symptoms are disguised fulfillments of the patient's erotic desires made neurosis seem simply a matter within the individual; Balmary, on the other hand, thinks it is inherently interpersonal (p. 128). Sexual desire and sexual trauma disturb the child not so much in and of themselves as because of the way their value is defined by those who speak with authority and represent the moral order in the child's eyes. When something important to the child's understanding of that order and his place in it is hidden, then a powerful drive to bring it to light is awakened and gives rise to symptom formation. The neurotic symptom itself, she believes, is an attempt to give expression to something that cannot be openly avowed, to bring it to utterance. This too is an idea she developed on the basis of her study of Lacan. "Men are the authors of symbols," she says, "but they are the spectators of symptoms. It is as though the symptom were a subsymbol, a chance return of what could not be symbolized. Does Lacan not say that what cannot be symbolized reappears in the realm of the real?" (p. 9).

As one illustration of this principle and of the way it may become connected with awareness of fault within a family, she cites a case history told by Lacan in his first seminar, for the year 1953–54, about a man of Muslim descent who showed "symptoms having to do with the use of his hands" and who did not respond to the usual Freudian analysis in terms of the effects of infantile masturbation.[34] The necessary clue came to Lacan when he explored the possibility of a connection with the Koranic law that a thief's hand should be cut off. It turned out that during his childhood the patient had heard someone say this about his father, who had been dismissed as a civil servant. The sentence had never been passed on his father, but Lacan says, "it nonetheless remained inscribed in the symbolic order of intersubjective relations which one calls the law." Returning to this case at the end of her book, Balmary comments: "Recall Lacan's clinical example: what the son knew all alone became strange to him. There was no one around him with whom to know that he knows. What does this knowledge concern? It concerns an unrecognized fault, something that his father concealed from him. . . . There is therefore a hole, an obscure zone, in the discourse that they share" (p. 161).

From this point of view, the "unconscious" as a source of psychological disturbance is primarily that which cannot be spoken and thereby brought into the open between people, and the symptom is an effort to accomplish this when all other possibilities of communication are closed off. Lacan said in his *Ecrits,* "The unconscious is that part of the concrete discourse, insofar as it is transindividual, that is not at the disposal of the subject in reestablishing the continuity of his conscious discourse. . . . The unconscious is that chapter of my history that is marked by a blank or occupied by a falsehood: it is the censored chapter. But the truth can be rediscovered; usually it has already been written down elsewhere," namely in the form of physical symptoms, of childhood memories, of the language one uses, of stories one tells about one's life, and of distortions in the other chapters of one's history.[35]

"When will all that return to consciousness?" asks Balmary.

---

34. Lacan, *Le Séminaire,* 1:221; quoted in Balmary, p. 21.
35. Quoted in Balmary, p. 132.

"When he meets someone—the analyst (here, Lacan)—with whom he can speak about it," so that he can pass from "he knows" to "he knows that he knows" (p. 160). In the case in point, "the son knows about his father's theft, but he does not know it *with* his father. This knowledge then assumes the status of the unconscious" because it is difficult not to repress information, however important, that one must bear alone. This points, she says, to another way, fundamentally different from Freud's, of interpreting the idea of "the unconscious": "that what one knows with the Other is conscious, and what is known without the Other is unconscious."

Freud himself came close to this way of thinking, only to back off from it, during that crucial time in 1896–97 when his thought crystallized in the form it was to retain throughout the rest of his career. In a letter of May 1896 to Fliess, Freud said of the process of becoming conscious [*Bewusstwerden*] "that, as regards memories, it consists for the most part of the appropriate *verbal* consciousness—that is, of access to the associated verbal images," and "that it is not attached exclusively either to what is known as the 'unconscious' sphere or to the 'conscious' one, so that these terms should, it seems, be rejected."[36] An implication of this line of thought, says Balmary, is that the categories of conscious and unconscious lose their interest because the more important distinction is between the utterable and the unutterable. This in turn has the further implication that " 'becoming conscious' is subordinate to the quality of the relation to the interlocutor and not to the physical status of the things repressed," a position that she says "is obviously easier to understand . . . after having read Lacan" (p. 109). Freud did not pursue these possibilities, however: "Having glimpsed the breach, Freud will nevertheless pass it by without venturing to go through it. Year after year, transmitted from one person to another, the metaphor of the unconscious gradually becomes solidified. It became the answer to everything, the type of response that definitively stops the development of what is really at work in every equation" (p. 110).

36. Letter 46 (May 30, 1896), *Origins of Psychoanalysis*, pp. 165–66; quoted in Balmary, p. 109.

In the sixth chapter of this study we will consider in detail what Balmary thinks the shape of a psychology centered on the quality of the interpersonal relation can be. For now the important question is why, according to her critique, Freud chose the particular path he did and why she thinks this was something more than a merely theoretical false turn. Considered simply in terms of theory, the turn Freud took during that critical period 1896–97 was from his hypothesis about the origins of hysteria and neurosis in the repressed memory of an experience of early sexual trauma (frequently called the "seduction theory") to that of the universal Oedipus complex. The first hypothesis he had worked on for several years, from approximately 1892 to 1897, on the basis of considerable clinical observation of cases of such trauma.[37] His public presentation of that theory took place in a lecture in May 1896, "The Aetiology of Hysteria," but the central thesis was already succinctly stated in two letters he wrote to Fliess in October 1895, in which he said that "hysteria is conditioned by a primary sexual experience (before puberty) accompanied by revulsion and fright; and that obsessional neurosis is conditioned by the same accompanied by pleasure" and also that "[h]ysteria is the consequence of a presexual *sexual shock*. Obsessional neurosis is the consequence of presexual *sexual pleasure* later transformed into guilt."[38]

Freud continued to hold this position until September 21, 1897, when he wrote to Fliess that he no longer believed it. One of the reasons he gave for abandoning it is "[t]he astonishing thing that in every case blame was laid on perverse acts by the father, my own not excluded, . . . though it was hardly credible that perverted acts against children were so general."[39] His other reasons were (1) that he had not yet found a way to bring an analysis "to a real conclusion," (2) that "there is no 'indication of reality' in the unconscious, so that it is impossible to distinguish between truth and emotionally-

---

37. For some examples, see Balmary, pp. 90–93, 111–13, 117.
38. Letter 29 (October 8, 1895), *Origins of Psychoanalysis*, p. 126; quoted in Balmary, p. 107. Letter 30 (October 15, 1895), p. 127; quoted in Balmary, p. 108.
39. Letter 69 (September 21, 1897); quoted in Balmary, p. 145.

charged fiction," and (3) that the most advanced cases of psychosis do not show signs of such unconscious memories. None of these last reasons would seem sufficient to abandon the hypothesis, especially since, with regard to the second, there were ways other than reference to unconscious memories to confirm the reality of the traumatic events, as in the case of a patient referred to in letter 69 of the Fliess correspondence (January 3, 1897) who had journeyed to his homeland "to check the genuineness of his memories for himself, and . . . got the fullest confirmation from his seducer, who is still alive (she was his nurse, now an old woman)."[40] Or there is the example of a young woman whose case Freud dropped immediately when her father "began to sob bitterly" after she had let fall "a single significant phrase": "Naturally," says Freud, who Balmary says always tended to back away from evidence of parental guilt, "I pressed my investigation no further; but I never saw the patient again."[41]

Only three weeks after abandoning the seduction theory, into which he had put years of research, Freud came up with the Oedipus theory. "With the end of the summer of 1897," as Balmary puts it, "comes the time for Freud to abandon the first foundations of his work and to lay down a new base. While the first were established on the bedrock of fact, however, the second rest upon the sands of myth" (p. 133). The first reference to the Oedipal theory comes in letter 71 (October 15, 1897), the same letter in which, as was mentioned above, he expresses surprise regarding what his mother told him about his nursemaid being a thief. It was written, said Freud, after three days of inner crisis. To have given up a theory that had been the work of years left him feeling a bit at sea and therefore in need of some other way of making sense of the phenomena that perplexed him. "Only one idea of general value has occurred to me," he writes. "I have found love of the mother and jealousy of the father in my own case too, and now believe it to be a general

---

40. Quoted in Balmary, p. 111. Oddly, Freud went on to say in the same letter that the patient, who was now feeling very well, was "obviously using this improvement to avoid a radical cure."

41. Freud and Breuer, *Studies in Hysteria,* quoted in Balmary, p. 93.

phenomenon of early childhood. . . . If that is the case, the gripping power of *Oedipus Rex* . . . becomes intelligible. . . . Every member of the audience was once a budding Oedipus in his phantasy, and this dream-fulfillment played out in reality causes everyone to recoil in horror, with the full measure of repression which separates his infantile from his present state."[42] Balmary comments regarding this sudden shift from clinical cases to myth: "There is nothing from reality here; no event is at the bottom of all this. . . . there remains no basis other than the dream emotions of Sigmund Freud. . . . Everything finally comes from the subject himself and from his desires" (p. 152).

The fault, above all, is no longer the hidden fault of parents, but that of children. Freud had decided that despite any confirming evidence from other sources, the stories of seduction were fictions made up by children and projected by them onto their parents. The shift was abrupt, and is all the more surprising because the Oedipus story is not really the story of a man who wanted, even unconsciously, to kill his father and marry his mother. When Oedipus received an omen that this fate awaited him, he did everything he could to avoid letting the prediction come true: he immediately left what he honestly believed was his homeland and the couple he believed were his parents, and he could have had no idea that the stranger he killed in a fight on the road was his father or that the queen of Thebes was his mother. Moreover, as Balmary points out, there are many features of the Oedipus story that point to the fault of the parents as the source of trouble rather than to any conscious or unconscious desires on the part of the child. "Freud, who does not want to recognize reality," she says, ". . . puts all his faith in this myth, which, moreover, he has misconstrued" (p. 127).

Before going into the aspects of the Oedipus myth that Freud failed to take into account, however, we should stop to consider why, according to Balmary's own interpretation, Freud may have been motivated to make this theoretical shift at precisely this time.

42. *Origins of Psychoanalysis,* pp. 223–24; quoted in Balmary, pp. 151–52.

Something else of great moment in Freud's life had happened not long before: his father died on October 23, 1896. He wrote to Fliess shortly after, "By one of the obscure routes behind the official consciousness the old man's death affected me deeply. I valued him highly and understood him very well indeed, and with his peculiar mixture of deep wisdom and imaginative light-heartedness he meant a great deal in my life. By the time he died his life had long been over, but at a death the whole past stirs within one. I feel now as if I had been torn up by the roots. . . ."[43] Balmary thinks this death affected Freud deeply enough that during the entire one-year period of mourning, Freud showed many signs of its effects, both in his dreams and in his thinking about psychological matters. To attempt to develop a universal psychological theory on the basis of a self-analysis conducted during a period of emotional upheaval regarding the death of a parent would be risky in any case, and especially when the theory one ends up with sets aside evidence and the testimony of patients, as did the Oedipal theory, and turns entirely to a combination of myth and analysis of one's own feelings about a parent who has just died. Such feelings commonly include some sense of guilt combined with exaggeration of the excellences of the departed parent. Balmary discusses numerous dream and other images that she thinks indicate that Freud experienced considerable inner turmoil during this period, especially with regard to early memories, and that he felt the effects of repressed suspicions that his father may have had something to hide.

None of these suspicions ever seem to have come to the surface in a way that Freud could recognize. We saw above how when he asked his mother for information about his nurse, he simply took her word for it that she had been a thief, even though it conflicted with his own earlier impressions. Freud seems generally to have had difficulty admitting any sense of possible fault regarding his parents or those toward whom he had a relation of similar respect. In her later book, *Le Sacrifice interdit: Freud et la Bible,* Balmary mentions in this connection his exaggerated respect for his mother: he

43. Letter 50 (November 2, 1896), p. 170; quoted in Balmary, p. 80.

said that the only love that did not contain any element of aggression was a mother's love for her male child—despite his manifest feelings of resentment regarding his mother's domination of him throughout her life and his expression of relief when she died (p. 53). Another example she mentions there is Freud's amazing reluctance to criticize Fliess regarding a clear case of gross malpractice. Fliess had the theory that nasal operations could clear up a variety of medical problems. In one instance he had performed such an operation on a patient of Freud's and had absentmindedly left behind in her nose fifty centimeters of gauze, which subsequently led to a painful infection and to hemorrhages that could have been fatal. Not only did Freud write to Fliess after this episode, "Of course, no one makes any reproach against you," but a year later he had even worked up a preposterous explanation of the incident to the effect that "her hemorrhages were of hysterical origin, brought on by unsatisfied desires."[44]

Nevertheless, Freud's imagination seems in dreams and elsewhere to have betrayed traces of buried suspicion regarding his father's secret. One example is a dream he mentioned in his letter to Fliess of November 2, 1896, in which, he said, "I found myself in a shop where there was a notice saying: 'You are requested to close the eyes.' "[45] Freud also mentioned this dream in *The Interpretation of Dreams* (1900), with the time given as the night before the funeral rather than after it: "During the night before my father's funeral I had a dream of a printed notice, placard or poster—rather like the notices forbidding one to smoke in railway waiting rooms—on which appeared either 'You are requested to close the eyes' or 'You are requested to close the eye.' "[46]

Another apparent hint pointing toward the family secret is the

44. Letters of March 8, 1895, and April 26, 1896; quoted in Balmary, *Le Sacrifice interdit*, p. 62. Fliess's botched operation on this patient (Emma Eckstein) is also discussed in detail by Jeffrey Moussaieff Masson in *The Assault on Truth: Freud's Suppression of the Seduction Theory* (1984), pp. 55–72.

45. *Origins of Psychoanalysis*, pp. 170–71; quoted in Balmary, *Psychoanalyzing*, p. 80.

46. S.E., 4:317; also quoted in Balmary, p. 80.

enigmatic phrase, "Rebecca, you can take off your wedding-gown, you're not a bride any longer," in the letter in which Freud says that he has abandoned the seduction theory.[47] Freud evidently intended it to refer ironically to himself, bereft of his long-held theory, as one left alone like a rejected bride, but Balmary points out that his rejection of the theory about the hidden faults of fathers and his adoption soon after of the theory that all such faults are figments of their children's imaginations had the effect of shielding his own father from the possibility of suspicion about another problematic Rebecca who would also be left husbandless if his father could no longer be suspected of having been married to her.[48]

Still another item that Balmary thinks may obliquely express repressed suspicions—and is also interesting because, like Freud's reading of the Oedipus story, it presents another example of misconstrued interpretation of a work of literature—is the quotation from Vergil's *Aeneid* that Freud used as an epigraph to *The Interpretation of Dreams*, but which he first referred to in a letter to Fliess of December 4, 1896: "Flectere si nequeo superos Acheronta movebo" ("If I cannot bend the higher powers, I will move the infernal regions," *Aeneid* 7.312). He evidently intended this to mean that if one cannot discover the meanings that are psychologically important to a person from the manifestations of his conscious thought, then one can turn to expressions of the unconscious—that is, dreams. It is not usually noticed, however, that in its original context this quotation has a meaning that brings it uncannily close to what Balmary thinks is the secret about his father's Rebecca. The speech in Vergil is by the

---

47. Letter 69 (September 21, 1897), *Origins of Psychoanalysis*, p. 218; quoted in Balmary, pp. 64, 145. See also the translator's introduction, p. xiii, for some further information about this phrase and its associations. Masson, *Assault on Truth*, pp. 107–10, also discusses this letter and refers to it as "bristling with obscurities" (p. 110), but he does not take up the question of the possible significance of this phrase.

48. Masson's hypothesis about Freud's reason for abandoning the seduction theory, on the other hand, is that it was due in part to the general opposition of Freud's professional colleagues in Vienna and also in part to the more particular opposition of Fliess, who Masson speculates may have been engaged in active sexual abuse of his own son, Robert, just at the time Freud was writing to him about the theory. See Masson *Assault on Truth*, pp. 138–42.

goddess Juno, who is expressing her anger and her determination to punish Aeneas for abandoning Dido, the queen of Carthage, after having seduced her. Aeneas abandoned her in order to continue to Italy and found Rome; when he left, Dido committed suicide. Juno's speech occurs on the occasion of Aeneas's arrival in Italy when he concludes an alliance with the king and his daughter Lavinia, who is to become his bride and found with him his Roman dynasty. Aeneas had been married before in Troy, and if one counts the night of love with Dido as a kind of secret marriage, Dido would count as his second wife and Lavinia as his third—which makes for a striking parallel to the story of Jakob Freud, Rebecca, and Amalie. None of this seems to have been consciously noticed by Freud, but Balmary thinks both his attraction to this quotation and his development of an interpretation that screened its true import from view were manifestations of his tendency to avoid giving voice to felt suspicions about people who were too important to him to be considered reproachable.[49] It served the same purpose, that is, as his misconstruing of the Oedipus story and his attribution of the effects of Fliess's bungled operation to the patient's hysteria.

Freud seems habitually to have misconstrued works of literature in a way that shifted suspicion and guilt to children and generally deflected attention—his own as well as ours—from parallels to the story of his family. At the same time, he seems to have been drawn to works exhibiting such parallels, as though he were flirting with

---

49. Carl Schorske, *Fin-de-Siècle Vienna: Politics and Culture*, pp. 200–201, offers another interpretation of the psychological implications of this quotation from Vergil, but one that similarly suggests an unconscious attempt on Freud's part to conceal its actual significance for him. He suggests Freud probably took it from a political pamphlet by Ferdinand Lassalle that he was reading at the time and that carried the quotation on its title page. Schorske associates it with an attempt on Freud's part to avoid acknowledging his own political rebelliousness, which he thinks developed in Freud to compensate for his sense of his father's weakness and failure to stand up to the anti-Semitism of his milieu. In this reading, the Acheronta represent the rebellious lower classes that could rise against the antiliberal elite currently in control of the imperial government. According to Schorske's interpretation, Freud turned to a psychological exposure of his own patricidal tendencies to avoid acknowledging his feelings of failure for having given up the efforts he had once intended.

self-knowledge but then fending it off through interpretations that pointed away from the danger zone. Another example of a skewed interpretation of a work with dangerous parallels to the family secret was his reading of Ibsen's *Rosmersholm*. The play is about true and false secrets leading to several suicides. At the end, Johannes Rosmer joins in a double suicide with the central female figure, Rebecca West, after she has confessed to him that she drove his wife, Beata, to suicide to get her out of the way so that she could marry him herself. Unlike Rebecca Freud, this Rebecca is hardly an innocent figure. But she is not guilty in the way Freud makes her out to be; he gratuitously interprets Rebecca West as having committed incest with her father, an interpretation for which there is no evidence at all in the play, and he then assumes that her feelings of guilt about incest constitute her principal motivation for suicide. It is true that Rebecca is disturbed to discover at one point that she is in reality the illegitimate daughter of the man she thought was her stepfather, but there is nothing to indicate she ever had a sexual relationship with him. Freud's highly speculative interpretation, however, is, in Balmary's words, "that she reveals one secret (Beata's murder) only to keep another (incest with her father) in silence" (p. 71).

In Ibsen's play, the "murder" of Beata, who was tormented by feelings of inadequacy due to her inability to bear her husband a child, took the form of Rebecca's driving her to suicide by insinuating to her that she herself was pregnant by Rosmer. Balmary suggests that several aspects of the Freud family secret may have found echoes here. For one thing, if she had lived, this Rebecca would have been a second wife, like Rebecca Freud. But more significant, the stories of Rebecca West and Beata Rosmer seem to blend again with that of Freud's own mother. Balmary wonders if Rebecca Freud, a considerably older and evidently sterile wife like Beata, may have been pushed toward suicide by her discovery of the pregnancy of the younger woman, Amalie. If so, "a new character would here be introduced into the history of the fault; if that is the case, the father would no longer be the only guilty party, even if he remained, by his infidelity the probable cause of feminine despair.

At his side is another woman, ready to marry him, perhaps even ready to execute not only her own desires to occupy the place of the wife but also, perhaps, the desire of the man himself . . ." (p. 74). She also says of Freud's idea of unconscious concealment in this story: "Freud says that she renounces happiness by confessing to a crime only in order to conceal another crime. He says that she confesses to murder to hide incest. Why would the reverse not be the case? Does Freud himself confess in his work that he carries out incest in his dreams in order to conceal a murder carried out before his birth? Or if not directly a murder, then a suicide, for which his parents would be responsible?" (p. 74).

Let us turn finally to what Balmary thinks Freud overlooked in the Oedipus story. Again she finds a strange blindness to the fault of the father. Whatever transgressions Oedipus committed were not only unintentional but contrary to his will, since he had done everything he could to prevent the oracle's prophecy from being fulfilled. His father, Laius, on the other hand, had committed quite conscious crimes in his youth, and the prophecy, which was originally made to Laius, either shortly before or shortly after the conception of his son (depending on the source), was connected with them.[50] Laius had been very young when his own father, King Labdacus, had died, and he had had to flee Thebes when the regent was killed. He found refuge with King Pelops, but subsequently kidnapped and raped the king's son, Chrysippus, who committed suicide out of shame. That Laius is fated to be killed by his own son is retribution for the death of Chrysippus and fulfillment of the curse of Pelops. This was Laius's first fault. The second, at least in one version of the story, was the begetting of a son after having been warned that his son would kill him. The third was the attempted murder of the son, Oedipus, by having his ankles pierced and having him left to die in the wilderness. In a manner that bears witness to the semiotic emphasis of her Lacanian training, Balmary interprets the resulting

---

50. Balmary's sources for the earlier story of Laius are principally *The Phoenician Women* of Euripides and the articles on Laius, Oedipus, and Chrysippus in Pierre Grimal, *Dictionnaire de la mythologie grecque et romaine*.

swollen feet of Oedipus, from which his name was taken, as a "symptom" resulting from his being deprived of the proper symbol that would have made him recognizable as the son of his true father: "Oedipus, to whom all symbols are refused, is therefore passively marked by a bodily symptom. . . . Instead of a symbolic name, Oedipus is given a symptomatic name. For Oedipus, victimized by a diabolic, divisive act that separates him from what is his own, there is only a symptom where there should be a symbol. Such is the result of the father's willful disavowal of his fault and of his effort to protect himself from its consequences" (pp. 9–10).

The Oedipus story, therefore, seems much more clearly suited to interpretation as the story of how a father's unacknowledged faults bear fateful consequences for his innocent child than to interpretation as a story about the secret guilt of the child. This seems clear enough, moreover, even in the shortened version presented by Sophocles, that even a small degree of attention to the story itself should have been enough to make Freud aware that his own reading of it was truncated and twisted. To the questions, "Why did Freud retain only that part of the legend which makes Oedipus the guilty one?" and "What made Freud retain less of Oedipus than Sophocles had?" Balmary replies: "Psychoanalysis itself . . . permits us to answer: When someone thus omits telling part of a story, it is because the omitted section resembles some repressed elements of his personal life. Freud himself often applied this very simple reasoning to his own failures of memory" (p. 27). But he did not apply it carefully enough.

On the basis of her own more inclusive reading Balmary develops what she describes as "a theory of the father's hidden fault and of its transmission across generations, through symptoms, violent acts, and unconscious faults of all sorts" (p. 27), and in her second book she applies this both to clinical cases and to an analysis of the family relations depicted in the book of Genesis. We will leave that until the sixth chapter for more extensive discussion. In the next chapter we will see how René Girard also reexamines the Oedipus story and finds in it other elements Freud overlooked.

One of these, however, should be mentioned briefly here, since it is a point of connection between Girard and Balmary that she herself notes in several places: the casting of Oedipus in the role of an "emissary victim" or scapegoat. Balmary says that with Freud's choice of the Oedipus story as the foundation for a new, comprehensive theory of human psychology, "[t]he history that was expelled returns disguised as myth. One will no longer speak of the father, Jakob, who doubtless led his wife Rebecca . . . to death; but one will speak of Oedipus, without saying what his father had done and without making too much of the fact that Oedipus also led his wife . . . to a similar death. From now on, the bearer of the fault will no longer be the father but the son . . ." (p. 144). She also goes on to say, in a manner that recalls both Lacan on "the symbolic" and Girard on victimizing, "Since the fault was not recognized, it becomes necessary, as it is for every fault without an author, to find someone who can be charged with it so that the symbolic order can be, if not reestablished, at least filled in. We are therefore entirely within what anthropologists describe to us as the mechanism of the 'emissary victim' " (p. 144). She attaches a reference to *Things Hidden since the Foundation of the World,* about which she also notes later, "At numerous points our work seems to cross and recross René Girard's thesis in *Des choses cachées depuis la fondation du monde* . . . of which we learned only late in the preparation of our research" (p. 183, n. 14). For Balmary, Oedipus was such a victim and so also were Rebecca Freud, the patients of Freud who had been molested as children, and also, ultimately, Freud himself, who would wander like the Oedipus he identified with, blinded to the fault of the father by his hastily constructed theory about his own hidden guilt and that of every son.

Before passing on to the next critic of Freud, Mikkel Borch-Jacobsen, who points more directly into Girardian thought, at least insofar as it has to do with mimesis, than does Balmary, it is worth mentioning that Balmary's theory of the transmission of faults from one generation within a family to another seems itself in need of a theory to explain it. One of Freud's cases that she cites can serve as an example.[51] It had to do with a male patient who had been seduced by his uncle and who had then seduced the uncle's eldest son and two of his own sisters. Freud wrote to Fliess that he had traced the uncle, who also suffered from symptoms of his own that Freud attributed to passive homosexual experiences. Freud included a chart showing the family trees on both sides with arrows indicating the pattern of sexual relations, with all arrows starting from the patient. Balmary points out that in view of the pattern of transmission, the appropriate path of the arrows should run from an unknown seducer of the uncle to the uncle, then from the uncle to the patient, and from him to the younger children: "One would then get a clear idea of the transmission of trauma across three generations. . . . The victim thus becomes perverse in his turn . . ." (p. 112). She does not attempt, however, to explain how the perversity reproduces itself. Her own approach throws light on important features of the pattern of seduction and the conflicts it gave rise to, and I will suggest in the sixth chapter that there are ways in which further aspects of her thought can serve as a valuable complement to the interdividual psychology of Girard and Oughourlian; but we will see that their theory of universal mimesis is better able to explain why such patterns would become repeated. First, however, we will consider still another approach to Freud that also attempts to explain why an alternative to his Oedipal theory is called for.

Mikkel Borch-Jacobsen

Like Balmary, Borch-Jacobsen asks, in *The Freudian Subject*, why Freud chose the Oedipal theory in preference to any other: "Why, among all the theoretical solutions available to him, the possibility of which he points to himself, does he systematically opt for 'Oedipal' solutions? What are the reasons for this deep-seated preference? What orients his choice? And what is it destined to preserve, to safeguard?" (p. 191).[52] His own answer is, "It preserves two

51. Described in Letter 55 (January 11, 1897) to Fliess, *Origins of Psychoanalysis,* p. 185, and discussed by Balmary, *Psychoanalyzing,* pp. 111–13.
52. First published as *Le Sujet freudien* (1982). Quotations are from the English translation by Catherine Porter, 1988.

things, which are one and the same: the Subject (and) Politics."
What this may mean will require some explanation, but first I
would like to point out some ways in which both this answer and its
question as asked by Borch-Jacobsen also bear on the psychological
factors that went into shaping Freud's thinking. Balmary, herself a
psychoanalyst, sought to psychoanalyze the psychoanalyst and turn
suspicion against the master of suspicion. Borch-Jacobsen, a philosophical theorist, aims at uncovering contradictions and aporias in
Freudian theory through a logical analysis of his texts. Even so,
however, his approach, too, reaches beneath the purely conceptual
aspect of Freud's arguments to probe the man and the motives that
gave rise to them.

The man he discovers seems perhaps less extensively subject to
self-deception than Balmary's Freud (even if he is not free from it),
but also somewhat less honest generally. Borch-Jacobsen hints at
disingenuousness on Freud's part in the way he twisted his theoretical formulations for strategic purposes and distorted the positions
of his opponents. He says, for example, that "there is a good deal of
bad faith involved" (p. 135) in the way Freud attempts in *Group
Psychology* to reduce Gustave Le Bon's position regarding suggestion in the psychology of crowds to something he can easily oppose,
while remaining actually much closer to him than he wants to
admit. He also points out a similar pattern in Freud's theoretical
formulations during the period of conflict with Jung, suggesting
that much of the logical incoherence he finds in "On Narcissism" is
the result of Freud's effort to make himself seem more different
from Jung than he really was by emphasizing the sexual character of
libido so as to oppose Jung's suggestion that libido should be conceived more broadly:

The entire discussion is organized as a forceful response to Jung, and it
cannot be understood properly if the stakes are not made clear. Freud
is manifestly concerned here with maintaining the gains of psychoanalysis: he is seeking to preserve its originality, in other words, to
establish differences—between dualism and monism, between psychoanalysis and non-psychoanalysis, between Freud himself (as science,

Cause, or Freudian "thing") and Jung. Anything that might attenuate or blur this difference, therefore, must be kept out of sight.

And yet what does Freud actually do in this text? As we look more closely, we find him doing exactly what he criticizes Jung for doing. Like Jung, Freud speculates freely (about a "primary narcissism"). What is more, he too, "expands" the concept of libido, by advancing the hypothesis of an ego libido. . . . Not only are all these developments dictated, then, by the pressure of the adversary . . . , they are rigorously modeled according to that pressure as well. (P. 57)

In this dispute, as Borch-Jacobsen sees it, Freud was pursuing two goals. One was to maintain his own claim to originality and the ownership of the psychoanalytic movement. The other was to defeat his rival while avoiding acknowledgment of the rivalry as such. Borch-Jacobsen's critique of Freud is based to a certain extent on the mimetic theory of René Girard, to whom he refers several times, and like Girard, as we will see, he considers rivalry to be both a central motive in the concrete psychology of human beings generally and a theme that needs more careful attention on the part of psychoanalytic theory than Freud gave it. "Jung was much more sensitive to the effects of rivalry on 'mental illness' (p. 74), he says, than Freud, who failed to notice not only its theoretical importance for psychoanalysis but also its practical role in his difficult relationship with Jung. Characteristically also, on the occasions when Freud did give attention to the combination of attraction and antagonism that can take place between "doubles," he tried to interpret this as an expression of homosexuality. Such an interpretation would not only serve to support the preeminence of the Freudian system by emphasizing erotic attraction but it would also cast the opposing figure in the role of an object rather than a rival subject. Thus, in his ruptures with his own "doubles," Jung and Fliess, Freud preferred to interpret the antagonism as rooted in homosexual desire rather than acknowledge how deep were his own feelings of rivalry. And yet, says Borch-Jacobsen, "once we have learned to what extent the friendship . . . between Freud and Fliess was confused with their 'common' theoretical and professional preoccupations—once we have learned, too, that their relations terminated over a question of priority—we can no longer mistake the very particular character of the 'homosexuality' Freud is thinking of here. Quite clearly it is a matter . . . of a *homosociality*, a *rivalrous* homosociality" (p. 78).

We saw how Balmary suggested that in his formulation of the Oedipus complex Freud confessed to murderous sentiments against his father in order to avoid what would have been psychologically more difficult for him: to admit clearly, even to himself, any incipient suspicions he may have felt regarding his father's rectitude. Borch-Jacobsen, in effect, suggests something similar about Freud's sexual interpretation of conflict with friends and colleagues: he would rather confess to unconscious homosexual attraction than acknowledge how deep was his concern with maintaining his image as an original genius, an image incompatible with the admission that he could have rivals worth taking seriously.

In fact, as Borch-Jacobsen sees it, Freud's extreme ambitiousness was the fundamental passion of his life, and the psychoanalytic theory he eventually developed served both as a successful instrument for gratifying it and as a device for disguising it as a motive. Freud's theory was that object-desire comes first and all other motives are disguised versions of that. Borch-Jacobsen's own theory, which is based in this respect more on his reading of Lacan and Roustang (who wrote the foreword to the English translation of his book) than on Girard, is that what comes first is mimesis in the form of imaginative identification, with object-desire following after. Regarding Freud's ambitiousness as an example of this, he refers particularly to Freud's response to two prophecies dating from his childhood. One, of lesser importance because it was comparatively late, took place when he was about eleven or twelve: a singer in a café in the Prater predicted the young Freud would one day become a cabinet minister. The more important prophecy was from what Borch-Jacobsen calls "the immemorial eve of his desire." Freud described it as "an anecdote I had often heard repeated in my childhood. At the time of my birth an old peasant-woman had prophesied to my proud mother that with her first-born child she had brought a great man into the world."⁵³ "And *that*," says Borch-Jacobsen, "is the source of Freud's tenacious megalomania, his undying thirst for greatness (*Grössensehnsucht*), which the second prediction only channeled in a secondary way. This prophecy, then, was to be Freud's family romance, the myth of his birth, the legend of his desire" (p. 47).

Borch-Jacobsen's way of relating this to his own theory of mimetic identification is as follows:

> And this makes it clear, finally, that identification (here with the "great man," later with the Minister, with *professores extraordinarii*, and so on) induces—*predicts*—desire much more than it serves desire. In the beginning is mimesis: as far back as one goes in anamnesis (in self-analysis, we might say, if the *self* were not precisely what is in question here), one always find the identification from which the "subject" dates (the "primary identification," as Freud later puts it). In the beginning is the apocryphal "subject" of fantasy as we have attempted . . . to delimit it.
>
> This is why the chronology Freud most frequently indicates has to be inverted. Desire (the desiring subject) does not come first, to be *followed* by an identification that would allow the desire to be fulfilled. What comes first is a tendency toward identification, a primordial tendency, which then gives rise to a desire: and this desire is, from the outset, a (mimetic, rivalrous) desire to oust the incommodious other from the place the pseudo-subject already occupies in fantasy. . . . no desiring subject (no "I," no ego) precedes the mimetic identification: identification brings the desiring subject into being, and not the other way around. (P. 47)

This, then, can serve us as a basis for understanding Borch-Jacobsen's answer to the questions we earlier saw him pose as to why Freud always chose the Oedipal solution at every crossroad and what this choice was "destined to preserve," namely "the Sub-

---

53. Freud, *The Interpretation of Dreams*, p. 192; quoted in Borch-Jacobsen, *Freudian Subject*, p. 47.

ject" and "Politics." With regard to the first of these, the idea of the subject, Borch-Jacobsen says that "the peremptory installation of the Oedipus complex at the origin of the history of the individual subject is a way of short-circuiting the investigation of the subject's genesis in a pre-individual identification with the other" (pp. 191–92). It protects "the autarchy of the subject"—providing theoretical legitimation for our desire to believe that we are "subjects" or "selves" from the very roots of our being. It also protects "the propriety of the subject's desire (its 'feelings,' its affects, and so on)" (p. 192). It protects one, that is, from realizing that the relation to an "other," a model of being and desire, is always the root of our actual identity.

Freud's personal megalomania, one might say, is less a flaw of character in Freud than a paradigmatic instance of something universal: what Borch-Jacobsen refers to as "the ineradicable megalomania of desire—which is, finally, nothing other than a will-to-be-a-subject" (p. 48). The idea of the "will-to-be-a-subject" in this context, it should be said, has much in common with Hegel's notion of the subject and nothing with Kierkegaard's, a point I will come back to in the last chapter.[54] To be a subject, in the context Borch-Jacobsen has in mind, means to be an absolute object of self-knowledge and self-ownership—in his terminology, "to-be-present-to-oneself" and "to-be-free, auto-nomous, ab-solute" (p. 48). His own position, which he thinks is more consistent with the fundamental logic of Freud's investigations than Freud's own, is that the subject is not a real entity but a fiction, an image that enchants and lures each of us, just as it did Freud.

Nor can there be any sort of substantial self independent of the mimetic rapport that links us with others. This is where the idea of politics comes in. To be humanly conscious is to be intimately interwoven in the depths of consciousness with the other. All of Freud's critical decisions, he says, "ultimately add up to exempting the

54. On the fundamental difference between objectivizing (Hegelian) and existential (Kierkegaardian) conceptions of the subject, see Webb, *Philosophers of Consciousness*, pp. 100–101, 259–60, 266.

subject from the question—an infinitely disturbing one, to be sure, for it is infinitely abysmal, collapsing—of its being-(like)-the-other," which is also "the question of its *being-'social'* " (p. 192). According to Borch-Jacobsen's own rather controversial interpretation,[55] the chapter on identification in Freud's *Group Psychology,* although it was conceived by Freud "as a sort of return to the individual foundations of society," led to the resurfacing of the "social psychology" Freud thought he had dispensed with in his dismissal of Tarde, McDougall, and Le Bon "at the heart of 'individual psychology,' in the form of the identification of the ego itself" (p. 192).

Borch-Jacobsen's reasoning is that even when identification is considered as a strictly internal relation (of self to itself, of ego to ego-ideal), it is by its very nature a relation to what is "other." For a brief statement of the essentials of his own argument we might consider his analysis of what he thinks is the implicit logic of Freud's essay on narcissism:

> In the beginning, then, is the ego. The ego? Yes, but also, and especially, the Self. This *Ich* is a *Selbst* (*autos, idem,* and *ipse*), and this substantial identity or *Einheit* is indeed that of a subject, of a consciousness of self—as it happens, a desiring or loving consciousness of self: the narcissistic ego loves itself, desires itself. (Had not Hegel already said the same thing? "Self-consciousness is Desire in general.") What does this mean, if not that the ego desires to present itself to itself, to exhibit itself to itself, and that it must consequently get outside itself, posit itself as other than itself before returning to itself, beside itself? This line of thinking has an inescapable logic: the *Selbst* can relate to itself (and desire itself) only if it is penetrated by an internal difference, an intimate exteriority—only if there is a difference, a difference produced within the element of the Same. This difference, in other words, must pass between me and myself: I must

55. For a sense of the controversy Borch-Jacobsen's interpretation of Freud has generated in psychoanalytic circles in France, see the volume edited by Léon Chertok, *Hypnose et psychanalyse: Réponses à Mikkel Borch-Jacobsen* (1987).

be other than myself, and that other must be another myself. I must, let us say, resemble myself.

    This logic . . . is not made explicit by Freud, of course. . . . All the same, he allows himself to be obscurely and implacably ruled by it as soon as he uses the word *Selbst,* as soon as he invokes the myth of Narcissus (that is, specular reflections, mirrors, and so on). (Pp. 84– 85)[56]

One can see with the invoking of this last image (the reflection in the mirror) the link between Borch-Jacobsen and Lacan, and also the main basis of what he considers his difference from Girard, whom he otherwise resembles in his emphasis on mimesis and the relation to the other. There is no need, he says, "to call—as Girard too often does, in our view—on a mimesis of appropriation that would cause me to desire the same object as the mimetic double and *as a result* to compete with him in hatred" (p. 89). Rather the relation to the other is inherently antagonistic because it is rooted not in competition for the possession of objects but in the structure of identification as such. It is, in other words (and in a formulation that shows, I think, that Borch-Jacobsen is really closer to Girard than he realizes, as we will see in the following chapter's discussion of Girard's idea of "metaphysical desire"), a competition with the other for the "being" of the self. In Borch-Jacobsen's own phrasing, "the hostility arises straight out of the relation to one's neighbor, from the very moment he presents himself to me as an adverse 'I'— an outsider—who is infinitely dispossessing me of myself" (p. 89).

    Borch-Jacobsen's basic idea, as he explains it in more detail in his discussion of Freud's *Group Psychology,* is that before one begins to imitate or identify with another person, one must first take shape as a self by mimetic identification with an image of oneself. This image is by definition, however, other than oneself, which implies that otherness is posited within the very structure of the self as such,

---

56. The quotation from Hegel is from *Phenomenology of Spirit,* trans. A. V. Miller, p. 105.

prior to any relation to anyone else: "Far from supplying an origin or basis for the relation to others, the *sameness* of the ego it*self* has very paradoxically brought to light the necessity of thinking the other 'before' the ego or, more precisely, 'in' the ego, *as* ego" (p. 192). This, however, also implies that identification tends inherently to seek the destruction of otherness as such: "Original identification with the other, if it is constitutive of the ego . . . , is likewise radical violence with respect to the other—a devouring mouth clamped down on the alterity of others . . ." (pp. 192–93). This in turn means to Borch-Jacobsen that human relations are inherently violent: ". . . the 'social' womb or matrix of the ego is simultaneously the matrix of violence (hence the quotation marks that have to surround this 'sociality')" (p. 192).

Freud failed, says Borch-Jacobsen, to grasp this, in part because his theory of object-love as the basic human motivation led him to believe naïvely that conflict only begins over objects, but also in part, and on a deeper level, because he hoped it was not true. Borch-Jacobsen's own theory implies that the clash of rival selves begins as soon as the image of a self takes shape. Conflict, therefore, is inevitable, and enduring social peace is impossible. Freud, the orderly citizen of Vienna, on the other hand, hoped and believed it was possible, even if, as he explained in *Civilization and Its Discontents,* it was difficult and demanded of each person a realistic willingness to tolerate a certain amount of inevitable frustration.

Borch-Jacobsen thinks that Freud was induced by this misguided hope to develop a theory that would justify it. This is what he means, therefore, when he says that the purpose of the Oedipal theory was also to preserve politics. Just as it was designed to enable Freud to believe, against what Borch-Jacobsen interprets as the true logic of his own thought, in the radical autarchy and autonomy of the subject, so it was also designed to enable him to believe that human psychology begins in a kind of peace with otherness that only becomes conflictual at a later point, namely the Oedipal stage: "By making everything begin—the ego and sociality—at the Oedipal stage, Freud thus makes everything begin with peace, and this is a way to preserve the possibility of a united society that would not be destroyed or sapped in advance by intestinal violence, violence internal to the social body. A myth of the origin of the subject, the Oedipus complex is consequently also a political myth, a myth with a political function. It is the myth of the Subject Politic . . ." (pp. 193–94).[57] As Borch-Jacobsen puts it, "primitive identification constitutes at once the condition of possibility and the condition of impossibility of the ego *and* of sociality" (p. 193).

In this last formulation one may notice, by the way, echoes not only of Lacan on the perpetual human longing for an impossible state of fusion but also of Sartre on man as a "futile passion" seeking an impossible state of ontological stasis. It may not be inappropriate to note in connection with his specifically "political" critique of Freud that Borch-Jacobsen, the youngest figure to be considered here, is the only one who could be described as a *soixante-huitard*, one who was young at the time of the 1968 student uprisings. Borch-Jacobsen entered the university in the aftermath of those events, which, as was mentioned in the first chapter, led to the subsequent vogue of psychoanalytic thought in France as people began to look for an alternative to Marxism and a way of understanding why the hoped for utopia had proved impossible. It is not surprising that a thinker formed in this tradition, when he reads Freud, would delight in finding paradoxes, especially paradoxes that explain why conflict is inevitable: paradox can itself serve as a symbol of what is irresolvably contradictory in human affairs, and a paradox that reflects paradoxically on that very contradictoriness would be the fulfillment of every deconstructor's dream, a paradox of paradoxes.

A further paradox of Borch-Jacobsen's can serve to lead us to a final consideration of the other main point in his critique of Freud. Explaining the way Freud found social psychology resurfacing "at

57. The word "intestinal" in this passage seems a mistranslation, even though the translation was reviewed by Borch-Jacobsen himself. The word in the French text (*Le Sujet freudien*, p. 240) is *intestin*, which means "internal, within a social body"; there is another French word, *intestinal*, which means "intestinal" in English, but that is not the word used in the original.

the heart of 'individual psychology,' in the form of the identification of the ego itself," as was noted above, Borch-Jacobsen says: "The group is thus at the origin (without origin) of the individual. Neither simply undivided nor simply divided, neither One nor Other (the One in differance from the Other, to borrow from Derrida), the ego is then inaugurated as (the) group" (p. 192). There can be no individual, that is, without at least an implicit involvement in a group—even if the group is paradoxically not a group, since its essential plurality is really found within the individual as a function of identity as such. Societies, from this point of view therefore, must be seen as made up of what one might call "group-individuals," each longing inwardly for an impossible solipsistic paradise. Rather than the compassionate truce of mutually respectful stoic sufferers that Freud had hoped for, the only social peace really possible would be that in which the inherent mutual hostility of devouring identifiers would take the form of a nondestructive engagement in something like parallel play—a kind of disillusioned 1980s version of the *soixante-huitard* dream expressed in the rallying cry "Sous les pavés, la plage!" ("Under the paving stones, the beach!"). Borch-Jacobsen does not spell it out in exactly this way, but this seems a fair summary of the essential tenor of his thought.

What one really ends up with, therefore, according to Borch-Jacobsen, by following out the implications of Freudian thought is group psychology *within* the individual. Never quite grasping the full implications of his discussion of identification, Freud too, to his own surprise, found himself driven back at the end of *Group Psychology* to social psychology and specifically to hypnosis as "the example par excellence of the relation to . . . the ego-ideal, and consequently of the relation to authority in general" (p. 232). He failed, however, to understand what hypnosis was, because "this example manifestly eludes the metapsychological 'formula' that it is supposed to illustrate, that is, the *theoretical* distinction between the ego and the ego ideal (Ego vs. Father, Ego vs. Leader, and so on)" and because "by persisting in enclosing hypnosis within the framework of his theoretical 'formula,' he closes off or inhibits all the questions that might have arisen in this regard" (p. 232). Although he dismissed his French predecessors in social psychology at the beginning of the book, Freud nevertheless ended up essentially where they did, but without either realizing or understanding it: "The constructions of Le Bon and Tarde are similarly bound up with the hypnotic power of the leader, so that it is difficult to see, in the end, in what way Freud's contribution is profoundly original. Far from finding some sort of resolution, the confrontation with social psychology opens, finally, onto a very spectacular identification with the adversary, and this inability to define its difference from its other marks an unmistakable *failure* for psychoanalysis" (p. 233).

This is rather similar to Roustang's idea that the ultimate problem for psychoanalysis has proved to be that of establishing a substantial difference between itself on the one hand and hypnosis on the other. Borch-Jacobsen's way of conceiving of this problem, however, is very much his own. Roustang, as we saw above, meant that psychoanalysis had sought without realizing it to maintain the patient (and everybody else) in an infantile dependency instead of fostering individuation. For him this was more a problem of inadequate practice than of theory as such; it was a function of the fact that psychoanalysis was committed to the therapeutic use of the transference relation, which Freud never noticed is essentially like hypnosis and exposes both patient and analyst to an unnoticed temptation to indulge in a relationship infused with the power of suggestion.

What Borch-Jacobsen means, on the other hand, is that psychoanalysis has failed to realize that there can be no fundamental difference between social and individual psychology, and the reason is that it has not noticed the theoretical paradox posed by hypnosis—a paradox parallel to and directly dependent on that which is constitutive of identity itself. Borch-Jacobsen's conception of hypnosis, that is, is as paradoxical as his conception of identification. The hypnotic relation, he says, "is a relation of non-relation, is not a relation to an *other*. In particular, it is not at all a relation of identification with a paternal figure or with an ideal model, as Freud attempts to imagine it . . ." (p. 231). Rather, "the hypnotized individual *is* the hypnotist—himself" (p. 231), so that the ego "comes to (be in) the place of the other, which thus will never be present to him as an object or ideal model—it will have been immediately 'absorbed' in and as (the) ego" (p. 232), a point that, as he says, "leads us back to . . . devouring identification." Where Roustang, as well as Balmary, asks psychoanalysis to stop dominating or devouring "the other," Borch-Jacobsen asks it only to develop sufficiently clear self-reflexivity to recognize that the desire to devour otherness is intrinsic to human psychology and inevitably also to psychoanalysis itself. For him, moreover, it is not mainly a problem of the analyst's wishing to dominate the patient but also, and preeminently, of the patient's desire to devour by incorporation the "other" he finds in the analyst.

In his recent essay, "L'Hypnose dans la psychanalyse," in the volume, *Hypnose et psychanalyse* (1987), Borch-Jacobsen explains further what this means.[58] To summarize briefly the argument of that essay, even if it means repeating some points discussed earlier, Freud had wanted to dispense with hypnosis and considered the abandonment of hypnosis to be the distinguishing mark of psychoanalysis, but without fully understanding what he was doing he brought it back again in the form of transference. Freud thought the reason transference was needed was to enable repressed feelings in the unconscious to be "acted out" in the relation with the analyst so that they might be brought to consciousness. The analyst was to remain silent and distant in this relationship so that it could become clear that the feelings in question really had nothing to do with him (or her) but rather with some figure in the patient's past, the famous "third person" to whom the emotions surfacing in transference are supposed actually to refer. The memory of this figure is buried in "the unconscious" along with other traumatic material that has to be brought to light for the patient to become free from symptoms. Freud had wanted, through the cultivated aloofness of the analyst,

---

58. This has been published in English in a translation by Angela Brewer as "Hypnosis in Psychoanalysis," in *Representations* 27 (Summer 1989):92–110. Quotations will be from the translation.

to keep suggestion out of the analytic process. However, he further developed a theory as to what it was in general that was to be found in the unconscious, namely memories involved in some way with the Oedipus complex. He also developed a theory to explain what went on in the transference relation as well as why the patient had difficulty recognizing the specifically Oedipal material in his unconscious: this was the theory of "resistance."

Resistance, as Borch-Jacobsen explains, was not for Freud simply a matter of the patient's ego, or conscious personality, resisting awareness of unconscious memories; it was a matter of the unconscious itself taking over and resisting consciousness of the memories buried in its depths. In the initial phase of Freud's application of the transference theory, as he explained in the beginning of the third chapter of *Beyond the Pleasure Principle,* he thought that to overcome the power of resistance, the analyst had to formulate explanations regarding the material being resisted and persuade the patient to accept them. He subsequently decided, however, that this was not fully effective as a means of "bringing into consciousness of the unconscious"; rather the patient has "to *repeat* as a current experience what is repressed, instead of . . . *recollecting* it as a fragment of the past."[59]

Borch-Jacobsen sees several problems here. One is that whether the analyst realizes it or not, the transference relation is structurally the same as the hypnotic; it involves, above all, identification of the hypnotized with the hypnotist. This is, in fact what Borch-Jacobsen meant when he said in *The Freudian Subject,* as we saw earlier, that "the hypnotized individual *is* the hypnotist—himself." In "Hypnosis in Psychoanalysis" the way he puts it is: "The other, in hypnosis, does not appear *as other,* and if the subject does recognize himself in the other, it is rather by totally *identifying* with him" (p. 100). The analyst's deliberate aloofness may actually serve to make him more fascinating to the patient and elicit all the more the urge to identification.

59. *S.E.*, 18:18. These passages from Freud are not actually quoted by Borch-Jacobsen; I am including them for the sake of explanation.

Another problem is that Freud's theory of the unconscious is, according to Borch-Jacobsen, fundamentally misconceived.[60] Freud conceived "the unconscious" as a sort of archive of representations, with the implication that it was actually a sort of "other consciousness," in which an "other subject" contemplated the repressed representations, a notion Borch-Jacobsen considers sufficiently problematic in itself that he suggests the concept needs to be radically revised, if not abandoned: "It is time to give up all this *imagery* of subjects embedded in each other, once and for all. If the concept of an unconscious is to be retained, it needs to be definitively liberated from the phantom of the *other subject* and the *other consciousness* inherited from late-nineteenth century psychology and psychiatry. . . ."[61]

The reason Freud's concept of the unconscious is false, moreover, is not merely that it involves a clumsy doubling up of subjects and consciousnesses, but that it cannot deal with the problem of mimetic identification. (This is an important point that in the fourth chapter we will see developed in a rather different way in the thought of Jean-Michel Oughourlian, who also suggests that Freud's concept of the unconscious is fundamentally unsound.) Freud could never have dealt adequately within the framework of his theory of the unconscious with the problem of identification, because Freud's conception of both consciousness and the unconscious has them inherently tied up with representation whereas, as Borch-Jacobsen puts it, "mimesis is, in a wholly new sense, nonreflexive, prereflexive" (p. 42). This, by the way, is a point regarding which, in another recent essay, "L'Inconscient malgré tout" (1988), he discovers an affinity with the phenomenological philosopher, Michel Henry, who, as we saw in the first chapter, criticized Freud for accepting uncritically Descartes's identification of consciousness as such with representation.

To return, however, to Borch-Jacobsen's discussion in "Hypnosis in Psychoanalysis," Freud's conception of the unconscious and its contents, coupled with his theory of catharsis and his theory of resistance, carried the implication that transference, even if it was

60. *The Freudian Subject*, pp. 5–6, 41–43.
61. Ibid., p. 41.

necessary as a first step toward bringing the buried representations into the light of day in the relation with the analyst, was also an impediment to their becoming conscious for the patient through "remembrance." The reason was that transference, Freud came to believe, was itself a form of resistance, indeed the major form of it (p. 106), because as long as the unconscious material was only being acted out in the transference relation, it could not become "represented" for consciousness. To put the issue in a slightly different philosophical language from Borch-Jacobsen's, as long as the patient was uncritically absorbed in his feelings, they would remain strictly subjective, whereas the problem was to enable the patient to develop adequate objectivity about them, which meant that they would have to be consciously imaged and articulated in language so that they could be reflected on with genuine critical awareness.

The other face of the same problem, on the other hand, which Freud was also trying to deal with through the method of transference, was that if merely objective representations of the disturbing material were presented for the patient's contemplation by the analyst, they would remain for the patient only ideas—even if he consciously assented to the theory that explained why they must be true. The problem Freud was trying to solve was that of rendering the subjective as such genuinely objective for reflection. The reason he thought it could be accomplished through "remembrance" is that he conceived of the subjective material in question as being really objective rather than subjective—objective, that is, as representations contemplated by that "other subject" whose consciousness constitutes the "unconscious."

Borch-Jacobsen's objection to all this is not simply that it is a muddle; he also thinks, in accord with his own theory of mimetic identification, that Freud's aim is impossible. Freud sought, through first exploiting and then dissolving the transference, to bring the buried representations of the Oedipus complex into consciousness through remembrance. But Freud himself was forced, says Borch-Jacobsen, mainly in the movement traced above from "individual" to "group" psychology, to recognize that the Oedipal ties are themselves inextricably rooted in "a more archaic 'emotional tie' " (p.

108), namely that of "primary identification" or "incorporation." "Yet this 'emotional tie,' " he says, "which certainly remains very close to the hypnotic 'tie,' still cannot be represented or remembered, if only because it precedes the Ego, the subject-of-representation" (p. 108). The self, that is, is born *in* and *of* that identification that devours the other: "Because 'I am the breast,' (in Freud's famous phrase), because I am nothing before this earliest identification and because such is my birth, affect comes about—in other words, my being affected [*affection*] by an otherness [*altérité*] that is my identity or selfness 'itself' " (p. 109). One's own birth, however, can never be remembered, nor can the primal affective bond that gives one birth ever be dissolved, as Freud wished it to be. Borch-Jacobsen's final conclusion from all of this is that the founding (identifying, hypnotic, transferential) relationship to the other who is myself can never end but can only be repeated: "In the end, in this strange rite of passage that today we call 'psychoanalysis,' perhaps the only stake is this: repeating, repeating the other in oneself, dying to oneself—to be reborn, perhaps, *other*" (p. 109).

This, it must be acknowledged, remains a bit cryptic, even if along the way Borch-Jacobsen has articulated a number of valuable questions about the aporias of Freudian theory. Evidently what he has in mind is that the process of psychoanalysis, even if it can never achieve Freud's goals for it, could, if more adequately conceived, serve as a kind of psychological initiation in which one might reenact with greater awareness (even if not representational "consciousness") the fundamental gesture of becoming a self (while seeking by that very gesture to absorb all otherness into oneself and thus annihilate it).

Another more recent article of Borch-Jacobsen's, "Talking Cure" (1989), throws further light on his conception of the goal of analysis and on his difference from Freud.[62] Freud had begun his psychotherapeutic efforts with experiments in hypnosis, but he soon dropped that approach for the same reason he later advocated the

---

62. *Psychanalyse à l'Université.* 55 (1989):3–27. Despite the title, "Talking Cure," the article is in French; I will quote from it in my own translation.

withdrawal of transference: because he wanted the patient to develop sufficient "ego" strength to function independently as a responsible person. Borch-Jacobsen argues, in effect, that in this Freud was pursuing a will-o'-the-wisp: not only can one never become independent of the other, but psychotherapeutic healing is actually found, when it *is* found, precisely in an identification with the other. This is the active principle in all effective therapies, he suggests, from the induction of possession-trances among primitive tribes, to Christian exorcisms, to neo-cathartic contemporary therapies, "passing by way of the magnetic cures of Mesmer, the 'artificial somnambulism' of Puységur, the medical hypnosis of Charcot and Bernheim, and even (let us dare to say it) the analytic 'transference' of Freud" (p. 21). "According to this hypothesis, which I believe to be true," says Borch-Jacobsen:

> the speech [*"parole"*] that cures [in the "talking cure"] would always be, under one label or another, *mimetic* speech—that is, in the definition given by Plato in the *Republic* (392c–398b), speech in which I speak "in the name of another." Not, therefore, a speech addressed or given *to* the other, but a speech (whether vehement or calm makes no difference) in which I *am* the other, without any distance or mediation at all. Nor would this be an inter-subjective speech, but rather the speech of no subject at all (be it even an empty subject), the speech of trance, in which the "I" is quite literally spoken by the "other" whom he incarnates—and at the same time experiences, as an integral actor, all the affects of his role. In brief, the speech that cures would be the very same one that Lacan . . . had excluded from the start in his "Au-delà du principe de réalité," under the double heading of (ineffable) affect and (unreflective) *mimesis*. It would be, to put it in one word, the mimetic and cathartic speech of hypnosis. (Pp. 21–22)

What this seems to come to, finally, is that the deconstructive critique of the psychological subject is carried to the point that Borch-Jacobsen advocates dispensing with it altogether and giving up any (presumably vain) effort to help the patient develop his or her own strength in order to become a reasonable and responsible, at least relatively independent person. This sets him not only against

Freud, however, but also against Roustang and Balmary and, as will be seen further in the chapters that follow, a number of other thinkers who have also been exploring the implications of a theory of mimesis for psychology.

In the next chapter we will go to the principal point of origin, in the thought of René Girard, of the recent French interest in the idea of a fundamental human tendency to imitate others—though in this case it will be others who are, or at least can be some of the time, genuinely other, not just paradoxically oneself. We will consider after that, in the work of Jean-Michel Oughourlian, another approach through a theory of mimesis to the riddle of hypnosis, but one that is worked out in considerably more detail and with reference to experimental evidence rather than only to theory in the abstract. We will also find in Oughourlian another conception of the process of analysis as a sort of mimetic initiation, but one that reaches, through the exercise of critical discernment regarding models to imitate, not backward to inescapable infantility but forward toward the possibility, at least, of responsible adulthood.

CHAPTER 3

René Girard and the Psychology of Mimetic Desire

THE most radical and far-reaching new approach in France to the understanding of both individual and social psychology is the one sometimes called *le système girard,* after René Girard, who gave it its first formulation and initial impetus. Girard's thought, along with that of other thinkers—such as Jean-Michel Oughourlian, Paul Dumouchel, Jean-Pierre Dupuy, Michel Aglietta, André Orléan, Raymund Schwager, and others—who have taken up his ideas and developed them in various domains, is sufficiently new, broad, and complex to require a variety of topical segments over a series of chapters. In the present chapter, I will begin my consideration of the Girardian school by discussing the central idea from which Girard's thought took its departure, the fundamentally imitative character of human desire, with its implications for either beneficent or conflictual modeling. In the next, I will proceed to a discussion of the way his collaborator on *Things Hidden since the Foundation of the World,* the psychiatrist Jean-Michel Oughourlian, has taken up Girard's approach and applied it to the analysis of some particular psychological phenomena—possession, hysteria, and hypnosis— that have proved resistant to earlier methods of analysis but are easily explainable in terms of the mimetic hypothesis. Then in the fifth chapter I will discuss the socioanthropological dimension of Girard's own thought as well as that of several other thinkers who have extended his approach to the field of political economy.

In this area as in others, of course, Girard and his colleagues have built upon foundations that were laid by the generation before them. Sherry Turkle said, for example, of Lacan's appropriation of Freud, "He insists, as did Frankfurt's critical theorists, that to talk of 'social influences' on the individual neutralizes one of Freud's most central contributions: the recognition that society doesn't 'influence' an autonomous individual, but that society comes to dwell within him."[1] In Lacan's case this was conceived in terms of the social nature of language: "Lacan's theory of the construction of the symbolic order when language and law enter man, allows for no real boundary between self and society: man becomes social with the appropriation of language, and it is language that constitutes man as a subject" (p. 74). From the Girardian point of view, on the other hand, language itself has to be understood as developing out of still deeper roots in universal mimesis; and one of the things that makes the Girardian school such an important and original movement in French thought is the shift this implies from a fundamentally idealistic approach to understanding human psychology through language and abstract logic, with roots in both Cartesianism and Hegelianism, to an approach that emphasizes the concrete actuality of human relations in ordinary life and in history. The various people who have taken up and developed Girard's ideas have had their own conceptions of what this must imply, but their common foundation is the psychology of mimetic desire.

As Freud did with his theory of the Oedipus complex, Girard developed his theory of human psychology on the basis of a reading of literature. In his case, however, the literary base for his explorations was far broader, and the theory he developed grew more organically out of a careful reading of the texts. If Balmary is correct, Freud's discovery of the Oedipus complex from his reading of Sophocles was virtually an accident. As we saw in the last chapter, she suggests that Freud felt a pretheoretical and ultimately quite personal need to find a way of understanding mental disturbances that would explain them on the basis of impulses within the disturbed individual rather than on the basis of problems stemming from the fault of others—and especially not the individual's parents. According to her interpretation as discussed in the preceding chapter, Freud happened upon *Oedipus the King* at a time when he felt particularly sensitive about questions regarding the failings of parents and was coming dangerously close to solidifying a theory of

1. Turkle, *Psychoanalytic Politics*, p. 74.

hysteria that traced its origin to that sort of fault. His clearly slanted reading of *Oedipus* enabled him to find in it a model of the family relationship—with the fault stemming from the sexual desires of the son—that could serve to exonerate parents and locate the source of disturbance within the child, although by a happy and convenient chance not in such a way that the child himself or herself could be "blamed," since that source was not in the conscious and responsible self, or "ego," of the individual but in the unconscious. This fact, as we will see Oughourlian pointing out, contributed greatly to the marketability of the Oedipal theory to prospective patients and to modern Western society as a whole. A psychologist other than Freud, with his peculiar family history, might well have found something quite different in the Oedipus story than he did. In fact Balmary suggests, as we saw, that a more careful reading of that play with attention to its context in legend would actually have lent support to Freud's earlier "seduction theory" rather than refuting it. And a professional literary critic, more widely read and more skilled in the interpretive analysis of imaginative texts, might well have come up with an entirely different conception of what the field of literature could contribute to an understanding of psychological relationships.

This is precisely what happened in the case of René Girard. Girard became interested in a pattern he discerned in the great French novelists of the nineteenth and early twentieth centuries, principally Stendhal, Flaubert, and Proust, and in a variety of other major novelists as well, especially Cervantes and Dostoyevsky. He found in their works an analysis of interpersonal relations that focused on rivalry and the nature of desire and brought to light the way these are connected with personal modeling—or in the Greek term Girard uses for it, *mimesis*. In his first book, *Deceit, Desire, and the Novel: Self and Other in Literary Structure*, Girard presented a theory of the novel organized around these themes.

To state the argument of that book briefly, Girard claims that the novel as a genre came into being as an effort of psychological analysis with emphasis on the universal human need to find models to imitate and on the implications of doing that either well or poorly.

One does well when one acknowledges this need in a more or less conscious manner, chooses appropriate models, and accepts in an appropriate spirit the relationship of modeling or *apprentissage*. One does poorly when one drifts unwittingly toward models who become sources of conflict and objects of rivalry. This is more likely to happen when one denies any interest in a model, or need for one, and is scarcely conscious of the mimetic process and therefore has no real power of choice in it. Girard believes that all of the genuinely great novelists have explored these issues, with varying degrees of insight.

There is, of course, a certain circularity here in the conception of what constitutes a "great novelist," and this should be acknowledged from the start. Greatness in literature, for Girard, is a function of wisdom. As Girard conceives it, there are novelists and novels that live up to the genre's potential for the elucidation of human reality, and there are others that fail to do so. The first he has termed "novelistic" (*romanesque*) in that they realize that potential, and the latter he has termed "romantic" (*romantique*) in that they do not face up to human reality but try to disguise it, masking it behind cultivated illusions and encouraging the reader not toward wisdom but toward the folly of mimetic conflict.[2]

Girard is unusual among contemporary critics, in France and elsewhere, in taking with such seriousness not only the question of moral truth but also that of cognitive wisdom. Where many critics now tend to turn literature in on itself in such a way that it seems to have little or no reference to reality, Girard considers literature at its best—"great" literature—to be a source of genuine knowledge. As he put it in *Deceit, Desire, and the Novel*: ". . . in the great novels aesthetics is not a separate area—it combines with ethics and metaphysics" (pp. 145–46). Girard is not completely alone in such an approach to literature, of course. There is a lineage of cognitively as well as morally serious literary critics running from Dante through

2. Girard, *Deceit, Desire, and the Novel*, pp. 16–17; the title of this work will be abbreviated as *Deceit*.

Samuel Johnson and others in earlier centuries to people like Julien Benda, Jean-Paul Sartre, F. R. Leavis, and Lionel Trilling in our own, and it has long been virtually a commonplace to speak of the genre of the novel as focusing particularly on the personal and social implications of the problem of the relationship between appearance and reality. Still, among contemporary French critics Girard is a very individual figure in this respect. As we saw in the preceding chapters, French theoretical thought in the various intellectual fields has tended in the past two decades more toward the canonization of paradox, dilemma, and impasse than toward a search for positive solutions. Girard, on the other hand, has been motivated in all his work by a passion to understand the concrete problems of human existence, and he has sought this not just for the sake of a purely intellectual or aesthetic satisfaction but in order to find a way to deal with these problems in practice.

As Girard conceives of literature, therefore, it is at its best an expression of the writer's hard-won knowledge of how to live humanly well. The essential core of this knowledge has to do with the problem of desire. This is a universal problem because each human being, as he or she becomes woven into the fabric of society, is caught up in a web of desires, most of which tend to be illusory—not desires one feels on the basis of a genuine inner appetite but desires one learns from others for objects one feels are important to certain individuals who have prestige in one's eyes. Because this problem is universal, its understanding also tends toward the universal, even if in practice it may become explicit and systematic only by degrees. "A basic contention of this essay," Girard said at the beginning of *Deceit, Desire, and the Novel,* "is that the great writers apprehend intuitively and concretely, through the medium of their art, if not formally, the system in which they were first imprisoned together with their contemporaries. Literary interpretation must be systematic because it is the continuation of literature. It should formalize implicit or already half-explicit systems" (p. 3). Writers intuit it concretely, that is, by way of their own suffering in the struggle for wisdom and personal freedom; and the works they then produce guide the reader through an imaginative reenactment of their struggle. "Cervantes," says Girard, for example, "could not have written *Don Quixote* if the same object had not been for him first an enchanted helmet and then an ordinary barber's basin. The novelist is a man who has overcome desire and who, remembering it, can *make a comparison*" (p. 232). "In reading," he says, "we relive the spiritual experience whose form is that of the novel itself" (pp. 221–22).

Doing so we can discover, to the extent that the novelist has done so himself and we are prepared to follow his path of discovery, that our desires tend not to be our own but those of the models we either consciously or else unwittingly admire and imitate. Girard terms such models "mediators" because they function as go-betweens linking us to our objects of desire as well as to our aspirations for personal being. This is why he uses the phrase "triangular desire." Desire, as Girard analyzes it, is not a single line of force running between the self and its object; rather it is a triangle of vectors, as in the following diagram:

The line running from self to object is drawn as a broken line to indicate that it is imaginary. The solid lines represent the real course of desire running from the self to the mediator and then from the mediator to the object. One desires, in other words, what one learns to desire by watching the example of the mediator.

This is a simple notion, but it has broad and complex implications—as does the theoretical kernel of an elegant and powerful theory in any domain of science. To begin with, it explains the obvious but otherwise perplexing fact that desire may not only cause rivalry but also depend on it—to the point that without rivalry, desire itself sometimes threatens to languish, as in the case Girard cites of the eager cuckold in Dostoyevsky's *The Eternal Husband,* who depends on the proximity of his wife's lovers to keep his own desire for her alive.[3] Or when rivalry as such is not in question, Girard's concept of the mediator explains why one so often finds an object banal until it is transfigured by the appreciation of another observer. Such is the case with Proust's Swann, who feels no interest in Odette de Crécy until he notices her resemblance to a figure in a painting by Botticelli; or Proust's Marcel, who is disappointed by the supposedly thrilling actress, Berma, until he hears her praised (in an actually very conventional, socially imitative way) by M. de Norpois and a reviewer in *Le Figaro*, after which he even believes that he was thrilled at the very performance that had left him cold.

In Girard's analysis there are two basic possibilities in mediation: (1) that which leads almost inevitably to conflict, because the self and its model are both competitors *within the same field of action*, and (2) that which does not, because the self and its model cannot be competitors, since their fields of action do not overlap. He calls the first "internal mediation" and the second "external mediation." Two good examples of the relationship of external mediation can be seen in *Don Quixote*. The Don speaks to Sancho Panza of his admiration for Amadis of Gaul as the perfect model of knighthood: ". . . Amadis was the pole, the star, the sun for brave and amorous knights, and we others who fight under the banner of love and chivalry should imitate him. Thus, my friend Sancho, I reckon that whoever imitates him best will come closest to perfect chivalry."[4] Imitation here cannot become emulation; there can be no question of rivalry because Amadis is represented as a figure in a romance. Even if the Don may believe that Amadis once lived and performed his deeds on the same earth he himself now rides with Sancho, he also knows that it was long ago in a golden age of knight-errantry that can only be imitated from afar. Don Quixote's attitude is essen-

---

3. Another good example, not cited by Girard, would be *The Key* (*Kagi*) by the Japanese novelist Junichiro Tanizaki, about an aging man who repeatedly pushes his young wife into adulterous relationships in order to stimulate his own sexual desires for her, a strategem she cooperates in for her own purpose, which is to precipitate his death through overexcitement.

4. Quoted in *Deceit*, p. 1.

tially one of religious reverence. "Chivalric existence is the *imitation* of Amadis," says Girard, "in the same sense that Christian existence is the imitation of Christ" (p. 2).

The other example is Don Quixote's relationship with Sancho, who adopts a pattern of desire he is taught by the Don. In himself Sancho is a simple person with ordinary peasant appetites, but in the company of Don Quixote he learns to aspire to those objects that accord with the ideal image of a squire the Don picked up from the chivalric romances: "Some of Sancho's desires are not imitated, for example those aroused by the sight of a piece of cheese or a goatskin of wine. But Sancho has other ambitions besides filling his stomach. Ever since he has been with Don Quixote he has been dreaming of an 'island' of which he would be the governor, and he wants the title of duchess for his daughter" (p. 3). What is important about this example is that Don Quixote is clearly an "external" mediator for Sancho, just as much as Amadis is for the Don, even though one might think at first that in this case the two operate within the same field of action, since they travel side by side through the landscape of La Mancha. The symbolic and social space of their lives, however, is marked by a clearly defined and insuperable social gulf between them. The Don's desires and goals are lordly; Sancho's are always those appropriate to a servant as defined within the social world of Cervantes's Spain. Even the island he dreams of he can only receive from the Don and as a reward for being a faithful squire. "Internal" and "external," therefore, refer to strictly symbolic spheres: ". . . it is not physical space that measures the gap between mediator and the desiring subject. Although geographical separation might be one factor, the *distance* between mediator and subject is primarily spiritual" (p. 9).

The relationships depicted in Stendhal's *The Red and the Black*, on the other hand, are exactly the opposite. One of Stendhal's essential points, in fact, is that the world of the nineteenth century is one in which the blurring of social distinctions has rendered rivalrous mimesis virtually inevitable. The book begins with Julien Sorel admiring Napoleon the way Don Quixote admired Amadis; but in the era in which Julien lives, warfare can no longer serve as the equivalent of chivalry and all the old distinctions are breaking down. He is soon drawn into a tangle of desire and rivalry that eventually destroys his will to live. At the very beginning we see the workings of emulation in the rivalry between two rising bourgeois, Rênal and Valenod, for the services of Julien as a tutor. Neither especially wants a tutor in the beginning, but all that is necessary to make them fight over Julien is for each to become infected with the idea that the other wants him. Then as soon as Julien enters the Rênal household, he makes a project of seducing his master's wife. That he can accomplish this, as well as the seduction of the aristocratic and disdainful Mathilde de la Mole later, and reach the point of being acceptable as a son-in-law to her father, the Marquis de la Mole, shows how completely the social domains that had been distinct in the world of Don Quixote have now had their boundaries blurred, so that both aspirations and potential rivalries are unlimited. This has become a world, therefore, of predominantly internal mediation.

When the self and the mediator compete for a common object, a lover, for example, or an honor, then the model becomes not just a guide to desire but an obstacle to its fulfillment—hence Girard's terms "rival model" and "model-obstacle." When the mediator is "internal" in Girard's sense but has such overwhelming power that serious rivalry is hopeless, he can become a particularly vicious obstacle, inciting imitation and forbidding it at the same time. Girard has borrowed Gregory Bateson's term "double bind" for this situation in which the mediator says simultaneously, in effect, "Imitate me" and "Do not imitate me."⁵ He cites Bateson as suggesting that it is this sort of conflicting imperative taught to a child that is the major cause of schizophrenia.

Then there is "double mediation" or "reciprocal mediation," in which the model becomes drawn into the play of mimesis, imitating in the other the desire the other first found in him. This is all the more likely in a world in which there are few effective cultural

---

5. See, for example, *Things Hidden*, pp. 291–94.

barriers to rivalry and in which each denies that he models himself on anyone else (*Deceit*, p. 99):

> In the world of internal mediation, the contagion is so widespread that everyone can become his neighbor's mediator without ever understanding the role he is playing. This person who is a mediator without realizing it may himself be incapable of spontaneous desire. Thus he will be tempted to copy the copy of his own desire. What was for him in the beginning only a whim is now transformed into a violent passion. We all know that every desire redoubles when it is seen to be shared. Two identical but opposite triangles are thus superimposed on each other. Desire circulates between the two rivals more and more quickly, and with every cycle it increases in intensity. . . .

For a vicious circle of this sort to arise, the initial imitation of desire need not even be accurate. The imitator always imitates the desire he feels to be present in the other, but that desire need not actually be there; it is sufficient for him to think that it is. In a case of double mediation a first person may begin by experiencing a desire he feels is present in a second, and the second may then begin to feel it himself by imitating the first. The rivalry between Rênal and Valenod in *The Red and the Black* referred to above is an example. Rênal had no keen interest in hiring Julien as a tutor until Julien's father slyly said they had a better offer (which was purely fictitious). Rênal then conjectured that his competitor must be his old rival Valenod, a supposition that turned his interest in Julien from a whim into a passion. The vicious circle then became closed when Valenod, on hearing that Rênal wanted to hire Julien, decided he had to have him for himself.

All of this has become further exacerbated in the modern world through the influence of the romantic cult of originality. The idea that originality and spontaneity are marks of superiority, thus imitation is servile or a mark of infantile dependency, leads those who seek distinction to indulge in "negative imitation"—seeking difference as such, even if this only means that they watch what the others are doing and then do the opposite, so that "the effort to leave the beaten paths forces everyone inevitably into the same ditch" (p. 100). This, of course, leaves mimesis intact beneath the surface but strengthens its denial and sets up an additional cultural barrier to its recognition.

The romantic cult of originality serves indirectly to make clear that what is fundamentally at issue in mimesis is never really the supposed object of desire but the "being" or mode of existence of the model. When one emulates originality, what one wants is not to wear the other's clothes or espouse his opinions or tastes but to enjoy a similar uniqueness, to share what one supposes is his "spontaneity." Mimetic desire is only superficially a desire to have what the other has or wants; on a deeper level it is a desire to possess not the other's objects but his qualities—to *be* what he is. Girard's term for this is "metaphysical desire."

Metaphysical desire is not a different kind of desire from that which seeks the objects of the other; rather it is the same desire understood on a deeper level. It is the mainspring in each person's life that gives rise to the particular desires for particular objects. "Imitative desire," says Girard, "is always a desire to be Another. There is only one metaphysical desire but the particular desires which instantiate this primordial desire are of infinite variety" (p. 83). The objects desired by the other seem attractive because one feels that the reason the other wants them must be that he feels their possession might give him a greater degree of ontological sufficiency. Each person comes into the world with a sense of deficiency and dependency, if only because he enters it as an infant surrounded by godlike "others," the adults in his life, and he always longs to possess for himself a sufficiency similar to what he supposes they enjoy. Throughout his life he continually comes across new "others" who seem to have something of that sort of sufficiency and who arouse in him a desire to win it for himself.

This feeling may be aroused by almost any other person to some degree, but it is aroused all the more forcefully by those who seem indifferent to oneself. In all of our relationships there is probably some degree of mutual dependency and imitation. This is why Oughourlian speaks of "universal mimesis," as will be further discussed in the next chapter. Now and then, however, we encounter figures who seem to be sublimely beyond that, or at least beyond it in their relations with us. Such figures can have a tremendous power of attraction.[6] We want what they *have* because we feel that it makes them what they *are*.

An excellent illustration of the dynamics involved can be seen in an advertisement for Rolls-Royce automobiles that appeared in magazines not long ago. Two men in the driver's seats of two automobiles are waiting side by side at a traffic signal. One automobile is a white Rolls-Royce convertible with the top down, the other a dark-colored Mercedes Benz sedan. Most of us would feel that either driver is enviable, and many of us have experienced a desire for such an automobile—more likely the Mercedes, since expensive as it is, it is probably not totally beyond our imaginations. Few of us, on the other hand, have actively lusted after a Rolls-Royce. For one thing, we rarely see them and so have less occasion for temptation; for another, most of us probably think of them as simply out of reach. Furthermore, since both automobiles are in the high luxury class, we probably do not think too much about discriminating between them but feel we would be gloriously satisfied with either.

The ad is designed to reorganize these feelings along lines more favorable to the distributors of Rolls-Royces. To accomplish this it employs the principles of triangular and metaphysical desire. The photograph shows us the driver of the Mercedes, a well-dressed, prosperous, competent-looking man looking wistfully toward the other car and its driver. The driver of the Rolls sits in a state of supreme, self-contained contentment, not looking at anything in particular—after all, what in this world could attract the interest of an example of such perfect self-sufficiency? The effect is to draw us into identifying with the man in the Mercedes in his desire to be like the man in the Rolls-Royce. The ad is cleverly designed to lead us to see that if even *he* can feel deficient compared with his neighbor in

6. A good example not cited by Girard can be seen in a recently rediscovered early story by Marcel Proust, *L'Indifférent* (1896, republished 1978), which tells how a woman falls in love with a man simply because he seems so completely indifferent to her.

the elegant Rolls, we should also desire what he desires—or at least what he thinks he desires.

What, then, is it exactly that he desires? Clearly he wishes he had an automobile of the glamour and status of the Rolls. If he were asked, he would probably say quite readily that he would love to have a Rolls-Royce like that one. The openness of his face suggests that he is not a reverse snob who would deny such a desire. But why does he want the automobile? As a utilitarian vehicle, there is nothing it can do for him that his Mercedes does not do as just well. The value of the Rolls lies primarily in its glamour, in the sense it evokes of a higher realm of refinement, elegance, wealth, achievement, social status, and so on. It is not just a vehicle but a symbol, and a symbol in particular of the sort of perfect self-sufficiency the man in the Rolls seems to embody and enjoy. When we see the look of self-contained satisfaction on his face, it is difficult not to feel drawn toward it as toward a magnet, and when we see the man in the Mercedes drawn in the same direction, the pull is all the more powerful because of his mimetic influence. What the man in the Rolls seems to display before all our eyes is not just the status of a possessor of elegant objects but fullness of being.

It is that plenitude that the man in the Mercedes ultimately yearns for; the object is only a means to that end. The makers of the ad, of course, would prefer that we not notice that the object, the Rolls, is in the final analysis accidental, one among others in the "infinite variety" of particular objects that "instantiate this primordial desire" as we saw Girard put it. What they want is that we should identify with the man in the Mercedes and with his desire, imitating it and carrying it forward into action by getting in touch with our local Rolls-Royce dealer as soon as possible in the illusory hope that possession of the object will accord us the social (and ontological) status it symbolizes and thereby satisfy the deeper longing we feel but tend to overlook. For us to realize what it is that ultimately moves us in desire would defeat the purposes of those who have objects to sell, especially those objects whose value lies largely in what they symbolize. Sancho could gain a concrete satisfaction from a piece of cheese, but the title of duchess for his daughter is an abstraction, and even if she had it, she might well feel less real satisfaction than before, since she would then become drawn into comparing herself with other duchesses and competing with them for other symbols of status. It is in the interest of much of society therefore—not only producers and clever marketers, but also enchanted consumers—that the truth of mimetic desire remain hidden, and both Girard and Oughourlian emphasize how much resistance one can expect to its exposure.

Not, of course, that this exposure is something very many have ever wanted to bring about, and in a world of egalitarian ideals that is also enthralled by the cult of originality it can be expected that it will be all the harder for anyone to admit that his or her desires have been learned from others. The simplest and most popular strategy for avoiding this knowledge is to attribute the source of one's desires to the attractive power of objects. That way one can both claim the desire as one's own when one wishes to and disclaim it as alien when one does not, but without ever having to acknowledge that dependency, envy, or emulation might have anything to do with it. The last thing any of us usually want to admit, particularly when all are supposed to be equal, is that we could feel deficient in comparison with any other person. That we all feel the attractive force of objects make us fellow sufferers and enhances our sense of equality, whereas the suggestion that we would like to possess the qualities and not just the objects of others would remind us of the possibility of inequality. If Girard is correct, however, we always remain haunted by the fear of deficiency in relation to others, and any doctrine of desire therefore that denies the presence of that fear will have an immediate appeal.

This may explain the irony that Freud's doctrine of desire as fundamentally sexual was received so quickly and willingly, especially in the "puritanical" United States, which he expected to welcome it like the plague, as he told Jung in a famous remark at the beginning of their trip there in 1905. In the light of Girard's analysis of social psychology, on the other hand, the result seems less surprising. At the time Freud arrived in the United States there was probably no country in the world more advanced both in the claim to general social equality, at least among the vast American middle class, and in commitment to the pursuit of happiness through acquisitions. Balmary may be correct in her hypothesis that Freud sought out a theory that would exonerate from fault parents and other figures of authority, but it was also a theory that explained desires as expressions of object-oriented impulses arising within the self. It is probably no accident that a capacity for uniquely powerful desire was one of the distinctive qualities of the romantic heroes Freud must have noticed in his beloved Goethe, and it can be no accident either that a doctrine of desire that gives such eminence to both the object and the desiring self should have wide appeal. Even for many of those who might at first have found its suppositions repellent, it may well have seemed a lesser evil, and for those who chafed against the remaining traditional cultural restrictions on desire, it must have seemed a liberation. For a society moving at an accelerating pace from stable hierarchy and self-restraint on the part of those lower down the ladder toward universal upward mobility, any doctrine teaching that desire is the fundamental fact of life would seem a welcome legitimation for changing moral and cultural attitudes. It is true that Freud himself had a basically tragic vision of culture and a stoic attitude toward desire, but it should hardly surprise anyone that his doctrine of desire won its warmest reception in that new world that was trying to leave stoicism and tragedy behind along with hierarchy and subordination.

To an observer of certain other trends in the modern Western world, however, this line of development might seem more ambiguous. From some points of view, at least in some social and intellectual circles, it is no longer the figure who experiences and realizes intense desires who seems to incarnate the modern ideal but rather his opposite, the "anti-hero," as he has been called—one who seems to feel scarcely any desire at all and who rejects the quest either for goods or for status. In the 1990s this particular attitude no longer has nearly the currency that it did in the two or three preceding decades, not even in France where it had been symbolized above all by the universal indifference of Camus's Meursault in *The Stranger,* but it still had a fair amount of prestige when Girard was writing *Deceit, Desire, and the Novel.* Girard considers it simply more of the same, a new romanticism that reverses the values of the old but preserves its essential structure: "The early romantic wanted to prove his spontaneity—his divinity—by desiring more intensely than Others. The latter-day romantic tries to prove exactly the same thing by totally opposite means" (p. 270). "Now it is Others who desire intensely," he says, "and the hero— oneself—has little or any desire at all! Roquentin [in Sartre's *Nausea*] desires less than the citizens of Bouville and what he does desire he desires less intensely. . . . Similarly Meursault has only 'natural' and spontaneous desires, in other words, limited, finite, and without any future. . . . Not a single desire escapes the demystifier who is patiently occupied in constructing on top of all the dead myths the greatest myth of all, that of his own detachment."

The demystification of desire is, of course, Girard's own project, but the late romantic type of demystification he speaks of in this passage he considers only apparent: "Whereas romantic readers used to identify with the hero who felt the strongest desire, today they identify with the hero who feels least desire. They are always docile in their identification with heroes who provide with *models* their passion for *autonomy* . . ." (p. 272). The modern anti-hero is just another persona adopted by metaphysical desire. What fascinated certain readers in Meursault was the sublime self-sufficiency that seemed to them to be expressing itself in his characteristic verbal gesture, "Ça m'était égal" ("It made no difference to me"). "The individual who is spiritually too limited to respond to our advances," says Girard, "enjoys, in his relationships with everybody, an autonomy which inevitably appears *divine* to the victim of metaphysical desire" (p. 283).

Sartre and Camus may have experienced some measure of the genuine disillusionment with desire experienced by the "great novelists," but Girard suspects that there was probably also a certain amount of sour grapes and pretense in their own claim to detachment and much more of it in that of their followers.[7] In fact, one might even think of it as an example of the reverse snobbism alluded to above. The man looking wistfully toward the Rolls-Royce and its owner is closer to the truth than the admirers of the antihero; at least he acknowledges the reality of his desire, even if he does not clearly understand it. The man in the Rolls and the antihero, on the other hand, are essentially the same figure: both embody a sort of "divinity." The one who desires nothing because he already possesses it all and the one who desires nothing because he disdains it all are twins under the surface—and both are figures sublimely remote from the rest of us, who remain haunted by a sense of our deficiency.

Snobbism is a theme Girard discusses at some length, since it is often considered a dominant trait of Marcel Proust, whom Girard considers preeminent among modern French novelists. He does not consider the charge justified, but the reason is that Proust was a *former* snob. As he puts it in *Deceit, Desire, and the Novel*, "The novelist who reveals triangular desire cannot be a snob but he must have been one. He must have known desire but must now be beyond it" (p. 220). Rather:

> The genius of Proust's novel derives from snobbism transcended. His snobbism takes the author to the most abstract place in an abstract society, toward the most outrageously empty pseudo-object—in other words, to the place most suited to novelistic revelation. In retrospect, snobbism must be identified with the first steps of genius; an infallible judgment is already at work, as well as an irresistible impetus. The snob must have been excited by a great hope and have suffered tremendous let-downs, so that the gap between the object of desire and the object of nondesire imposes itself on his consciousness, and that his

7. For an analysis by Girard of Camus's *The Stranger* and its place in the culture of the 1960s, see *"To Double Business Bound": Essays on Literature, Mimesis, and Anthropology*, pp. 9–35. Girard also suggests in that essay that Camus eventually did come to realize the romanticism of *The Stranger* and corrected it in his last novel, *The Fall*.

consciousness may triumph over the barriers erected each time by a new desire. (P. 221)

The novelist who begins as a snob, in other words, is one who both feels keenly the pull of metaphysical desire and also senses intimations of the ultimate emptiness toward which it draws him. Putting that desire to the test and experiencing its inevitable disappointment, he learns through trial and suffering what most of us never quite discover, so that when the process of his education is complete, as it became in Proust's case, he is in a unique position to speak from experience about a disease that none of us is really immune to. He is not worse than we; rather he shares an affliction that is common to us all even if it rarely manifests itself in such extreme ways. But pursuing our common false hope to the end— the hope that by becoming like some prestigious other we will become free from our weakness and ordinariness—he experiences its ultimate vanity more bitterly and more consciously than the rest of us usually do, and is therefore in a position to create for us, through his knowledge and art, a map of the terrain that can guide us to a similar insight.

Proust's novelistic exploration of the Faubourg Saint-Germain, therefore, is able to offer the ultimate analysis and elucidation of the metaphysical desire underlying snobbism precisely because he experienced it there himself and was able eventually to come to see through it. He is also able to offer an unusually lucid analysis of mimetic and metaphysical desire in general because snobbism is a particularly pure expression of it. "The snob," says Girard, "seeks no concrete advantage; his pleasures and suffering are purely *metaphysical*. . . . When the concrete differences among men disappear or recede into the background, in any sector whatever of society, abstract rivalry makes its appearance, but for a long time it is confused with the earlier conflicts whose shape it assumes" (p. 220).

Girard's conception of snobbism here resembles that of Lionel Trilling, who defined it in *The Liberal Imagination* as "pride in status without pride in function" and said it was something that tended to arise when an elite no longer had any positive role to play in society.[8] In the earlier world of functioning aristocracy, its members could strive for honors that represented recognition of real achievements and contributions. In Proust's Faubourg Saint-Germain, on the other hand, they had nothing left to do but remember their ancestry and display their status, or, more likely, to strive for it or struggle to maintain it. It is in precisely such a world that snobbism flourishes. "Snobbism does not belong to the hierarchies of the past as is generally thought," says Girard, "but to the present and still more to the democratic future. The Faubourg Saint-Germain in Proust's time is in the vanguard of an evolution that changes more or less rapidly all the layers of society" (*Deceit*, pp. 220–21). Its value for the analyst of desire is that in that world the objects pursued are so purely abstract that the metaphysical core of desire becomes clearly manifest: "The novelist turns to the snobs because their desire is closer to being completely void of content than ordinary desires. Snobbism is the caricature of these desires. Like every caricature, snobbism exaggerates a feature and makes us see what we would never have noticed in the original. The Faubourg Saint-Germain is a pseudo-object and thus plays a privileged role in novelistic revelation" (p. 221).

What is ultimately revealed by the greatest novelists is something much subtler and more profound than merely that the objects and pseudo-objects we spend so much time desiring fail ultimately to satisfy. Although Girard does not mention this particular example, that is the sort of insight André Gide points to in *The Immoralist* with his image of North African fruit that looks succulent but turns to ashes in the mouth when you bite into it, and it is because he leads us no further than that that Girard would probably consider Gide a lesser writer than Proust (whose *Du côté de chez Swann* Gide found boring and turned down for publication when it was first submitted to Gallimard). Rather what the greatest novelists, such as Proust or Dostoyevsky, the two Girard admires most, reveal is that metaphysical desire leads toward a far more sinister end than mere disappointment with objects: it leads toward nothingness—

8. Trilling, *The Liberal Imagination*, p. 209.

toward empty violence, destruction, and nonbeing. "The truth of metaphysical desire," says Girard, "is death. This is the inevitable end of the contradiction on which that desire is based" (p. 282).

The source of this contradiction is that in fleeing from one's own emptiness into the supposed being of the other, one actually hurtles oneself into the abyss, sacrificing one's possibilities of life in the vain hope that fusion with the other will confer a plenitude and power that are only an illusion: "In the experience which originates the mediation the subject recognizes in himself an extreme weakness. It is this weakness that he wants to escape in the illusory divinity of the Other. The subject is ashamed of his life and his mind. In despair at not being God, he searches for the sacred in everything which threatens his life, in everything which thwarts his mind" (p. 282).

There are two reasons why Girard says that "[t]he will to make oneself God is a will to self-destruction which is gradually realized" (p. 287). One is that to lose oneself in an illusory Other is, obviously enough, a loss of real possibilities. The other reason is less obvious, but its effects are more dramatic and destructive not only of the individual but also of society: that in one's quest for an Other with real power, one will seek out increasingly powerful figures to try to win it from, and this will result in increasingly violent conflicts. As one pursues the objects and relationships that seem to promise the elusive metaphysical fullness, one inevitably experiences disappointment after disappoinment. The more successful one is, the more frequent and bitter the disappointments. There are two possibilities that then open up. One is to give up the chase because one has realized its hopelessness. The other is to redouble one's efforts. The latter alternative, however, leads not only to greater frustration but also to greater violence:

> The master has learned from his many different experiences that an object which can be possessed is valueless. So in the future he will be interested only in objects which are forbidden him by an implacable mediator. The master seeks an insurmountable obstacle and he almost always succeeds in finding one. . . . The *masochist,* for that is whom

we have been describing, may be originally a master who has become blasé. Continual success, or rather continual disappointment, makes him desire his own failure; only that failure will indicate an authentic deity, a mediator who is invulnerable to his own undertakings. (P. 176)

Masochism and sadism are, of course, terms that derive from the milieu of Freud. They were coined by Richard von Krafft-Ebing, a senior colleague of Freud's at the University of Vienna, who considered them the paradigmatic forms of sexual deviation.[9] Both Krafft-Ebing and, subsequently, Freud sought to understand and explain them in purely sexual terms—Krafft-Ebing as expressions of sexual hyperaesthesia and Freud as the result of sexual pleasure being bound to pain, at least before he developed his idea of the death-instinct, which he later considered to offer a more direct and comprehensive explanation: that masochism was a result of the death-instinct being directed toward the self, while sadism resulted from its being directed toward others. Girard, on the other hand, explains both the sexual deviation and the supposed death-instinct in strictly mimetic terms as the results of the model-obstacle relation: the object of mimetic desire becomes desirable not for its own sake but because it is desired by the mediating other, whose desire for it is taken to be an indication that he feels it can contribute further to the super-sufficiency he seems to enjoy. The more violent the conflict over it, the more powerful the mediator seems and the more desirable the object. There is no need, therefore, to suppose a "death instinct" as such any more than there is to suppose a sexual appetite for pain. Both can be understood simply as expressions of the tendency to seek out increasingly resistant obstacles in order to heighten the appearance of value in both the object and the model-obstacle. "The brutalities demanded by the masochist," says Girard, "are always associated in his mind with those to which a truly divine model would probably subject him" (p. 184). The individual who inclines either toward sadism or masochism is simply identifying mimetically with

9. Sulloway, *Freud, Biologist of the Mind*, pp. 283, 287.

the mediator: either positively—by identifying with him directly in his power to inflict pain—or negatively—by abasing himself before the mediator in order to believe in and worship his godlike power.

Here we can see the power of Girard's mimetic hypothesis to explain psychopathological phenomena: sadism and masochism are simply different ways of acting out, in sexual and other forms of dramatized modeling, the various ways one can relate to one's mediator as a model-obstacle. They are not special sexual appetites; rather, when they take on a sexual form, they are expressions through sexuality of a dynamic that pervades every aspect of our lives:

> Sexual activity mirrors the whole of existence. It is a stage upon which the masochist plays his own part and imitates his own desire; the sadist plays the role of the mediator himself. This change of roles should not surprise us. We know that all victims of metaphysical desire seek to appropriate their mediator's being by imitating him. The sadist wants to persuade himself that he has already attained his goal; he tries to take the place of the mediator and see the world through his eyes, in the hope that the play will gradually turn into reality. (Pp. 184–85)

Or as Girard put it in *Things Hidden,* "In the *mise-en-scène* which he creates of his relationships with the model, the subject can play his own role—the role of the victim—and this is the so-called secondary masochism. He can also play the role of the model and persecutor, and this is what is known as sadism. In this case the subject is no longer imitating the desire of the model, but the model himself . . ." (p. 333).

Sadism and masochism are not clinical essences, Girard explains in that work; they are simply terms for tendencies that are present wherever mimetic desire is present—that is, in all of us at all times to varying degrees, unless we have come to share the insights of those who have explored the twists and turns of that desire and thereby won a certain degree of freedom from it through clarity of consciousness. Rather, a "sadist" or a "masochist" in clinical terms is simply a person who has become habituated to playing these roles to an extreme degree: "After changing its models into obstacles, mimetic desire in effect changes obstacles into models. Since it is observing itself, it takes note of the transformation that has occurred . . . [and] makes what was initially no more than the result of its past desires, the precondition of any future desire. Henceforth desire always hastens to wound itself on the sharpest of reefs and the most redoubtable of defences" (p. 327).

Traditional Freudian thought has noticed the obviously theatrical character of sadistic and masochistic behavior. But with its bias toward biological and especially sexual explanations, it has treated the theatrical aspects of the phenomena as accidental—hence the terms "secondary masochism" or "secondary sadism." The mimetic explanation, on the other hand, reverses the priority, since theatrics is simply another term for the imitation of models: "Mimetic behaviour of a more or less theatrical kind is not something secondary, in the service of libidinal impulses that are specifically sadistic or masochistic. The very opposite is true. Mimetism is the motive force, and the specifically sexual appetite is taken in tow" (p. 335). The deeper thrust of the mimetic, says Girard, must always be understood as a drive toward the metaphysical: "To invite brutal treatment from a love partner who plays the role of the model, or conversely to treat the partner brutally—making him submit to the ill-usage one believes oneself to suffer at the model's hands—is always to seek to become a god mimetically. The subject increasingly aims at the model in preference to the object it initially designated . . ." (p. 334). Girard would not deny that there can be a sexual appetite, just as he does not deny that Sancho Panza can have an appetite for a piece of cheese or a drink of wine. What is important, however, is that in its more dramatic manifestations sexuality is a phenomenon not primarily of biological appetite but of mimetic and metaphysical desire; it is not a physical good from which we seek a physical satisfaction but a symbolic good through which we hope to attain a purely ideal power and sufficiency.

The same dynamic explains narcissism and the fascination we feel for the narcissistic personality, a topic Freud also found already being discussed in his Viennese milieu and which he explained in terms of sexual libido, either as a matter of the subject's feeling sexual desire for his own body or for another body like his own (in the case of homosexuality) or else as a sort of damming up of libido within the ego so that it cannot flow outward toward objects.[10] Girard comments on Freud's tendency to divide desire into an essentially "masculine" object-desire and an essentially "feminine" ego-oriented, narcissistic desire. Freud thought the latter type of desire was most often found in women of what he called the "eternal feminine" type, and he believed that it added greatly (beyond the merely biological pull) to their power of appeal, just as it does in the case of children and other self-absorbed beings:

> For it seems very evident that another person's narcissism has a great attraction for those who have renounced part of their own narcissism and are on the search of object-love. The charm of a child lies to a great extent in his narcissism, his self-contentment and inaccessibility, just as does the charm of certain animals which seem not to concern themselves about us, such as cats and the large beasts of prey. Indeed even great criminals and humorists, as they are represented in literature, compel our interest by the narcissistic consistency with which they manage to keep from their ego anything that would diminish it.
>
> It is as if we envied them for maintaining a blissful state of mind—an unassailable libidinal position which we ourselves have since abandoned.[11]

Something that should be immediately obvious about this passage from Freud is that while it describes the power of a narcissistic personality to attract a non-narcissist, and Freud himself in particular, it actually offers no explanation for this pull. Freud's "explanation" of narcissism as a matter of oddly directed libido on the part of the narcissist does not explain at all why a non-narcissistic observer of narcissists should find them any more attractive than other specimens of libidinal eccentricity. "It is as if we envied them," says

10. Laplanche and Pontalis, *The Language of Psychoanalysis*, p. 255.
11. Freud, *S.E.*, 14:89; quoted in *Things Hidden*, p. 369.

Freud—but what is the mechanism of the envy, what exactly is that "blissful state of mind" that exerts such a pull? Girard suggests that if this passage from Freud's *On Narcissism* is submitted to a "mimetic analysis," it will show "not only the inadequacy of narcissism as a concept, but the reason for this inadequacy, which lies in his partial blindness to his own desire" (p. 370).

"At no point," says Girard, "does Freud admit that he might be dealing not with an essence but with a *strategy,* by which he himself has been taken in" (p. 370). The strategy Girard believes is at work in narcissism is essentially coquetry, the enticing of desire from others by one who does not intend to respond to that desire but to make use of it for his or her own ends:

> The coquette knows a lot more about desire than Freud does. She knows very well that desire attracts desire. So, in order [to] be desired, one must convince others that one desires oneself. . . . If the narcissistic woman excites desire, this is because, when she pretends to desire herself and suggests to Freud a kind of circular desire that never gets outside itself, she offers an irresistible temptation to the mimetic desire of others. Freud misinterprets as an objective description the trap into which he has fallen. What he calls the self-sufficiency of the coquette, her blessed psychological state and her impregnable libidinal position, is in effect the metaphysical transformation of the condition of the model and rival. . . .
>
> The coquette seeks to be desired because she needs masculine desires, directed at her, to feed her coquetry and enable her to play her role as a coquette. She has no more self-sufficiency than the man who desires her, but the success of her strategy allows her to keep up the appearance of it, since it offers her a form of desire she can copy. . . . To sum up: in just the same way as the admirer caught up in the trap of coquetry imitates the desire that he really believes to be narcissistic, so the flame of coquetry can only burn on the combustible material provided by the desires of others. (Pp. 370–71)

Only in fiction, in other words, could there actually exist a Meursault. Behind the image of sublime indifference that enchanted some readers of *The Stranger* lay the real coquetry of its author, who in his early years, before *The Fall,* was probably taken in by the persona of Meursault just as much as his readers were.

Girard does not use the term in the passage just quoted, but what he is talking about can be analyzed as a variant of what was discussed above under the heading of "double mediation": the coquette's desire for herself is mediated for her by those she attracts, while their desire for her is mediated by what they think is her purely independent self-desire. He explicitly described coquetry in this way in *Deceit, Desire, and the Novel* in a passage that can serve to clarify what was meant above by the phrase "the metaphysical transformation of the condition of the model and rival":

> To imitate one's lover's desire is to desire *oneself,* thanks to that lover's desire. . . . The favor she [the coquette] finds in her own eyes is based exclusively on the favor with which she is regarded by Others. . . . she encourages and stirs up her lover's desires, not in order to give herself to him but to enable her the better to refuse him.
>
> The coquette's indifference toward her lover's sufferings is not feigned but it has nothing to do with ordinary indifference. It is not an absence of desire; it is the other side of a desire of oneself. The lover is fascinated by it. He even believes he sees in his mistress' indifference that divine autonomy of which he feels he has been deprived and which he burns to acquire. This is why desire is stimulated by coquetry, and in its turn desire feeds coquetry. Thus we have a vicious circle of double mediation. (Pp. 105–6)

Freud was "taken in" by the coquetry of the narcissist's pretense to desire himself or herself in an unmediated way. In reality, says Girard, that kind of desire can never be unmediated, but Freud was enchanted by the perpetual dream of every human being for an impossible self-sufficiency. Naïvely thinking himself free from metaphysical illusions, Freud set himself up to be their victim by providing them with a new "scientific" and apparently antimetaphysical suit of clothes: "Freud views his discovery of narcissism as analogous to the discovery of a chemical element. But an examination of his demonstration that this psychic entity really exists reveals an illusion based on an uncritical acceptance of the narcissistic phantasm, on Freud's own desire. At one extreme, his narcissism consists in falling into the snare of coquetry, while at the other extreme it is supposed to be deeply rooted in biological realities; it is one with individual self-apprehension. . . . To put it in a nutshell, Freud confuses the most delusory blandishments of metaphysical desire with the basic life force" (*Things Hidden*, p. 376).

This was, of course, the fundamental Freudian strategy: to reconceive all psychological desires as epiphenomena of or disguises worn by biological impulses. Both Freud's intentness on explaining all psychology in terms of biological object-attraction and the clumsiness he was led to in that effort can be seen in the *locus classicus* of his thought, the theory of the Oedipus complex, where all of the threads of his speculation about biological object-attraction (at least before his development of the idea of the death-instinct) can be seen to come together. Girard examines the Freudian theory of the Oedipus complex at some length in *Violence and the Sacred* and *Things Hidden*, approaching it from the start by way of its most obviously problematic feature, the difficulty Freud had explaining a son's admiring love for his father. By tracing the evolution of Freud's ways of dealing with this problem, he shows both how close Freud originally came to a positive conception of modeling and how he eventually felt it necessary to turn away from that in order to maintain, however awkwardly, his hold on the libido theory.

As an example of how Freud's early formulations of the Oedipal theory tended toward something like the mimetic conception, Girard cites in particular a passage from the chapter entitled "Identification" in *Group Psychology:* "A little boy will exhibit a special interest in his father; he would like to grow like and be like him, and take his place everywhere. We may say simply that he takes his father as his ideal. This behavior has nothing to do with a passive or feminine attitude towards his father (and towards males in general); it is on the contrary typically masculine. It fits in very well with the Oedipus complex, for which it helps to prepare the way."[12] Commenting on the final sentence of this passage, Girard says, "What

12. *S.E.*, 18:105; quoted in Girard, *Violence and the Sacred*, p. 170.

can this sentence mean, if not that identification directs desire toward those objects desired by the father?" (*Violence and the Sacred*, p. 170). This is, of course, a way of saying in Girardian terms that the child undergoes mimetic influence from the father and *thereby* learns from him to desire the mother. This indicates, says Girard, that "there already exists in Freud's thought, at this stage, a latent conflict between this mimetic process of paternal identification and the autonomous establishment of a particular object as a basis for desire—the sexual cathexis toward the mother. This conflict is all the more apparent because identification with the father is presented as fundamental to the boy's development, *anterior to any choice of object*" (p. 171).

Initially, therefore, Freud saw the Oedipus complex as having two sources that worked in parallel until a certain age: the mimesis of the father as a model for desire and the biological attraction to the mother as object of desire, with the latter eventually becoming predominant. It later became clear to him, however, that to remain consistently biological and object-centered his theory would have to adopt the latter source exclusively and rule out the mimetic. In a later summary of the Oedipal theory in *The Ego and the Id*, Freud speaks again of two parallel processes, identification and "object-cathexis," but this time he leaves out the idea of the anteriority of identification and any suggestion that it could "prepare the way" for the Oedipus complex.[13] Girard suggests that here "Freud saw the path of mimetic desire stretching out before him and deliberately turned aside" (p. 171).

An approach in terms of the mimetic theory would, on the other hand, be both simpler and more realistic. For one thing, it would be able to take account of the simple fact of a boy's admiration for his father without having to try to find a way to explain this as a specifically sexual fascination, as Freud attempts to do by way of a theory of universal latent homosexuality (*Things Hidden*, pp. 362–64). And for another, it would avoid the equally ridiculous error of projecting into small children an attitude that would require a

13. Freud, *S.E.*, 19:31–32; *Violence and the Sacred*, pp. 172–173.

higher degree of enculturation—regarding such ideas as exclusive sexual "property," for example—than they can realistically be supposed to have attained at their age, even if the child should imitate the father's choice of a sexual object by desiring his mother:

> If there is a stage of human existence at which reciprocity [of violence] is not yet in operation and at which reprisals are impossible, that stage is surely early childhood. That is why children are so vulnerable. The adult is quick to sense a violent situation and answer violence with violence; the child, on the other hand, never having been exposed to violence, reaches out for the model's objects with unsuspecting innocence. Only an adult could interpret the child's actions in terms of usurpation. Such an interpretation comes from the depths of a cultural system to which the child does not yet belong, one that is based on cultural concepts of which the child has not the remotest notion. (*Violence and the Sacred*, p. 174)

To connect the problem of the Freudian Oedipal triangle with Girard's discussion of external and internal mediation as described earlier, one might say that the child's own first inclination is basically toward external, nonconflictual mediation. The child looks to its parent first of all for a model from whom to learn about the possibilities of a full and happy life. There is a "metaphysical" thrust to this from the start, due to the obvious discrepancy between the child's relative weakness and the parent's strength. But there is no necessary reason why under normal circumstances this relationship of modeling and discipleship should have to become conflictual. The family is, probably more than any other milieu in most social worlds, a place in which the potential for internal mediation in Girard's sense is minimized. The son's imitation of his father's love for his mother need not lead in the direction of specifically sexual rivalry; at its best it can take the form of the imitation of an attitude of intersexual respect and friendship. If, in a particular case, the family becomes a world of internal rather than external mediation, it is far more likely that the cause of this will be found in the attitudes of the parents than in those of the young child, to whom adoring discipleship could be expected to come naturally and rivalry rather unnaturally.

Here, then, is another place besides the theme of victimization where Girard's and Balmary's readings of Freud converge, in that Freud's hypothesis of a rivalrous attitude of the child toward the father is a characteristic way of shifting blame from the parent to the child. Like Balmary, Girard points out that in the original Oedipus story the source of conflict lay in the world of the father:

> The "father" projects into the future the first tentative movements of his son and sees that they lead straight to the mother or the throne. The incest wish, the patricide wish, do not belong to the child but spring from the mind of the adult, the model. In the Oedipus myth it is the oracle that puts such ideas into Laius's head, long before Oedipus himself was capable of entertaining any ideas at all. Freud reinvokes the same ideas, which are no more valid than Laius's. (P. 175)

Where else might Girard's thought be said to connect with that of some of the other thinkers besides Balmary discussed in the preceding chapter? One obvious point of connection is with Kojève, as is indicated in the reference quoted above, from *Deceit, Desire, and the Novel,* to "the master" who seeks to do combat with an implacable rival so as to establish his own value and that of his objects of desire. Like Roustang, Girard does not refer explicitly to Kojève, but he has told me in conversation (at Stanford University, August 1989) that he read Kojève at the time he was writing *Deceit, Desire, and the Novel,* and there could hardly be a more direct comparison than that between Girard's emphasis on the centrality of desire in human psychology and Kojève's idea (or his interpretation of what he considered Hegel's central idea) that "The (human) I is the I of a Desire or of Desire" and that human desire is not desire for objects but rather "Human Desire must be directed toward another Desire."[14]

---

14. Kojève, *Introduction to the Reading of Hegel,* pp. 4, 5. I should mention, however, that in the same conversation Girard emphasized that he did not consider either Kojève or Hegel to have made a contribution toward what he himself considers his major original insight, his theory, which will be discussed in the first section of chapter 6, of the resolution of violence through its polarization on a single victim; both Hegel and Kojève, he says, remained bound to the idea of a perpetual dialectic of violence.

Another point of connection, even if it may be more indirect, is with Lacan.[15] If the fundamental Freudian strategy was to reconceive all psychological desires as disguised expressions of biological impulses, the characteristically French recasting of Freudianism, on the other hand, as exemplified for two or three generations of French intellectuals by the thought of Jacques Lacan, placed its emphasis on the symbolic element in desire and on the way it was tied up with imaginative identification with an "other" or "Other." Lacan conceived of the latter as inherently fraught with an inevitable potential for conflict. Roustang summed him up on both points in terms that, after the preceding discussion, should make it clear how direct is the line running from Lacan to Girard: "If, as Lacan says, desire is always the desire of the other" then to become completely free of transference would require that "the other who makes me desire must become nobody" (*Dire Mastery*, p. 19). In this respect Lacan could be described as having sketched out some of the basic elements both of the mimetic theory and its corollaries regarding internal mediation and metaphysical desire.[16]

For the most part, however, the French recasting of Freud has remained precisely that: a revisionism that remains tied to the Freudian framework. Lacan presented himself as the only adequate interpreter of Freud, and even thinkers like Roustang and Borch-Jacobsen who have been strongly critical of Freud have tended to remain closer than Girard to the fundamental Freudian and Laca-

---

15. Girard has told me that, unlike Kojève, Lacan was not someone he especially studied at any point; the parallels, however, remain signficant, even if only as demonstrating the unfolding of a pattern of ideas that may grow less out of the influence of one French thinker on another than out of a common matrix of French thought that both have shared. It is also, of course, important that many of Girard's French readers (as I have also discovered in conversations with them) spent their early adulthood steeped in Lacan, in many cases attending his seminars, so that at the very least Lacan may be said to have played a major role in preparing for a certain reception of Girard's thought among French intellectuals.

16. Cf. also Lacan, *Ecrits* (French), p. 181, where Lacan clearly rejects Freudian biologism and draws on Hegel to assert that "man has no object constituted for his desire without some mediation" because the real object of every desire is the desire of another (by way of the demand to have one's own desire recognized by the other).

nian conceptuality, even when they use it as a point of departure for critique and revision. Girard and those who have adopted his alternative approach, such as Oughourlian, are the only French thinkers to have broken not only fundamentally but also explicitly and completely with the Freudian framework. The others have sometimes departed from it considerably as well, but for the most part they have not been inclined to commit themselves too openly or unreservedly to a radical break with Freud, even though their criticisms of Freudian object-orientation and biologism are often very close to Girard's.

Borch-Jacobsen, as must have been evident from the discussion of his work in the last chapter, is a good example. His many references to Girard as well as his emphasis on imitation and the relation to "the other" make clear how close he is to Girard, but he still insists on differentiating himself from Girard in favor of Lacanian emphasis on the theme of identification. As was mentioned there, he says that there is no need "to call—as Girard too often does, in our view—on a mimesis of appropriation that would cause me to desire the same object as the mimetic double and *as a result* to compete with him in hatred" (*The Freudian Subject*, p. 89). Rather the hostility between individuals "arises straight out of the relation to one's neighbor, from the very moment he presents himself to me as an adverse 'I'—an outsider—who is definitely dispossessing me of myself." I mentioned earlier that we would eventually be able to see that Borch-Jacobsen is closer to Girard than he either thinks or his Lacanian language allows him to acknowledge. The discussion of Girard's concept of "metaphysical desire" should already have made it clear why this is true: Borch-Jacobsen's idea that the neighbor is inherently "an adverse 'I' . . . indefinitely dispossessing me of myself" is simply another formulation, for all its Lacanian provenance, of the concept of metaphysical desire; and it is not true, as Borch-Jacobsen seems to be implying, that in Girard's framework this is conceived of as merely an appendage to appropriative mimesis. Girard clearly considers the metaphysical thrust of desire to be what is fundamental in it while the appropriative element, though so common as to be virtually universal, is comparatively superficial.

It is the supposed ontological sufficiency of the model that from Girard's point of view is the real source of that figure's personal magnetism *as well as* of that of the objects that shine in the light he casts upon them.

There is something else, however, that really does differentiate Girard from Borch-Jacobsen even if the latter never remarks on it, just as it also differentiates him from Freud. This is Girard's distinction between external and internal mediation as cooperative or benign modeling on the one hand and conflictual or destructive modeling on the other. Borch-Jacobsen's interpretation of every neighbor "as an adverse 'I' " can be analyzed in Girard's terms as a universalizing of internal mediation—the supposition that there can be no mediation that is not, at least implicitly, a prelude to mortal combat. In this respect Borch-Jacobsen is an heir of Lacan's, and even more of Kojève's: identification tends always to be conflictual because it tends toward fusion, and fusion must end either with the other being absorbed into and consumed by the self, or it will end with the loss of the self in the other. He differs from Girard, and, as we shall see shortly from Oughourlian, for both of whom the tendency to identification, if it is consciously acknowledged and the model is chosen with appropriate discrimination, can be pacific and life-giving—when it takes the form, that is, of what Girard calls "external mediation" and Oughourlian, as will be explained, "adorcism."

CHAPTER 4

Jean-Michel Oughourlian and the
Psychology of the Interdividual

JEAN-MICHEL Oughourlian has a special place in the present study of French psychological thought because, of the various
contemporary figures discussed here, he is the only one who is not
only a practicing psychotherapist but also a medical psychiatrist
(Lacan, of course, having died in 1981), and he brings to the fore
themes and phenomena that tend to be more central to psychiatric
work than to lay analysis. Roustang and Balmary are lay analysts
and Borch-Jacobsen an academic theorist. Girard is a literary and
cultural critic of very broad scope, and psychological thought is
only one of his many interests. Oughourlian, who is also a professor
of psychopathology at the University of Paris V (the Sorbonne) and
holds doctorates in both medicine (with a residency in neuro-
psychiatry) and psychology, brought to the Girardian school the
special perspective of a widely experienced clinician with an interest
in the history of medicine as well as of psychology. In addition to
being coauthor of *Things Hidden since the Foundation of the
World,* on which he collaborated with René Girard and Guy Lefort,
he is the author of two books of his own, *La Personne du
toxicomane: Psychosociologie des toxicomanies actuelles dans la
jeunesse occidentale* ("The Drug Addict as Person: The Psycho-
sociology of Addiction in Western Youth Today," 1978) and *The
Puppet of Desire,* on the psychology of trance, possession, hysteria,
and hypnosis.

The title and subtitle of the first of these indicate the way the
Girardian perspective has focused Oughourlian's special approach
to psychiatric problems. Although he has a great deal to say in *La
Personne du toxicomane* about the physiological aspects of chemical dependency, he does not approach the subject primarily from a
physiological angle, as his background in medicine might have led

him to do. Rather he emphasizes the psychological needs that lead potential addicts to affiliate themselves with social groups that use drugs. He also emphasizes the social factors that contribute to chemical dependency at least as much as the physical effects of the chemicals themselves. His explanation for his use of the term *personne* in his title makes clear why he thinks this is so. One reason he gives is that the contemporary problem of drug addiction cannot be understood except on a psychosociological level, since the addictions of today, unlike those of the nineteenth century, for example, are group affairs, and the notion of a "person" in his usage expresses the interdependency of the individual and his communities; a person seeks communion with others and "can accomplish his *I* only in a *we*" (*Personne,* p. 12). Another reason is that the term has implications of universality, so that, as Victor Hugo said, "When I speak of myself, I speak of you," an idea that Oughourlian also associates with Girardian conceptions of personality. Still another, also deriving from Girard, is that aggressivity and violence play a central role in the life of both the person and the group, and much of the culture of drugs has to do with ways of managing or resolving these forces through their use in accord with the operative norms of the group involved.

In the foreword to his second book, *The Puppet of Desire,* Oughourlian says that the broad cultural implications of his earlier research into drug addiction led him into the study of general anthropology, ethnology, sociology, the history of religions, and philosophy—fields so wide that he might have been in danger of becoming utterly lost if he had not met René Girard and received from him two clues that enabled him to discover an underlying order in the phenomena he was investigating: "In his hypothesis about mimetic desire he offered an instrument for the systematic deciphering of psychological issues; and he also offered a key for sociological and cultural analysis: the mechanism of victimization. These have served as two lanterns that have enabled me to pass through the labyrinth of the human sciences without getting stuck in it" (*Puppet,* p. xxiii). There will be more to say in the next chapter about Girardian ideas regarding violence and the victimizing mechanism and their central role in both group formation and the maintenance of group identity. The present chapter will concentrate on more strictly psychological aspects of the interdividual relation, especially as these are discussed in *The Puppet of Desire,* of which they are the primary focus.

Oughourlian begins that book with what he considers the most fundamental question of psychology, that of why there is specifically psychological movement or activity at all. What is it that impels a small child to commence mental activity? How, for example, does one teach a small child to say "Papa" or "Mama" or "cookie"? How does one teach him to speak the language of those around him and what makes him reach out to learn it? Oughourlian believes that the Girardian concept of mimesis provides the essential clue: "Answering these questions does not require complicated experiments. There is no need for measuring instruments or for statistical calculation. Immediate observation, everyday experience, and plain good sense are sufficient to answer them. All one need do is repeat the word to the child a sufficient number of times to trigger him to repeat it" (p. 1). He subsequently refers to studies of child development that show how fundamental repetition and imitation are to learning, and especially to a study by Andrew N. Meltzoff and M. Keith Moore in 1977 that demonstrated that learning through imitation takes place much earlier than previous theorists had thought possible (pp. 7–8).[1]

Likening his own psychological question to Newton's about physical motion, Oughourlian attributes the causality of psychological movement to the force of mimesis, which he says is as fundamen-

---

1. Oughourlian cites Meltzoff and Moore, "Imitation of Facial and Manual Gestures by Human Neonates," *Science* 198 (October 7, 1977): 75–78, which reported on experiments showing that imitation of facial gestures, which Jean Piaget and others had thought could take place only after about eight to twelve months, could in fact take place within two to three weeks. Since Oughourlian wrote his book, Meltzoff, who teaches in the Child Development and Mental Retardation Center at the University of Washington, has pushed back the starting point for such learning much earlier, to the first few days after birth.

tal and universal in the psychological domain as gravitation is in that of physics:

> No one, to my knowledge, has ever thought of naming or defining the force which draws the child into reproducing what an adult says or does, this force of attraction, interest, and attention of which I spoke above—so much is it taken for granted, so much is it a part of the fabric of humanity. A young child has no power to resist that attraction. To feel such attraction is the child's very nature, to the degree that he or she is "normal." A child lacking this capacity would be deprived of something basic to his humanity; he would become isolated, autistic. That natural force of cohesion, which alone grants access to the social, to language, to culture, and indeed to humanness itself, is simultaneously mysterious and obvious, hidden in and of itself, but dazzling in its effects—like gravity and the attraction of corporeal masses in Newtonian space. If gravity did not exist, life on earth would be impossible. Without it, there would be chaos. Similarly, if this remarkable force that attracts human beings to one another, that unites them, that enables children to model themselves on adults, that makes possible their full ontogenesis and, as I just said, their acquisition of language—if this force did not exist, there would be no mankind. (P. 2)

Carrying further the analogy of "universal mimesis" to the theory of universal gravitation, Oughourlian goes on to say that there is also something fundamentally like Newton's conception of "mass" at work in it and that this can be helpful in explaining both small-scale interactions and the problems of group psychology:

> . . . it could be said that the mimesis between two individuals is the force of attraction that each simultaneously exerts on the other and submits to. This force is proportional to the mass, as it were, of each and inversely proportional to the distance between them.
>
> What, however, is it that one can refer to as "mass" in psychology? For a young child in his or her relation to an adult, the notion of "mass" can be interpreted almost literally: the mass of the adult in

comparison with that of the child explains the latter's tendency to seek and submit to the adult's influence. Between adults there is also a force of attraction, but in this case the notion of "mass," which is to say, that which each represents for the other and the capacity each has to influence or attract the other, becomes more complex. Mass also correlates closely with quantity. The mimesis that a crowd triggers, the power of influence a group has, is proportional to the number of individuals in it. It is this prodigious magnification of the force of mimesis that explains the difference between the psychology of individuals and mob psychology and the stupendous transformations that the former can undergo when influenced by the mimetic power of a group, a crowd, or a mob. (Pp. 3–4)

Taking his cue from Girard's discussion of mimetic rivalry, Oughourlian also goes on to speak of how, like gravitation, "mimesis is at once a force of attraction and a force of repulsion: imitation begins as discipleship, in which the model is taken simply as a model. But before long, the imitation of a gesture will cause the model and the disciple to grasp at the same object: the model will become a rival, and mimesis will take on the character of conflict. In this way mimesis engenders both attraction and repulsion" (p. 4). This is a major reason why mimesis in the form of identification does not end in fusion, just as two corporeal masses drawn together by the force of gravity do not necessarily collide.

Mimesis also has both spatial and temporal dimensions as imitation and repetition. The former, the imitation of the gestures and attitudes of others, the capacity for communication and empathy, is central to the formation of society; while the latter, as the source of habit formation and memory, is fundamental to the psychological development of the individual:

Universal mimesis, considered as a principle of gravitation, binds people together and constitutes the human being as a "social" animal essentially through its spatial dimension, which is to say, imitation: this is man's *sociogenesis*. . . . by its temporal dimension mimesis holds a person together and constitutes him as "psychological" man: this is his *psychogenesis*. These two absolutely inseparable dimensions, the spatial and the temporal, together cause our ontogenesis. (P. 6)

This is why Oughourlian says, as was mentioned in the preface, that human ontogenesis is "as dependent on psychology as it is on sociology—two sciences that are artificially separated, but which in reality make up a single science" (p. 7).

One of the most important implications he derives from this conception is "that mimesis precedes consciousness and creates it by its action" (p. 6). The psychological "self," that is, is a function of imitation and repetition, a result of mimetic learning, and it is organized particularly around patterns of desire, which Oughourlian agrees with Girard in conceiving of as completely mimetic. Like Girard, as I mentioned in the first chapter, Oughourlian distinguishes between desire on the one hand, which is an artificial appetite aiming at purely symbolic goods that one learns to desire by imitating the real or supposed desires of others, and on the other hand the natural appetites, which aim at real but limited goods, like Sancho Panza's piece of cheese (which is not to say that, depending on its context, even a piece of cheese cannot sometimes become less food than symbol). Girard usually contrasts "desire" with "appetite" while Oughourlian uses the sort of language specific to the field of psychology: "One must keep in mind my definition of desire and avoid confusing it with need and instinct, a habitual way of thinking that one can easily slip into" (p. 175 n.). But the distinction they refer to is the same. It is desire, in this mimetic sense, that becomes the nucleus, according to Oughourlian, of what he terms the "self of desire" (*le moi du désir*).

Because patterns of desire may change over time, a given individual or "holon" (to use the term Oughourlian took from Arthur Koestler, as was explained in the first chapter) may have a multiplicity of personalities or selves, some of which may be radically discontinuous with others. This is a theme Girard took up as well, in his discussion of Proust in particular in *Deceit, Desire, and the Novel* (pp. 90–91), where he linked it with the theme of mediation.

Every mediation projects its mirages; the mirages follow one another like so many "truths" which take the place of former truths by a veritable murdering of the living memory and which protect themselves from future truths by an implacable censure of daily experience. Proust calls "Selves" the "worlds" projected by successive mediations. The Selves are completely isolated from each other and are incapable of recalling the former Selves or anticipating future Selves.

Girard also discusses Stendhal and Dostoyevsky in this connection, the first as describing a lesser degree of discontinuity of personality than that depicted in the work of Proust and the latter a greater degree:

> The first signs of the hero's fragmentation into monadic Selves can be seen in Stendhal. The Stendhalian hero's sensibility is subjected to abrupt changes which foreshadow the successive personalities of *Remembrance of Things Past*. The personality of Julien Sorel remains an unbroken unity but this unity is threatened at the time of that temporary aberration which is his love for Mathilde. . . . The greatest suffering is reserved for Dostoyevsky's hero. The underground man's mediators succeed one another so rapidly we can no longer even speak of distinct Selves. The periods of relative stability, separated by violent crises or intervals of spiritual emptiness, which we have seen in Proust, are supplanted in Dostoyevsky by a perpetual crisis.

Where Girard took his data bearing on this point from imaginative literature, Oughourlian took his primarily from classic studies of hypnosis, particularly Pierre Janet's accounts of his hypnotic experiments. Or perhaps it would be more precise to say that Girard's discussion of multiple personality is drawn from the insights of imaginative authors, while Oughourlian's discussion of the self of desire is an attempt to draw upon Girard's formulation of those same insights to explain data that were turned up in experiments by Charcot, Bernheim, Janet, and other investigators of hypnosis but that they were unable to explain. What the experimentalists found were odd facts, but apart from a few rudimentary concepts, such as suggestion, influence, trance, and so on, they had no explanation for them and no way of integrating them with the rest of their thinking about personality.[2]

What Janet observed in experiments with posthypnotic suggestion was that subjects in the deepest stage of hypnosis, termed "somnambulism" by Bernheim, developed new "selves" that were quite distinct from the ordinary or waking self and had different sets of memories. As Oughourlian summarizes Janet's account, he "could cause a new self to develop by way of somnambulism, for example, new personalities for Lucie 1 and Léonie 1, which he called Lucie 2 and Léonie 2. When state 2 was well established, he hypnotized Lucie 2 and Léonie 2 again. Another hypnotic swoon took place, marking the dissolution of [self] S^2 and putting an end to state 2, and then after that a state 3 took shape, more or less rapidly, giving birth within a deeper state of somnambulism to another new self, a new personality posterior to the prior ones, a Lucie 3 and a Léonie 3" (Puppet, p. 237).[3] Janet formulated three laws of memory to describe these phenomena:

1. Complete forgetfulness during the normal waking state of everything that took place during somnambulism.
2. Complete remembrance during a new state of somnambulism of everything that took place during preceding states of somnambulism.
3. Complete remembrance during somnambulism of everything that took place during the waking state.[4]

But these laws were only descriptions of regularities; they were not in themselves explanatory. Oughourlian found, as will be explained shortly, that his hypothesis regarding the organization of conscious-

---

2. See Sulloway, Freud, Biologist of the Mind, pp. 43–50, for a concise account of the history of hypnosis and hypnotic theory among such seminal figures as Auguste-Ambroise Liébault (1823–1904), Jean-Martin Charcot (1825–93), and Hippolyte Bernheim (1840–1919), as well as Freud. Pierre Janet (1859–1947) was a student of Charcot's and his successor at Salpêtrière.

3. Referring to Janet, L'Automatisme psychologique, pp. 98–103.

4. Ibid., p. 88; quoted in Oughourlian, Puppet, p. 235.

ness through mimetic desire was able to offer an explanation for these phenomena that was both simple and complete.

To step back for a moment, however, from the special problems of somnambulism to the broader theory of universal mimesis and state Oughourlian's hypothesis in the most basic terms: its starting point is the idea that human beings are both involved in and themselves constitute, by their innate mimetic tendencies, a field of forces which impinge on all simultaneously, although with varying degrees of intensity. On the level of a pair of individuals, A and B, one might say: A has a tendency to imitate the actions, the thoughts, the feelings and attitudes, and so on of B; while B has the same tendency with regard to A, although more weakly or strongly, depending on the state of relative deficiency or power.

Depending on the angle from which one considers the process to which this tendency gives rise, one may speak of it either as imitation or as influence. One and the same mimetic process, that is, may be viewed as imitation if one thinks of it as something A, for example, is doing to B, or as influence, if one thinks of it as a corresponding pull or attractive force exerted on A by B. To picture it in terms of diagrams, one may say that what appear to be two different vectors indicated by the two arrows (influence and imitation) in the diagram at left, are actually aspects of a single process, mimesis—so that the two can be equally represented as a single two-directional arrow in the equivalent diagram on the right:

In the normal course of events, moreover, both A and B experience the tendency to imitate the other (or, to put it the other way around, each exerts a certain degree of attraction with regard to the other), so that comprehensively considered, the two-directional arrow of mimesis in the right-hand diagram should be viewed as including not only both influence and imitation but also each flowing in both directions. To state the matter in terms of Oughourlian's analogy between mimesis and gravitation, there is normally a relative balance between the forces of velocity, inertia, and gravitation that keeps one entity or holon from colliding with or being engulfed in the other. And there is also a possibility of imbalance. In the Newtonian analogy, a smaller body such as an asteroid may collide with a planet and merge with it, or else if it retains enough of its own inertial velocity not to collide with the planet but lacks enough to escape its gravitational pull, it will become a satellite of the larger body—and perturb its orbit to some degree through its own residual force.

The interdividual relation operates similarly. It is common for some individuals or holons to exert greater influence on others and thereby make satellites of them, but not without some corresponding influence coming in return from the other. The relations between a parent and child or a teacher and student can serve as examples. The parent has more psychological "mass" than a young child; a mother has less need of the child than the child has of her, at least until the child grows older and their respective positions of need, power, and influence gradually reverse. But even while the child is quite young, the parent feels some responsiveness to the feelings and attitudes of the child. A young child's anger might not feel as painful to his mother as hers does to him, but it is usually not without at least some effect, and the affection between them is similarly reciprocal. So also a teacher normally is in a position of superior knowledge and authority, but a student's questions, if they reach into new territory or bring to light unrecognized problems, may stimulate further thought in the teacher, perhaps even leading him to adopt a whole new approach to the subject at issue.

During the course of a person's life, there are all sorts of relationships that he or she develops with other individuals and with the society and culture as a whole—or, as Oughourlian terms them, the "other" and the "Great Other." Everyone feels the force of the opinions, attitudes, and feelings of others and of the group to which he or she belongs. Sometimes the relationship may also be with a culturally defined figure representing qualities that the group wants to encourage, as in the Christian's imitation of Christ—a pattern that is, of course, familiar already as Girard's "external mediation." Sometimes the mimetic rapport may take on a special intensity and lead to what has long been called "possession," which from this point of view consists essentially of an imitation so powerful that one loses one's ordinary sense of independent selfhood in it, identifying one's thoughts, feelings, and desires with those of the other, or Other. When this is unwanted, one may undertake an "exorcism" to become free from it. Or if it is wanted, as in the case of various African and Caribbean possession cults, shamanism, Christian "dying into Christ" in Baptism and Holy Communion, and so on, then one may engage in rites of what Oughourlian calls "adorcism" to encourage it. To state it in terms of the astronomic analogy, adorcism is the process by which one seeks to become a satellite of some approved figure, and exorcism is the process by which one who has become such a satellite tries to break free from the orbit imposed by the greater effective mass of the other.

Hypnosis, therefore, is a case in which the mass of one holon, the hypnotist, is so great in comparison with that of the hypnotized, especially in the deeper degrees of hypnosis classified as somnambulism, that the hypnotized loses his own personality proportionately in that of the hypnotist. This is like an extreme case of possession, though with differences that will be explained below. Oughourlian also uses the same principle to explain the power with which individuals in a group are drawn to share a single pattern of attitudes, merging, as it were, into a single collective mentality (*Puppet*, pp. 227–28):

In a crowd . . . the force of mimetic attraction and suggestion will increase enormously around each holon, drawing out of him his self of desire. The desire of each holon then dissolves into that of the crowd and submits to it. Here psychological mass blends with numerical. Holons caught up in a crowd are in a state of somnambulism; this somnambulism is plural and has nothing to do with sleep. It takes over right away and quite forcefully, without passing through the clinical phases of lethargy and catalepsy, because . . . the force of mimesis is so heightened in a crowd that in this case the other-self-of-the-other-desire substitutes itself immediately for the dissolved self of desire of the individual.

The result, Oughourlian goes on to say, is "a collective self of a collective desire": "A new reality is born, a new self: the mass or crowd, this gigantic protoplasm, this monstrous polynuclear cell, each nucleus of which, having lost the membrane that surrounded it and gave it a semblance of individuality, is immersed in the mimetic torrent that pulls it along with all the rest" (p. 228).

The reader will remember how in the second chapter, in the section on Borch-Jacobsen, Freud was seen to have raised, in his *Group Psychology,* the subject of Tarde's hypotheses of social imitation and Le Bon's of "the mutual suggestion of individuals and the prestige of leaders" only to dismiss them in favor of his own libido theory as an explanation of the tendency of people in crowds to think and feel alike and to become highly susceptible to influence. In the continuation of the passage just quoted, Oughourlian, on the other hand, explicitly recalls his French predecessors and carries forward within the framework of his own theory of mimesis the approach they initiated (pp. 228–29):

Plural somnambulism, fusion of desires, mimetic gigantism, dissolution of the self of desire of the individual holon—this is a crowd. Le Bon puts it in almost the same terms: "The fading out of the conscious personality and the orientation of thoughts and feelings in a single direction" are the first marks "of a crowd in the process of organizing itself." There then manifests itself "the psychological law of the mental unity of crowds," which consists in the abandonment of individuality and the birth of a *"collective soul. . . ."* The captive of a psychology of consciousness and fascinated by Freud, Le Bon characterized plural somnambulism by reference to the unconscious personality. Now it is evident . . . that the determining factor is actually the other's desire, that is, mimetic desire.[5]

5. The references to Le Bon are to *La Psychologie des foules,* new edition, edited by Otto Klineberg (Paris: Presses Universitaires de France, 1963), book 1, ch. 1, p. 10 and p. 11 respectively.

Freud also sensed—correctly, Oughourlian would say—that there was a significant parallel between the phenomena of group psychology and those of hypnosis, but his only explanation for either was in terms of libido: an erotic attraction either to the group's leader or to the hypnotist. In chapter 2 we also considered a passage from Freud's *Group Psychology* in which he likened hypnosis to being in love, with the hypnotized showing "the same humble submission, docility, absence of criticism, toward the hypnotist as toward the loved object, the same absorption of the subject's own initiatives," so that "the hypnotic relation is the unlimited devotion of someone in love, but to the exclusion of sexual satisfaction." I said there that if Oughourlian were to comment on that passage, he would probably suggest that it would be more illuminating to try to understand both hypnosis and being in love as functions of sympathetic involvement in the subjectivity of the other. In love, there is normally a mutual interpenetration of subjectivities that gives psychological substance to the saying that in a marriage the spouses "become one flesh." The major difference, which Freud seems to have overlooked, between being in love and hypnosis is to be found precisely here: that between lovers the subjective interpenetration is reciprocal whereas between the hypnotized and the hypnotist the relation is unidirectional.

From the point of view of the mimetic hypothesis, the essential element in hypnosis is that the hypnotized feels a powerful urge to imitate the attitudes and desires of the hypnotist. This explains why, as we also saw Freud observe, the hypnotized takes his cues as to what is real from the hypnotist, as well as why the hypnotized feels impelled to carry out the hypnotist's commands: his mimetic impulsion leads him to experience *as his own* the beliefs and desires he perceives or feels to be present in the hypnotist. The hypnotist feels no such urge with regard to the hypnotized, and one may assume that if he did, he would probably prove to be rather ineffective as a hypnotist. It is precisely the hypnotist's aloofness and imperviousness to mutuality that give him the power to elicit from the hypnotized so powerful and one-sided a mimesis.

Hypnosis is also, of course, what Girard would call an example of external mediation, since there is no question of rivalry between hypnotized and hypnotist, at least for the duration of the trance. This is why, as Oughourlian states it, "*direct* suggestions are possible in somnambulism because the model functions simply as a model and progressively forms the self; the self is in a learning mode, watching the actions and desires of the model in order to reproduce them, and the model does not set up any resistance to this mimesis, but willingly remains a model" (p. 234). In ordinary life, on the other hand, suggestion has to do its work indirectly, because the subject usually tends to see the model as a rival and does not want to learn from him but rather to take what he has, while the model himself usually does not want to be imitated but prefers to retain exclusive ownership of both his objects and desires.

That the hypnotized actually experiences the other's wishes as though they were his own explains in a clear and straightforward way, therefore, why hypnotic commands are effective. The hypnotized "obeys" the commands not, strictly speaking, as "commands" at all; rather, imitating subjectively the desires he finds, or feels he finds, in the hypnotist, he experiences them as his own desires, so that when he acts, he is, as far as his experience of it is concerned, simply doing as he himself wishes. Although Oughourlian does not put it in exactly these terms, one might say that here the analogy to gravitation shifts from Newtonian conceptions to those of Einsteinian relativity, in which astronomic bodies do not, as in the Newtonian framework, curve in their trajectories to move around another body, but always move straight ahead *relative to their own spatial frame of reference*. The new self of desire that forms in the hypnotized has no other desire than that which he finds in the hypnotist, because "[m]imesis is the physiological mechanism that presides over the formation of the self and therefore of the consciousness that is its attribute" (p. 232). (Oughourlian is here using the term "physiological" in the medical sense, to mean normal as compared with pathological; he does not intend a biological reductionism, though he recognizes that mimesis has to have a neurological foundation.) The ordinary self of desire, with the organization of consciousness defined by its ordinary desires, "swoons or fades out" and a "new self then comes to birth" in the hypnotized that is "progressively generated by the other's desire," the desire of the hypnotist (p. 234). The hypnotic subject "is *constituted* and *moved* by the other's desire" in such a way that "[t]he new self that takes shape is a self-of-the-other's-desire, of the other-desire now present within the holon" (p. 234). The hypnotized therefore has no need to subordinate "his own" desires to those of the other in order to obey his commands; rather the other's desires have become, in effect, his own. Relative to his experiential frame of reference, to use the Einsteinian analogy, he is proceeding in a straight line, the line indicated to him by what he experiences as his own inclinations.

This means that strictly speaking it would probably be more precise not to use the term "command" with regard to hypnosis at all. There is a fundamental difference between a command and a hypnotic suggestion. Whereas a command is addressed to an already established self of desire formed by an earlier, independent psychogenesis and requires that the hypnotized's "memory must maintain at each moment a recollection of the other and his desire" so that "if, for any reason, it becomes distracted and forgets either one or the other, the action stops and the execution of the command is interrupted" (p. 232), hypnotic suggestion works in just the opposite way. Instead of imposing the will of the other on an already existing self, it exploits the mechanism of mimesis in order to elicit in the hypnotic subject the formation of a new self of desire organized around the hypnotist's desire. Constituted and moved as it is by that desire, then, the subject is incapable of apprehending the hypnotic suggestion as a "command," since this would require memories that are no longer present because they have gone into eclipse with the old self of which they were a function. As Oughourlian explains the process:

> Consciousness cannot grasp a suggestion in the moment it is produced by that suggestion; memory cannot help progressively forgetting a suggestion as that suggestion constitutes it, just as the egg and sperm lose their individuality, progressively effacing the traces of their origin as they constitute a new being. . . . The difference between a command ("Move your arm") and a suggestion ("Now your arm is mov-

ing") resides in the fact that to execute the command, the holon must *remember,* throughout the action, both the command and the one who gave it, whereas, in suggestion, it is both necessary and sufficient that the holon progressively *forget the suggestion in proportion as he enacts it.* (P. 232)

He must experience the suggestion, that is, not as a command, nor even as "a suggestion," but as a volition arising spontaneously within himself. Enacting it, he will then have no need to overcome any inner resistance but will have the feeling of doing exactly as he pleases. The new self of desire simply proceeds straight ahead, fulfilling the other's wishes indirectly and accidentally, one might say, as it aims at what it interprets as its own personal goals.

This constitutes a simple and complete explanation for the effectiveness of hypnotic and posthypnotic suggestions. It is, moreover, the first genuine explanation of these phenomena; it does not just say that hypnosis is the result of "influence" but explains what influence or suggestion themselves must be and how they must operate if they are to produce the effects observed. Anton Mesmer's eighteenth-century theory of "animal magnetism" is the only other one that tried really to explain hypnotic effects, and Oughourlian expresses his respect for Mesmer for having made that effort, even if the theory itself had drawbacks that made it only too easy for the standard science of Mesmer's time to discredit it. This had the unfortunate result that subsequent research into hypnosis has tended to be rather shy of theory. Post-Mesmerian discussion, in consequence, never managed to pass, until now, from an essentially descriptive approach in terms of "suggestion," "suggestibility," and "influence" to a genuinely explanatory one.

Oughourlian's mimetic theory of hypnosis, therefore, offers a major theoretical advance in accounting for phenomena that have long been observed but never adequately explained. It is certainly more explanatory than to say, as we saw Freud do in the passage from *Group Psychology* referred to earlier, that "the ego experiences as a dream whatever the hypnotist requests and asserts." There is a certain similarity between dreaming consciousness and deep hynosis in that in both the subject accepts appearances at face value as reality, but the resemblance between the two states is actually rather slight, as Bernheim himself noted in *De la suggestion* (1886): "There have been reports of a hypnotic type of lethargy, but I have never been able to verify this. In the deepest of induced sleeps, when the patient is inert, immobile, indifferent to what happens, and seems to have been reduced to a vegetative state, he still knows what is happening around him; he hears me, since I am able by stimulating him . . . to obtain from him a response or gesture."[6]

Bernheim's impression has since been confirmed by the modern method of the electroencephalogram, which shows that "the brain-wave patterns of hypnotized subjects are practically identical with those of people who are awake" (*Puppet*, p. 207). In the hypnotic state, therefore, even if what is presented as real is not critically questioned any more than it is in sleep, this is not for the same reason. Rather the reason no question arises is that the new hypnotic self of desire already has what he feels is a sufficient answer, having assimilated as fundamental elements in his own consciousness the beliefs as well as the desires displayed by his hypnotist-model—who precisely as a model could be said, of course, to function as an "ego-ideal," to use Freud's phrase but with greater explicitness of meaning.

The assimilation of the attitudes of the hypnotist, it should be noted, is not immediate and total, but takes place by degrees. As somnambulism replaces catalepsy, "[t]he nascent self, the other-self of the hypnotized holon (*h*) constitutes itself gradually, at widely varying speeds and to similarly varying degrees, with its different attributes, especially consciousness, speech, and memory" (p. 215). "The progressive development of autonomy in the nascent self of *h*," says Oughourlian, "sketches out before our eyes the evolution of the mimetic movement. The cataleptic wax passively received a form directly impressed on it by the model. The other-self comes to birth by actively modeling itself—by first modeling its gestures, its attitude, and then its feelings and reactions, in a simple and immedi-

6. Bernheim, *De la suggestion*, pp. 77–78; quoted in Oughourlian, *Puppet*, p. 207.

ate way, on the model's appearance, and later, in a more complex and mediated manner, on the model's *desire*" (p. 216). In the process, the new self of desire acquires its own set of memories shaped by its experience and organized around its own newly acquired desires. This is why, as we saw above was suggested by both Proust and Janet, a single holon may consequently have several "selves," each with its own attitudes, consciousness, and memories and each a function not only of the individual holon but also of the interdividual relation with whatever "other" serves as his model.

The psychological "self," therefore, is always a "self-between"— a point that Oughourlian brings to a greater degree of theoretical clarity than any other thinker discussed here. The individual holon that serves as its base, one might say, is only the starting point for the formation of the self, which is constantly being formed and reformed by the shifting pattern of its interdividual relations with the real others in its life as well as with the idealized models (the saint's Christ, Don Quixote's Amadis of Gaul, Julien Sorel's Napoleon, and so on) offered to it by its culture. Under normal circumstances the changes are gradual and continuous enough that they do not result in complete discontinuity of consciousness. This is why, although we experience change, we continue to retain our memories and experience a certain unity of psychological selfhood over time, despite the fact that, as Proust described so perceptively, the hand that early in the morning still reaches over to the other side of the bed toward Albertine a year after her death can be spoken of as the hand of an earlier self discontinuous with the one who will come to the fore on full waking.

That a single individual or holon may serve as the juncture of multiple selves may seem surprising to the ordinary way of looking at things, but it is not only consistent with Oughourlian's theory of interdividual psychology, it is also consistent with the experimental observations of Janet regarding somnambulism that were referred to earlier. In fact Oughourlian's theory alone is able to account for the fact that led Janet to formulate the three laws of memory quoted above. In this respect, hypnosis serves not only as an illustration of Oughourlian's hypnotheses regarding mimesis and the organization of consciousness around a fundamental pattern of desire but also as its experimental confirmation.

Janet, as was mentioned, found in experiments with somnambulism (1) that the hypnotized would, on "awakening," or return from the hypnotic state, show complete amnesia with regard to everything that happened during it; (2) that when rehypnotized he would remember everything that happened during previous states of somnambulism; and (3) that he would also then be able to remember the events of the "waking" state as well. He also found that a hypnotized person could be subjected to another, new state of hypnosis in which an additional new personality (self S^3) would form that would also be forgotten by S^2 on return to the first state of hypnosis but that would return with a subsequent second hypnosis and would then remember its own experiences as well as those of both S^2 and the normal waking self, S^1. It has also been observed by many investigators that after a posthypnotic suggestion has been carried out, the person who did it will have no memory of having done so or of the suggestion ever having been made. If asked afterward why he did whatever it was, he will give some other, quite fictitious, explanation. If he is interrupted in the process of enacting it, on the other hand, he will be able to recognize what he has been doing and will remember the suggestion.

Oughourlian's explanation for Janet's first two observations—about amnesia regarding what happened under hypnosis and recovery of the memory under subsequent hypnosis and about the possibility of distinct successive selves (S^1, S^2, S^3 . . .)—is simply that in a case of somnambulism the old pattern of desire, and hence of consciousness, becomes so diminished as it is replaced by that of the hypnotist that a new, radically discontinuous "other-self-of-the-other-desire" forms with new experiences and memories, which is to say a new consciousness, that are not shared by the previous self. With regard to Janet's third observation—that S^2 can remember the experiences of S^1 while S^3 can remember those of both S^1 and S^2—his answer is that each successive self lives in a later time than that of those before: "Psychological time is the time of desire, just as the self is the self of desire, which is to say that it is formed by desire.

This time is not subject to the laws of physical time. It is movement that constitutes time. The movement of universal gravitation constitutes physical time. The movement of universal mimesis constitutes psychological time and memory, as well as sociological time, that is, History" (p. 237).

This means that each "later" self is in a position to remember the experiences of "earlier" selves, while the latter, of course, are not— since for them it would be a matter not of remembering but of foreseeing. The same principle applies also in the case of post-hypnotic suggestion and explains the odd tricks of memory associated with it:

> We can see, then, that during the physical time that a post-hypnotic suggestion is being carried out, it is self S^2 who takes, who has *eclipsed* self S^1, and returns with its memory m^2 and his sensibililty s^2. . . . Once the post-hypnotic suggestion has been carried out, S^2 goes into eclipse, and self S^1 resumes its normal course. The latter is obviously unable to *foresee* psychologically what S^2 *did* physically. If asked about it, the subject does not recognize the elapsed time as *his* past and reacts, as in all cases of this type of memory failure, by fabricating a compensatory story. (Pp. 240–41)

Janet's own tentative effort to explain posthypnotic suggestion was the source of the highly influential idea of the "subconscious" or "unconscious," which was subsequently taken up and made one of the most widely known *idées reçues* of the twentieth century by Freud. Oughourlian considers this not only no genuine explanation but a begging of the question that has served only to obscure the real issue and mask still more effectively the truth of the interdividual relation:

> The crucial problem for a theory of hypnosis, as Janet emphasized, is how to understand the post-hypnotic execution of a suggestion. Janet posited a subconscious, where the suggestion would abide while awaiting the moment of its realization. Freud drew on this same phenomenon in concluding that there is an unconscious. These explanations seem to me tautologous. To say that a suggestion remains unconscious

is simply to restate the fact that the subject has neither memory nor consciousness of it; it does not say why he does not have them. We should not forget that the suggestion comes from the other. And, generalizing from this, we should recognize that *the unconscious is the Other.* (P. 241)

What Oughourlian means by this last phrase is that the invisible controlling factor in somnambulism, as also in other cases in which a person performs acts that do not proceed from an original volition of his own, is the mimetic force in the holon appropriating the desire of the mimetic other, his model. To say that the cause is "in the unconscious" is to say no more than that it is obscure both to the one acting and to the observer. Rather than supposing a hypothetical entity functioning somewhat like a computer cache for the instructions of a program reserved for later execution—instructions that remain themselves in need of an explanation for how they actually take effect—it would be more appropriate to attend to the dynamics of the interdividual relation between the holon and whatever real or imaginative other is pulling the puppet strings that make him move.

The same principles of explanation are also valid, Oughourlian suggests, for cases of possession. Somnambulism is not the only example of a case of the extinction or eclipse of habitual patterns of desire and consciousness. The same thing occurs in possessions. Oughourlian devotes a whole chapter of his book to the history and ethnography of possession, a topic often avoided—like hypnosis—because of its frequent association with occultism. Oughourlian believes the phenomena of possession are equally in need of scientific analysis and also equally susceptible to it when approached from the point of view of the mimetic hypothesis. The basic explanation was already mentioned above: possession consists essentially of a mimetic operation so intense that one loses one's ordinary sense of independent selfhood in it, identifying one's thoughts, feelings, and desires with those of another—either a real other, such as a local sorcerer, or a culturally defined imaginative other, such as a god or demon. Depending on the circumstances and the way the phenomenon is culturally interpreted, it may either be encouraged and culti-vated through rites of adorcism or discouraged and opposed through rites of exorcism.

In the Western cultural tradition, possession is almost always thought of as a negative phenomenon, either pernicious or patho-logical, but this is the result of the cultural orientation imposed on our imaginations by the heritage of the Christian Middle Ages, for which "demonic possession" became, says Oughourlian, the princi-pal way of explaining strong inner conflicts acceptably—that is, in such a way as to minimize the disturbance to society that would be caused by a more direct acknowledgment of such conflict. It func-tioned both to mask the mimetic mechanism—as Oughourlian thinks every society has sought to do in various ways—and to deny that there is real conflict between the interests of the individual and the predominant institutions of the society as a whole.

As an example of this, Oughourlian analyzes in considerable detail the history of one of the last major cases of possession, and one of the best documented: that of the Ursuline nuns of Loudun in 1632. One of the things that makes this case so interesting is that in it the mimetic character of the possessions is particularly clear, since the person with whom it all started, Sister Jeanne des Anges, the prioress of the convent, had never seen or heard, let alone met personally, the supposed sorcerer, Father Urbain Grandier. "Mother Jeanne des Anges's desire for Urbain Grandier," says Oughourlian, "was *purely mimetic*. The movement that bore her toward Grandier was copied from the Great Other, that is, from the surrounding culture, or if you prefer, fashion: it was mimetism and nothing else. . . . all witnesses—and they are many—agree on the fact that Mother Jeanne's object of desire was not directly known to her; indeed she had never even seen him" (p. 85). She had only heard of Grandier from visitors to the convent, who talked about how young, good-looking, eloquent, and generally impressive he was and how successful in attracting the amorous interest of women. The prioress's own interest was aroused by this gossip, but as it was a cloistered order and he declined her subsequent invitation to become the spiritual director of the convent, she had no opportunity to meet him.

Still, she found herself unable to get Grandier out of her mind and began to have elaborate fantasies about him as well as physical symptoms. When she talked about it to the other nuns in the convent, they started to show the same symptoms. Exorcists were called in, who happened to have political reasons of their own for wishing the demise of Grandier. Soon an elaborate panoply of demons—each the cause of some particular symptom, or "sin"—was identified. After an inquisition that served not only to identify Grandier as the sorcerer behind it all but also, conveniently enough both for the exorcists and for Cardinal Richelieu, to implicate and disgrace some prominent members of the local Protestant community, Grandier was burned at the stake and the possessions came to an end.

Another feature of this case, beside the purity of its mimetism, that makes it especially interesting from Oughourlian's point of view is that there is extensive documentation of the ways the possession as such was interpreted by the principal parties involved. These show how it was both culturally defined and rendered culturally useful. The nuns were required, for example, to identify their demons by name—or, to look at it from the exorcists' point of view, the demons were required to identify themselves by name when talking through the nuns—which they did when supplied with the names by their exorcists from lists in standard manuals of exorcism. To believe that a convent of nuns might collectively go crazy or take up sinful desires was culturally unacceptable, and in this case it was all the more so because at that time the Catholic tradition of monasticism was subject to criticisms of just this sort from its Protestant rivals. It was imperative, therefore, that the clearly erotic desire the nuns were experiencing for Grandier be interpreted as not originating in them. The theory of demonic possession seemed made to order for this purpose:

> They [the ecclesiastical authorities] affirmed that Mother Jeanne was not the subject of her desire. This desire did not belong to her. They had to support this belief for the sake of maintaining, at any cost, their misunderstanding of the mimetic relation. Any recognition of that

relation would have the effect of making it clear that the prioress of the Ursulines was the plaything of worldly desires, like a sort of Proustian heroine. The existence of the Devil would thereby be put in question and—who knows—perhaps even that of God Himself. The culture of that age was not ready to bear this sort of truth or to receive this sort of revelation. . . . Mother Jeanne was declared to be the plaything of her desire: she could not be its subject. . . . she must belong to it, be its captive, be *possessed* by it! In mythic language culture declared that Mother Jeanne des Anges was possessed by the Devil. The Devil, that is, mimetic desire, is the Other's desire, contaminating, invading, possessing the self of desire. (Pp. 88–89)

It is also worth noting that over a period of time Jeanne des Anges herself developed several different interpretations of the possession episode. Oughourlian thinks that they represent the beginning of the broad European shift from demonism as an explanatory (and masking) principle to something more modern that could still serve both purposes. The problem with the demonic explanation was that, useful as it was for the denial of responsibility, it also took away from the individual too much that was cherished: "In certain respects the remedy was worse than the disease. The Devil, in fact, deprived the self of both its claim to the ownership of its desire and its belief in the desire's anteriority. The mythic figure of the Devil pressed too close to the truth; that cultural entity translated reality too literally" (pp. 92–93). Although demonism served to mask the interdividual relation, it did so by wearing too many of its features: it hid the real "other" behind the mask of the mythic "Other," the devil and his demonic agents, but in the process it seemed to eclipse volition. At first the prioress reveled in the freedom from responsibility her state of possession granted her, but later she can be seen trying to reclaim some of the autonomy it also took from her. "The gradual elimination of the Devil began in an insidious way in 1642," says Oughourlian, "in the autobiography that Mother Jeanne composed at the command of the Superior General of the Ursulines, which describes her experiences between 1633 and 1642" (p. 93). By this time she was safe from any accusation of blame, so she no longer needed to cling so strictly as she had before to the idea that she had had no personal involvement in her state of possession:

> Rather timidly Sister Jeanne began to lay claim to her ownership and the anteriority of her desire, as my italics in the following passages emphasize: ". . . I almost always felt some remorse in my conscience, and with good reason, because I usually knew quite well that I was the *first cause* of my disturbances and that the demon never acted except *in accord with the opportunities I gave him*" (p. 77). And again, recounting the episode in which she spat the host in the curate's face: "I know quite well that I did not do that act freely, but I am also *quite sure*, to my great confusion, that *I gave the Devil the opportunity* to do it and that he would not have had that power *if I had not got myself* bound up with him in the first place" (p. 79). And then again: "*my nature* with all its tricks and *my egoism* functioned as demons within me . . . for these evil spirits are admittedly very weak when we do not ourselves give them weapons with which to make war upon us" (p. 113). And finally: "I was therefore, by the grace of Our Lord, firmly established in my resolve *to take upon myself* the responsibility for all my disturbances and no longer regard the demons as their authors . . . after having reflected upon all my inclinations . . . I recognized immediately that *the evil came from me*" (p. 128).
>
> Thus, in the course of her confession and her autobiography, Sister Jeanne gradually laid claim to her desire. In this way, she gradually separated herself from the cultural myth she had rather profitably exploited and also from the psychological truth of her desire, that is, from the reality of the mimetic origin of the movements that animated her and from the real otherness of her self. (*Puppet*, pp. 93–94)[7]

It was mentioned above that this reinterpretation by Jeanne des Anges of her possession represents the shift from medieval demonism to something more modern. Oughourlian says that "the

---

7. Italics added by Oughourlian. The page numbers refer to an undated manuscript by Sister Jeanne des Anges, published in Legué and de La Tourette, *Soeur Jeanne des Anges, supérieure des ursulines de Loudun.*

type of claim she made has since become that of all neurotics and especially of hysterics: '*I am manipulated, but I am manipulated by myself* " (p. 94). He believes that Western culture's efforts to explain mental problems deriving from disturbances in the interdividual relation have gone through three great historical phases, each of which has also served as much to mask the interdividual relation as to make it possible to speak of it: (1) the medical theory of hysteria in the ancient world, (2) the medieval theory of demonic possession, and (3) the modern Freudian theory of neurosis. The ancient theory of hysteria, which derives from the Greek word for "womb," attributed mental illness to the effects of the womb's having come loose and taken on an independent life of its own within the body, causing it to behave strangely and suffer various physical symptoms as it knocks about inside. There was also, according to the same theory, a male equivalent involving the idea of excessive independence on the part of the male sexual organ and intracorporal migration of the semen. One of the standard prescriptions in both cases was to employ sexual gratification as a cure.

This approach naturally lost its cultural acceptability as a result of the spread of Christianity, which replaced it with the theory of demonism. Both functioned in similar ways, however, in that they explained the disturbances as resulting from an otherness within. The Freudian theory of the unconscious as a seat of complexes is parallel in this respect to its two predecessors, says Oughourlian, and serves the same kind of simultaneous explanatory and masking function. Commenting on the common claim of hysterics, demonics, and neurotics to be manipulated, but manipulated by oneself, Oughourlian says:

That defense and the illustration of that sort of claim came to blend, down to our own day, with psychology and psychopathology. Culture, long perplexed in the face of that aporia, would throw itself into the arms of Freudian psychoanalysis, which has saved it by enclosing the Other definitively within the self. The origin of desire is seen as completely within the holon: a novel satisfaction for an eternal claim. Yet at the same time, the holon is not responsible for its desire, much less guilty, since the origin of that desire is unconscious: the holon is the proprietor of its desire, but it is not aware of it. It is therefore doubly reassured. It has "the best of both worlds." (P. 94)

In this connection it is interesting to note that as demonism declined, hysteria became a fashionable complaint once again, and it was hysteria in particular, of course, that Freud was trying both to treat and to theorize in his early work. Although Oughourlian himself does not mention it, it also seems pertinent that in the last months of his effort to explain hysteria through his seduction theory Freud began, as Balmary points out, to take an interest in the theme of possession: "Freud then begins to get interested in books dealing with the devil and sorcery. He sees the great resemblance between possession and neurosis, but he does not truly explain it to himself." Balmary goes on to say, in words that could almost have been spoken by Oughourlian, "After September 1897 and the abandonment of the theory of seduction, however, perversion and neurosis will be viewed as gathered up together in the interior of the individual psyche; henceforth, the phenomenon of interindividual transmission will, for the most part, be hidden from sight in Freudian theory."[8]

If Oughourlian is correct in his claim that Freudian neurosis has become the modern equivalent of its two major predecessors, this would explain the mysterious clinical diminution of cases of hysteria since Freud's time remarked on by Sulloway.[9] If mental disturbances are particular expressions of disorder in the mimetic function of the interdividual relation, it could be expected that they too would have their fashions, so that hysteria and neurosis could both be learned the same way Oughourlian says Jeanne des Anges " 'caught' a desire that was in the air, in the discourse of the city" (p. 87) and her sisters "caught" it in turn from her. In the late nineteenth and early twentieth centuries, however, possession had become so thoroughly out of style that it was not a very good

8. Balmary, *Psychoanalyzing Psychoanalysis*, pp. 113, 114.
9. See Sulloway, *Freud, Biologist of the Mind*, pp. 59, 82, 97, 208.

candidate for being caught any longer, and hysteria was not really much more useful as an explanation because its theoretical element, the idea of the freely floating sexual organ moving around inside the body, was impossible to maintain in the light of modern anatomical science.

By the time of Freud, the concept of "hysteria" had ceased to be much more than a vague catchall for various sorts of nervous illness accompanied by psychosomatic symptoms. What Freud was trying to do in his early research into hysteria was to order this rather messy field by developing a new theory to replace those of classical hysteria and possession as a way of dealing with the gamut of problems then lumped under that heading. In this sense it certainly seems true that the Oedipus complex has served as a modern re-placement for the displaced womb and the demon. What made Freud's new theory catch on in the culture, says Oughourlian, is that the culture had been waiting for something of exactly the sort Freud offered it:

Culture and neurosis share a common interest. Neurosis leads the holon to lay claim to ownership of *his* or *her* desire and its anteriority in relation to that of the other. Neurosis affirms the originality of the desire, its specificity, its *difference,* and it is in this that it links itself to culture's special preoccupation. When reality obtrudes, neurosis recog-nizes it; "I am manipulated," says Sister Jeanne des Anges, but she immediately claims ownership of that animation: "I am manipulated by my own self." This is why the history of hysteria blends with that of its culture. It is also why the disappearance of the Demon as a cultural entity, the banishment of the Devil from Western civilization, posed so sharply and so prominently the problem of hysteria. . . . It was not until 1893, with the *Preliminary Report* of Sigmund Freud and Josef Breuer, and then 1895, with the appearance of their *Studies on Hysteria,* that culture's demand was fully satisfied: by hiding the Other *inside* the subject in the guise of the *unconscious,* Freud pre-served and protected its anonymity. . . . Thus the Other, after having been Sex (an intra-physical Other) and then the Demon (an external Other), became the Unconscious (an intrapsychic Other). For four thousand years, these three masks have served as amazingly successful disguises, and even now the masquerade goes on. (Pp. 150–51)

The Freudian theory of traumatic memories and buried conflicts contained in "the unconscious," in other words, has become just one more device for avoiding a direct confrontation with what Oughourlian thinks is a much more disturbing reality: that the selves in which we take such pride and their supposedly spontaneous, self-originating desires, are actually functions of our relations with real or imagined others in relation to whom we feel a dependency or inferiority that is the very last thing we will ever be willing to acknowledge, either to others or to ourselves. This, again, is why Oughourlian, if he were to use the term "unconscious" at all would say, as we saw him do above, that "the unconscious is the Other":

The origin of our own desire, the fact that its source is in that of the other, has always been misunderstood. . . . In this sense one might indeed say, within the framework of my theory, that the origin of our desire is unconscious. But I refuse to speak in this way, because I am not willing to hypostatize the unconscious. I say bluntly, and will say it again and again: the Freudian unconscious, that mythic hypostasis peopled with all sorts of occult mythic forces in conflict with one another and to whose quarrels we have to submit as inevitably as to bad weather, simply does not exist! (P. 152)

To reject the idea of the "unconscious" altogether would perhaps be a bit extreme, especially since there is considerable experimental evidence that the mind can have information present to it that is not consciously adverted to but which can have a distorting influence on mental functioning.[10] It is not that conception of the "unconscious" that Oughourlian opposes, however. What he has in mind is the specifically Freudian conception of the unconscious as a kind of hypostatized inner entity that is supposedly the seat of spontaneous desires that are simultaneously one's own and not one's own and

10. See, for example, Daniel Goleman, *Vital Lies, Simple Truths: The Psychology of Self-Deception* (1985).

that serves, like its predecessors (hysteria and demonism), to hide the truth of the interdividual relation. It is in terms of this understanding that he goes on to say: "The Freudian unconscious does not truly exist, any more than did the Demon that it succeeded as the mask of the Other. The Id, the Superego, Eros, Thanatos, and the rest, have neither more nor less actual existence then Asmodeus, Beelzebub, Leviathan, and the various other demons. The figures of the traditional demonology, like the more abstract figures of the psychoanalytic pantheon, have only a cultural existence" (p. 152).

What Oughourlian favors instead of Freudianism or any other system of thought that would deny the centrality of the interdividual relation in human psychology is its clear recognition and guarded, circumspect acceptance. This is why he says, in opposition to the medicalizing tendencies not only of Freudianism but of psychiatric thought generally, that properly understood "the opposite of madness is not 'health' but wisdom."[11] It is also why he thinks that traditional rites of adorcism have on the whole been beneficial in the context of their cultures and deserve more consideration from Western psychologists. Traditions of adorcism have the advantage, suggests Oughourlian, that they acknowledge the role of the other in human psychology and try to help the individual to manage the dynamics of the interdividual relation in ways that can reduce individual and interpersonal conflict. Adorcism can also encourage personal growth through identification with helpful models.

Identification, of course, as we saw in the last chapter, especially in the discussion of Roustang and Borch-Jacobsen, has tended to be a sensitive topic in the psychoanalytic tradition in France. Lacan and the Freudian revisionists inherited the theme of problematic identification from Freud himself, who, in accord with the logic of the premises of his libido theory, associated it with narcissism as the opposite of Oedipal object-love. In the context of interdividual psychology, on the other hand, it has quite different associations. There the problem is not one of turning libido outward but of learning to understand one's personal involvement in the dynamics of the in-

11. In conversation with the author, Paris, July 1988.

terdividual relation and above all of learning to relate well to one's models, since modeling in some form is part of being human. This means relating to them in nonconflictual ways, as in what Girard calls external mediation, rather than with hidden, unacknowledged rivalry and hatred. That is why I referred above to a "guarded, circumspect acceptance" of the mimetic rapport: that acceptance must not be a matter of romantic infatuation but of realistic self-awareness and intelligent, critical appreciation. Identifications of the right kind, with appropriate models and in a spirit of love and respect, rather than envy and emulation, may be enriching and liberating rather than diminishing and enslaving.

The purpose of psychotherapy as Oughourlian conceives and practices it is to assist the patient in understanding this and in extricating himself from the tangles of internal mediation. As he expressed it in the conclusion of *The Puppet of Desire*, "Complete healing and ultimate wisdom will be found in the renouncing of all *rivals* and *obstacles* in order to keep only *models*" (p. 245). Depending on the case, the process of such therapy will probably involve at least to some degree the encouragement of some form of external mediation, if only in the form of the therapist himself's representing for the patient a model of wisdom. Again depending on the case, it may also involve the therapist's making direct or indirect suggestions designed to help the patient discover a more adequate way of dealing with his problems.[12] A therapeutic practice so conceived would, of course, make great spiritual as well as intellectual demands on its practitioners, since it cannot be merely a matter of objective information and technique but must require substantial

12. In this connection Oughourlian has expressed admiration for the techniques of therapeutic use of suggestion and hypnosis developed by the American psychiatrist Milton Erickson. In a conversation in Paris in July 1988, Dr. Oughourlian told me that he considers Erickson the psychotherapist who most clearly exemplifies wisdom of the sort he has in mind and that he hopes to continue his research into the theory of hypnosis drawing on Erickson's *Advanced Techniques of Hypnosis and Therapy* and also, on the level of therapeutic practice, to pursue clinical research along the lines of Erickson's *Strategies of Psychotherapy*. For a discussion of Erickson, see Jay Haley, *Uncommon Therapy: The Psychiatric Techniques of Milton H. Erickson, M.D.*

maturity and insight on the part of the therapist if he is to initiate the patient into wisdom:

> The formation of the new psychiatrists and psychologists who will be needed to practice and do research into this interdividual psychother-apy cannot be a simply pedagogical matter. I will also require a sort of initiation. . . . as we know from all cultures that have learned to treat mimetic psychopathology, this treatment requires a special kind of wisdom. The therapist will have to be more advanced, in this respect, than the patient if he is to lead him, through the light of his own experience, into the path of liberation and surrender—of submission to reality and recognition of the mimetic rapport. (P. 244)

The future acceptance and success of the interdividual psychother-apy Oughourlian has in mind may well depend, therefore, on some-thing much more difficult to develop and communicate than what one usually thinks of as scientific understanding. Like the Girardian movement generally, as we will see further in the next section, Oughourlian's thought implies a virtual revolution in the ways we have learned to think about ourselves and all our social interac-tions. This is indicated by his declaration that in the centuries-old history of hysteria, possession, and neurosis, "psychosociological history blended with cultural history to provide people with a suc-cession of ways to mask the mimetic relation, until now, at the end of the twentieth century, we have been brought to the kind of unveiling attempted here" (p. 88).

CHAPTER 5

The Social and Political Dimension
in the Girardian School

A S discussed in the first chapter, an important element in the dynamics of French thought in the mid to late twentieth century has been an effort to deal with the tension between the individualistic thrust of the Cartesian heritage and a general tendency to conceive of the individual as embedded within and largely determined by the social matrix. Sartre's swing from an extreme emphasis on radical autonomy of thought and action in his earlier, existentialist phase to the collectivistic orientation of his later, Marxian phase was mentioned as an example. In *The Scapegoat* (1982), Girard alludes to what he believes is a rather sinister aspect to this side of Sartre's social and political thought. Referring to the high priest Caiaphas's suggestion in John 11:50 that "it is better for one man to die for the people, than for the whole nation to be destroyed," he says:

> Caiaphas's statement triggers to a certain extent the effect of the scapegoat it defines. It not only reassures his listeners [that is, that their action is sanctioned by his "serene certainty" as their leader and model], it galvanizes them into action; it "mobilizes" them in the sense that we speak of mobilizing the military, or the "militants" who must be *mobilized*. What is at work? The formation of the famous group in fusion that Jean-Paul Sartre dreamed of, without of course ever saying that it will produce nothing but victims. (P. 113)

This tendency in French thought to idealize collectivity goes back well before Sartre, as does the equally characteristic insistence on the individual in opposition to the group. Both elements were, of course, prominent in Jean-Jacques Rousseau. But without going back that far, one may consider the set of thinkers in the late 1930s known as the College of Sociology, whose members included such subsequently prominent figures as Roger Caillois, Georges Bataille, and Denis de Rougemont. Its special focus of interest might well be described as "the group in fusion," which they hoped would somehow also be compatible with the fullest development of individuality. In his introduction to *The College of Sociology, 1937–39,* Denis Hollier quotes a passage from Hegel's *Aesthetics* that expressed for them their central concern: " 'What is the sacred?' Goethe asked. And he answered, 'That which unites souls.' "[1] Hollier then goes on to say, "The College of Sociology went back to Goethe's question. It too wanted to find out what united men and to study the sacred, that is—as Bataille declared in one of his first lectures—human activities 'as they create unity' " (p. xi). This is an idea that clearly foreshadowed Girard's conception of the sacred as well, as we will see.

But not all the members of the circle were equally optimistic or enthusiastic about the ideal of social cohesion through the sense of the sacred, even if it did preoccupy them generally. Alexandre Kojève, an older, already highly distinguished figure among this group of young admirers, was openly skeptical regarding their project of restoring the sacred deliberately. "Kojève listened to us," said Caillois, "but he dismissed our idea. In his eyes we were putting ourselves in the position of a conjurer who wanted his magic tricks to make him believe in magic" (p. 86). De Rougemont, on the other hand, knew the trick could be done, having witnessed some of Hitler's sacred ceremonies, and their effects, during a visit to Germany. But he was suspicious of the goal, saying he did not believe in the "collective soul" the others did: "Is it not a grandiloquent phrase for denoting the *absence* of a personal soul in individuals swept up in the mechanical movements of a crowd?" (pp. 165–66).

Sartre, in the years after the war, was an intellectual and spiritual descendant of the College of Sociology in both the collectivistic and individualistic aspects of his thought, but he went further than they had in identifying violence itself as the key agent for producing the group identification Bataille and Caillois had hoped for. Girard, of course, is not the only person to have noticed the romanticizing of

1. Denis Hollier, *The College of Sociology 1937–39,* p. x.

violence in Sartre. In her essay "Reflections on Violence," Hannah Arendt also pointed to it when she said that in his preface to Franz Fanon's *The Wretched of the Earth,* Sartre was "unaware of his basic disagreement with Marx on the question of violence, especially when he says that 'irrepressible violence . . . is man recreating himself,'" that it is 'mad fury' through which 'the wretched of the earth' can 'become men.' "[2]

Girard shares something with both Arendt and Sartre here, and he would probably also find a certain naïveté in both as well. He shares Arendt's wariness of the romanticism of violence in Sartre, but he would also say that Sartre has a point, even if he approaches it from the wrong angle. Just as Girard has been the only important thinker to take a really serious interest in Freud's hypothesis, expressed in *Totem and Taboo* and *Moses and Monotheism,* that society began with a founding murder on the part of a primal horde, so Girard is also probably one of the few who would still take seriously Sartre's idea that there is an essential link between group formation and "irrepressible violence" and "mad fury." The difference is that whereas Girard thinks that this is indeed how group formation, as well as the social and political regeneration of communities, has taken place historically, he also argues that violence should not be cultivated but renounced.

Girard believes, that is, that violence has been as important for the past of mankind as Sartre thought it should be for the future, but he also thinks that if the human race is to have a future in a world in which the destructive possibilities of violence have become so greatly magnified, it must now renounce both violence and its roots in conflictual psychology. The present chapter will focus primarily on Girard's idea of the role of violence in society and on the ways some other thinkers in the Girardian school have adapted his

2. Hannah Arendt, "Reflections on Violence," *Journal of International Affairs,* 23 (1969): 4. The disagreement with Marx she had in mind was specifically that in Marx it was not through violence but through labor that man produced himself. The belief in violence itself as spiritually regenerating has its roots rather in Bakunin and Kropotkin. Cf. Eric Voegelin, *From Enlightenment to Revolution,* pp. 195–239.

analysis, in ways often rather different from his own, to deal with issues in political economy. Girard's thought on the possible transcendence of violence will be left for the next chapter.

The roots of violence, according to Girard, lie in unreflective mimesis, which gravitates ineluctably toward conflict as the desires of individuals come to converge on common objects. The emphasis in his *Violence and the Sacred* and the first part of *Things Hidden* is on the way society as such—as well as much of what makes man specifically human—grows out of the stages of this process as they proceed from particular to generalized conflict and then to a resolving crisis by way of what he calls "the victimizing mechanism." As evidence for the universal presence of a tendency to acquisitive mimesis that will spontaneously generate conflict, he refers to experiments in which a number of children are placed in a room with an equal number of identical toys.[3] In principle, since there is nothing to distinguish one toy from the other, there is no reason why each child should not go right over and take one of the toys and then play happily with it. What typically happens, however, is that the children will hang back as though waiting for a cue. Then one of the children will begin to move toward one of the toys. That becomes a signal that that particular toy is desirable. Soon several others will make a grab for it, quarrels will start, and general pandemonium will ensue.

An equivalent situation rarely occurs among civilized adults, Girard says, because they have learned to suppress mimetic rivalry, "at least in its crudest, most obvious and most immediately recognizable forms."[4] Children have less self-control, but fortunately they also have less capacity to do each other damage. If we hypothesize, on the other hand, a situation among adults before the development of society and therefore without the restraints of civilization, we have a case in which the behavior we saw in the children could be

---

3. See *Things Hidden*, p. 9, and Thomas F. Bertonneau, "The Logic of the Undecidable: An Interview with René Girard," *Paroles gelées, UCLA French Studies* 5 (1987): 17–18.
4. *Things Hidden*, p. 9.

expected to lead to a bloody free-for-all, especially if we consider the "metaphysical" element that is always present in mimetic desire. This, it will be remembered, is the attempted imitation of the "being," which is to say, according to Girard' analysis, the *power* of the other. The object, that is, is desired not just in simple imitation of another's desire but with the additional felt supposition that the other desires it because he seeks from it an enhancement of his power. This has the implication, says Girard, that one becomes most attracted to precisely those objects that are claimed and defended with the strongest violence. "Violent opposition," he says in *Violence and the Sacred,* ". . . is the signifier of ultimate desire, of divine self-sufficiency, of that 'beautiful totality' whose beauty depends on its being inaccessible and impenetrable" (p. 148). It also implies that if an opponent can be defeated and his object won from him, then he must not have had the power one thought and his object must not therefore be worth what one hoped. This means that the desirer, as long as he never realizes the insidious dynamics of the process he is caught up in, will "turn to an even greater violence and seek out an obstacle that promises to be truly insurmountable" (p. 148). "Desire," says Girard, ". . . is attracted to violence triumphant and strives desperately to incarnate this 'irresistible' force. Desire clings to violence and stalks it like a shadow because violence is the signifier of the cherished being, the signifier of divinity" (p. 151). And of course violence itself can become mimetically self-feeding, as the raging antagonists, imitating each other's fury, become the "monstrous doubles" of one another.

Girard thinks it reasonable to assume that there have been times, at the dawn of human life as we know it, when such a state of self-exacerbating generalized violence must have occurred, perhaps repeatedly, before resolving itself in the birth of society. The resolution, he suggests, must have come about through the same mechanism—mimesis—that caused the violence. Just as mimetic desires can come to bear on the same objects, so the mimetic violence and the hatred that go with it can converge on a particular person, perhaps one who catches the attention of the others by some peculiarity of appearance or who has a defect that renders him vulnerable. All that is necessary is for some two or three to turn on him for their violence to become like a magnet drawing the others to attack him as well. This "polarization of violence onto a single victim who substitutes for all the others" (p. 161) will have the effect of generating a sense of unanimity and brotherhood among the attackers, deflecting their hatred from each other onto him. Their collective violence will culminate in a paroxysm of murderous rage against the victim which will be followed by a new stillness and peace as the allies stand over his dead body. He who was first hated as the source of the evil among them may now seem to be the source of the peace and brotherhood they are experiencing. It is Girard's hypothesis that it is in this attribution to the "surrogate victim," or scapegoat, of the ambiguous power to generate both violence and peace, hatred and love, that the idea and the experience of the sacred originates—and with it religion.

Girard's hypothesis about origins extends still further. He suggests not only that society was born from the resolution of a crisis of generalized violence but also that hominization, the birth of specifically human life, had the same origin. In his hypothetical scenario, the victimizing process became not only the source of the group as such but also of signification and language, along with the human mode of intelligence that they require:

I think that even the most elementary form of the victimage mechanism, prior to the emergence of the sign, should be seen as an exceptionally powerful means of creating a new degree of attention, the first non-instinctual attention. Once it has reached a certain degree of frenzy, the mimetic polarization becomes fixed on a single victim. After having been released against the victim, the violence necessarily abates and silence follows the mayhem. This maximal contrast between the release of violence and its cessation, between agitation and tranquillity, creates the most favourable conditions possible for the emergence of this new attention. Since the victim is a common victim it will be at that instant the focal point for all members of the community. Consequently, beyond the purely instinctual object, the alimentary or sexual object or the dominant individual, there is the cadaver of the collective victim and this cadaver constitutes the first object for this new type of attention. (*Things Hidden*, p. 99)

The victim, therefore, becomes the first sign, the source of all cultural meaning: "The signifier is the victim. The signified constitues all actual and potential meaning the community confers on to the victim and, through its intermediacy, on to all things" (p. 103.) This meaning is primarily a complex of further significations designed to preserve the effects of the originating sacrifice: "The sign is the reconciliatory victim. Since we understand that human beings wish to remain reconciled after the conclusion of the crisis, we can also understand their penchant for reproducing the sign, or in other words for reproducing the language of the sacred by substituting, in ritual, new victims for the original victim, in order to assure the maintenance of that miraculous peace" (p. 103).

In this aspect of his thought Girard runs counter to one of the major trends in French intellectual life in the 1960s and 1970s: structuralism. This school of thought, as represented by both Lévi-Strauss and Lacan, tended toward an absorption of contingent reality into an ideal world of meaning constituted by the inherently linguistic structure of the human mind. Whereas for Girard the various images of a founding murder or sacrifice in myths of origin were reflections of actual events that have played a formative role in history, for structuralist thought the shape of myths was determined by the structure of mental categories and the rules of their combinations. Girard says in *Violence and the Sacred* that "structuralism is itself locked into the structure, a prisoner of the synchronic, unable to perceive a change in terms of violence or fear of violence" (p. 242) and that "Lévi-Strauss always views the production of sense as a purely logical problem, an act of symbolic mediation," with the result that for him "the role of violence remains hidden" (p. 244).

Girard's emphasis on the historical reality of violence underlying the violence depicted in myths is one of the things that has made him such a controversial and individual figure among French intellectuals, who have tended in this respect to share a Cartesian, essentially idealistic philosophical orientation and therefore to feel more comfortable with a world in which meaning is determined by logical laws and supratemporal categories, than one in which signification takes its rise from contingent experience, with all the accident and arbitrariness that that typically involves. Generally speaking, French intellectuals have been inclined not so much simply to disagree with the kind of particular affirmations Girard makes regarding the historical reality of the victims he talks about as to reject in principle the idea that the proper business of thought is to move from hypothesis to contingent affirmation. Roustang reflects this general tendency of French thought when he says that "what distinguishes madness from theory is precisely that theory is recognized as fiction," and especially when he follows this with the paradox that "the theoretical fiction can exist only if it tends to assert itself as a reality. . . ."[5]

It may be that the reason Girard feels the need to move from theory to what he claims is historical fact is that having made his academic career in a different culture with a more empirical orientation he has had occasion to reflect in a different way on the goals of theoretical thinking. Girard is not naïve, moreover, in the way he understands the connection between theory and reality—not at all someone who could legitimately be accused of slipping into the uncritical "madness" Roustang was warning against. His occasional remarks on methodology show that he has a clear sense of the limits of hypothetical affirmation as well as its importance. In *Violence and the Sacred*, for example, with reference to such myths as that in *The Bacchae* of Euripides, he acknowledges that "the apparition of the monstrous double cannot be verified empirically; nor for that matter can the body of phenomena that forms the basis for any primitive religion. . . . the monstrous double remains a hypothetical creation. . . . The validity of the hypothesis is confirmed, however, by the vast number of mythological, ritualistic, philosophical, and literary motifs that it is able to explain, as well as . . . by the coherence it imposes on phenomena that until now appeared isolated and obscure" (p.

5. Roustang, *Psychoanalysis Never Lets Go*, pp. 20, 21.

164). His comment at the beginning of *The Scapegoat* on his procedure in interpreting Guillaume de Machaut's *Judgment of the King of Navarre* as a "persecution text"—that is, as an account of real violence "told from the perspective of the persecutors, and therefore influenced by characteristic distortions"—reflects clearly both the critical realism Girard thinks must direct serious thought and the difference he sees between himself and the more typical French intellectual of his generation:

> Another contemporary notion suffers in the light of Guillaume de Machaut's text . . . and that is the casual way in which literary critics dismiss what they call the "referent." In current linguistic jargon the referent is the subject of the text; in our example it is the massacre of the Jews, who were seen as responsible for the poisoning of Christians. For some twenty years the referent has been considered more or less inaccessible. It is unimportant we hear, whether we are capable or not of reaching it; this naïve notion of the referent would seem only to hamper the latest study of textuality. Now the only thing that matters is the ambiguous and unreliable relationships of language. (P. 9)

In the case of the *Judgment of the King of Navarre*, the referent is the contingently real collective victim, the massacred Jews whom Machaut and his readers treated as a scapegoat; and for Girard, to uncover this referent and do justice to it is a matter of both moral and scholarly urgency.

One can understand, therefore, Girard's sympathy with Freud's speculations about a founding murder on the part of the primal horde of brothers. He says that Freud, "is unique in having understood the necessity of real collective murder as a model of sacrifice" (*Things Hidden*, p. 25), although he differs with Freud fundamentally on how this can be imagined as happening and how it is to be interpreted. Freud had said that first there was the murder (of the father, who had prohibited his sons from sexual contact with the women), then came imitation in the form of sacrifice, which was motivated by a compulsion to reenact the events that made the community feel guilty. (In accord with his Lamarckian evolutionism, Freud believed the memory of this act could be biologically inherited and that it would produce in the unconscious of the group the same sort of compulsion toward the "return of the repressed" that a problematic memory does in the unconscious of the individual.)

Girard argues on the other hand that first there was mimesis itself, producing an initial state of chaotic violence, and then came the murder as its product and resolution. He also argues that the sacrificial rites that subsequently developed were motivated not by a sense of guilt but by a desire to rekindle the original unanimity of the group and to express reverence and gratitude with regard to the saving events that generated it. "The idea that a group would gather to immolate any sort of victim in order to commemorate the 'guilt' they still feel for a prehistoric murder is purely mythical," says Girard. "What is not mythical, by contrast, is the idea that men would immolate victims because an original, spontaneous murder had in fact unified the community and put an end to a real mimetic crisis. In this light, ritual becomes comprehensible as an attempt to avert the real threat of crisis . . ." (p. 25).

A new crisis, that is, could arise at any time if mimetic rivalry were to become intense enough and the barriers to violence were to erode. The most important such barriers for society are the distinctions that mark out who is entitled to what objects and symbols of status and respect, what kind of violence is ritually correct and what kind "impure," and so on. Religion is designed to maintain these distinctions: "For in the final analysis, the sole purpose of religion is to prevent the recurrence of reciprocal violence" (*Violence and the Sacred*, p. 55). If these distinctions become blurred, the result can be a "sacrificial crisis," in which it is no longer clear what is permitted and what forbidden, who is entitled to what and why. Girard says that a "cultural order is nothing more than a regulated system of distinctions in which the differences among individuals are used to establish their 'identity' and their mutual relationships" and that a "sacrificial crisis can be defined . . . as a crisis of distinctions" (p. 49). This is specifically a *sacrificial* crisis both because in the normal course of events it can be resolved only through a new operation of the victimizing mechanism and because when the system of distinctions breaks down it is no longer clear who is to be the saving victim whose sacrifice will restore order and community.

This theory of human and social origins is one of the more controversial aspects of Girard's thought, but it is not, it should be clear, just a matter of speculation about events that presumably happened long ago. The breakdown of the old order in Germany after World War I produced a particularly clear example of a modern "sacrificial crisis" of the type Girard talks about, and it was resolved, at least within Germany, in part through the Nazis' instinctive, and unfortunately all too unreflective, sense of the need for a collective victim—for which the Jewish members of the population, with their clear signs of difference and vulnerability, were a readily identifiable set of candidates. Horkheimer and Adorno, writing in the 1930s, offered an analysis of that process in terms remarkably like those of Girard, even emphasizing the role of mimesis in it—the vicitimizers' "mimesis" of one another and their suppressed mimetic attraction to their victim as well.[6] Our century had seen the same sort of thing happen again and again: in Stalin's purges, in the McCarthy hearings, in the Cambodian massacre of suspected elites, and in the use by Iranians of American embassy personnel, then their enemies in the war with Iraq, and most recently the novelist Salman Rushdie as scapegoats to direct hostility away from themselves so as to encourage a sense of collective dedication and community within their own country. Girard's book, The Scapegoat, has to do with the way this pattern has been repeated again and again over the centuries, and also continually hidden behind myths and "texts of persecution."

Although this is far from being a strictly modern problem, it is nevertheless one that Girard thinks becomes exacerbated under the conditions of modern cultural change, with the breakdown of distinctions that have come with it. In Deceit, Desire, and the Novel, Girard emphasized that the social tensions arising from internal mediation were becoming increasingly acute in the world of the nineteenth century because, as he put it, "increasing equality—the

6. See Max Horkheimer and Theodor W. Adorno, Dialectic of Enlightenment, pp. 183–86.

approach of the mediator in our terms—does not give rise to harmony but to an even keener rivalry" (pp. 136–37). On initial reflection it might seem that egalitarian democracy and the opening up of free markets for economic expansion would lead to greater general social harmony, since more goods would be produced and more desires satisfied. Girard, however, believes his theory would predict just the opposite:

> Although this rivalry is the source of considerable material benefits, it also leads to even more considerable spiritual sufferings, for nothing material can appease it. Equality which alleviates poverty is in itself good but it cannot satisfy even those who are keenest in demanding it; it only exasperates their desire. . . . The passion for equality is a madness unequalled except by the contrary and symmetrical passion for inequality, which is even more abstract and contributes even more directly to the unhappiness caused by freedom in those who are incapable of accepting it in a manly fashion. (P. 137)

Nor is the modern problem simply one of greater tensions and more widespread conflict; it is also one of more dangerous and less controllable conflict. As Girard emphasizes in *Things Hidden,* the course of history has led us to an unprecedented unmasking of the mimetic and victimizing mechanisms, but this offers both hope and danger. The hope comes from the fact that when these mechanisms are effectively unmasked they are also disarmed. When one realizes that a particular desire is not simply and spontaneously one's own but grows out of imitation of some other person's desire, one tends to lose interest in it fairly quickly, and when one realizes that a hated enemy is not really the source of one's problems but only a scapegoat, it is difficult to feel that same enthusiasm for his murder. Trying deliberately to believe in the guilt of a scapegoat would be another example of a conjurer trying to use his own tricks to convince himself of the reality of magic. Hitler had to be sincere to make the victimizing mechanism work effectively; the reason he could believe in his Jewish scapegoats and impart that belief to his followers was that he was not a Machiavelli, at least in that area, but only a fool.

The special danger in the modern situation, on the other hand, comes from the fact that as the scapegoat mechanism becomes more transparent it also becomes less effective at resolving conflict. This has the ambiguous implication that although "any increase in our knowledge of the victimage mechanism, anything that tends to disengage or reveal violence, represents considerable progress, at least potentially, in intellectual and ethical respects," it also tends to go hand in hand with ever-increasing virulence in the search for believable scapegoats and in the levels of violence with which they are attacked: "human beings, confronted with this situation, will be tempted to restore the lost effectiveness of the traditional remedy by forever increasing the dosage, immolating more and more victims . . ." (*Things Hidden*, p. 128). As Oughourlian summarized the issue in that volume, "In sum, the mechanism becomes recognizable only with the development of sufficient critical intelligence to hinder its functioning. The arbitrariness of the victim becomes apparent, and a reconciliatory unanimity is no longer possible" so that "spontaneous collective violence no longer possesses its founding capability" (p. 129)—to which Lefort added, "the only true scapegoats are those we cannot recognize as such." Understanding itself, therefore, has impaled humanity on the horns of a dilemma: it may liberate us from the necessity for blind violence, but at the same time it deprives us of the only mechanism in history that has so far functioned effectively for its resolution.

For Girard, the only exit from this situation can come through a truly radical renunciation of violence and transcendence of the mimetic mechanisms on which it is founded. We will consider his ideas on this possibility in the next chapter. Before finishing the present one, however, it will be appropriate to consider another view within the Girardian camp. Girard's basic theory of the dynamics of society, as we have seen, is that social development normally takes place by way of a movement that begins in the chaotic violence of the sacrificial crisis and then proceeds through the identification and persecution of a victim to the founding of society and culture, and especially of religion as a device by which to perpetuate the effects of the resolution of the crisis. Some of his colleagues, on the other hand, although they share his premises regarding the mimetic mechanism and the way it generates desire and conflict, nevertheless think that there are other ways short of chaos and victimization by which conflict can resolve itself. This was a theme of the conference on "Disorder and Order" at Stanford in 1981 as well as *L'Enfer des choses: René Girard et la logique de l'économie* (1979) by Paul Dumouchel and Jean-Pierre Dupuy.

Dupuy and Dumouchel are economists, and they share the belief that the psychology of mimetic desire can offer a great deal to the field of economics in explaining the problems of competition and scarcity in the social world, but they also believe that Girard's conception of social dynamics as it applies to the sphere of political economy needs to be supplemented by the perspective of the economist. As Dupuy puts it in his section of *L'Enfer,* entitled "Le Signe et l'envie," the breakdown of differences that Girard sees in the modern world has indeed "left the field entirely free for the unbridled expansion of mimetic desire," but at the same time one needs to ask a question Girard has not considered: "what is it that gives modernity the capacity to confront that liberation of desire and to nourish itself on it?" (pp. 111–12). As he and Dumouchel see it, the economic arena is indeed a battleground, but it also has its own built-in mechanisms for the resolution of specifically economic conflicts, and its particular type of combat provides society as a whole with a functional substitute for the type that would otherwise threaten to tear it apart or at least force it to an endless destruction of sacrificial victims. First we will consider what these thinkers believe Girardian psychological thought can contribute to the field of economics and then what they think Girard overlooks.

Economics is usually conceived in objectivistic terms. Generally economists have assumed that scarcity, for example, is a function of lack of economic goods. They have also believed that it is scarcity that causes conflict and that an increase in economic production will therefore, by reducing scarcity, also lead to a reduction of conflict. In the political arena, these assumptions have been shared by both the right and the left. Paul Dumouchel's section of *L'Enfer,* entilted "L'Ambivalence de la rareté," proposes that the opposite is really the case: "Contrary to the liberal tradition [which Dumouchel traces from Hume, Locke, and Malthus through Paul Samuelson], which believes that natural limitation of resources forces desires to converge on the same objects, our hypothesis claims that the mimetic convergence of desires on the same objects is what causes the parsimony of nature" (p. 191). He also argues that only this way of thinking can explain the fundamental aporia of traditional economics, "the fact that scarcity does not correspond to any particular real quantity of goods and disposable services" (p. 191)—that is, that the only way one can distinguish, even within the framework of traditional economics, between extreme and moderate scarcity is by way of the intensity with which the lack of certain goods is felt rather than by any purely objective measure of deficiency. To the objection that the actual physical deprivations to be found in primitive societies would amount to an objective state of lack and therefore of scarcity, Dumouchel responds that it is precisely in modern, relatively wealthy societies that people are most convinced that they suffer from scarcity, whereas in primitive societies both the sense of need and the distribution of goods are managed in such a way that there is little or no experience of scarcity.[7] "Scarcity is a social institution," he says. "It founds the modern world as the sacred founded primitive societies" (p. 179). It founds it, that is, by using the sense of need to generate competition and productivity.

Dumouchel's Girardian revision of the idea of economic scarcity is paralleled by the approach of André Orléan, another economist, to the concepts of "wealth" and monetary "value." In his 1986 essay, "La Théorie mimétique face aux phénomènes économiques," Orléan suggests that the objectivizing approach of traditional economics to the idea of value amounts to a kind of "fetishism" that only an analysis in terms of Girardian psychology can break through.[8] According to Orléan there is a close parallel between

---

7. Dumouchel cites Marshall Sahlins's *Stone Age Economics* (1972) as support for this view.

8. In *To Honor René Girard*, pp. 128–29.

Girard's idea of the ontological incompleteness of the subject and the state of uncertainty that the economic producer-merchant finds himself involved in: "Both are confronted with the same basic situation: a desire that cannot be resolved into a more or less lengthy list of objects, a desire opaque to itself and subject to perpetual reinterpretations" resulting from endlessly repeated disappointments as people discover that what they sought turns out not to offer them the satisfaction they had hoped it would (pp. 124–25). The economic concept of "wealth," he suggests, developed as a device for dealing with this situation; it is the economic equivalent of what in Girardian terms would be the concept of "the absolutely desirable" (p. 126). Orléan says that the merchant's desire for wealth is proportional to his sense of a lack of subjective being, and that all economic significations proceed from its exteriorization in the form of money as the fetishistic sign of some presumably intrinsic property of value (p. 128). This is a theme Orléan also took up in *La Violence de la monnaie* (1982), where he and his coauthor, Michel Aglietta, say that "mimetism is the key process that makes intelligible the way needs evolve in a being marked by inconstancy and indeterminacy of desire. Unable to find in himself a rule that will enable him to make a choice of objects, he turns toward others to guide him in his search."[9] Whereas classical economics has assumed that preferences are the results of private, individual, basically utilitarian calculations of pleasure and pain and are therefore prior in principle to any exchange or social relations, Orléan and Aglietta think that the workings of mimetism precede all valuations and therefore establish the imperative necessity of social relations at the very heart of economic activity.

Dupuy makes a similar point in his criticism of Max Weber's sociological analysis of capitalism. Weber, says Dupuy, falls into a naïve materialism in characterizing capitalism as based on an unbounded appetite for worldly wealth; rather, capitalism constitutes the most "spiritual" of universes because what moves it is not really the desire for objects but "envy," the fundamentally ontological

9. Michel Aglietta and André Orléan, *La violence de la monnaie* (1982), p. 5.

fascination with the "human Mediator" hidden behind those objects (*L'Enfer*, p. 73). The objects the capitalist pursues are not simply utilitarian instruments for the satisfaction of natural appetites but spiritual symbols, the signs of envy to which his title, "Le Signe et l'envie," refers. Girard's theory of "double mediation," he says, offers the only adequate explanation of the underlying energy of capitalism and of the nature of the spiritual world it generates under modern conditions, with the breakdown of barriers to internal mediation:

> It is neither the subject nor society that determines what is desirable, but the *Other*. Or rather, since the subject and his *alter ego* have become perfectly interchangeable doubles, it is their involuntary cooperation that makes the object spring forth from nothing. Each discovers in the desire of the Other the absolute proof of the reality and value of the object. As these rival desires increasingly exacerbate one another as their human bearers become closer, they become capable of creating a world more real and desirable than any object of physical and social reality. (P. 70)

Dupuy has also suggested, in his 1981 essay, "Shaking the Invisible Hand," that Adam Smith's openness to this perspective was an important element in his special greatness as an economist. Smith is often read as having introduced, in his concept of the "invisible hand," an idea of purely impersonal economic mechanism that has fed directly into the modern tendency toward the "one-dimensionalization of people" and the "trivialization of their relationships," but Dupuy says this is based on a shallow reading.[10] He interprets Smith's idea of "sympathy" in *The Theory of Moral Sentiments* (1759) as having to do with "the 'contagion' of sentiments and values"—making his thought, in effect, an anticipation of Girardian mimetic theory and something quite different from the standard economic theory that both before and after Smith has always tended to assume that there could be "pure" economic interests: "Traditional thought held that interests could *contain*, i.e., could stem the flow of passions. Smith,

10. In *Disorder and Order*, ed. Paisley Livingston, pp. 134–35.

for his part views interests as *containing* passions, in the sense that they are infected by them. The bug of contagion is within them. And if Smith sees economy as *containing* violence—and this is what is meant by the 'invisible hand'—it is in this double meaning of the verb 'to contain' " (p. 136).

It is precisely to Smith's invisible hand, therefore, that Dupuy and Dumouchel look for an alternative form of resolution of violence from that which Girard believes is normally the only effective one. Dupuy suggests that whereas the objects of mimetic rivalry tend to be viewed by Girard as unique, indivisible, and therefore unshareable, "the object conceived by economic thought and fashioned by economic reality is of a palpably different sort. It is an item of *merchandise,* in the precise sense that Marx gave that term. It has no value and does not exist at all except in relationship to other objects for which it can always be exchanged" (*L'Enfer,* pp. 112–13). Although Girard offers an important insight, Dupuy believes, into "the logic of appropriative mimesis" as having to do with unique objects that "have no price" and therefore give rise to murderous conflict, nevertheless "the abstract logic of equivalence and of exchange value" is able in practice to counteract the first logic and deflect it from its destructive course:

My hypothesis is that the economy brings about a conjunction of these two logics and that it is here one must look for the key to the surprising resistance of the modern world to runaway mimetic conflict. The economy is certainly the place of a war of all against all, perhaps the most violent there has ever been, but it also serves as an ever expanding means of channeling the overflow of mimetic energies and preventing the reservoir of human antagonisms from exploding destructively. . . . In the universe of merchandise, the imitation of the Other's desire does not necessarily cause the Subject to hurtle, head lowered, against the obstacle that his model constitutes. Direct conflict can be avoided by a simple lateral move. It suffices for the Subject to acquire *the equivalent* of the object possessed or desired by the Other for him no longer to feel the torments of envy. Since all items of merchandise are commensurable with one another, mimetic rivalry becomes reduced to the struggle of each person for his share of a cake called "the national wealth," the dough of which is an indistinct mixture of all exchangeable goods. (P. 113)

His colleague, Paul Dumouchel, means essentially the same thing when he says that in the economic marketplace, "[t]he intensification of rivalries diminishes the chances of polarization and catastrophic implosive conflict" because "no polarization can take place if the lateral displacements are universal" and therefore remain in equilibrium (p. 187). One must distinguish, he says, between two different ways in which a society can break out in turmoil: "An implosive outburst, which characterizes the sacrificial crisis, and an explosive one, proper to scarcity, which is simultaneously the mechanism of growth and the mechanism that produces exchange-value" (p. 187 n.). The implosive outburst is a progressive polarization against a single victim; the explosive one is the opposite. In this respect, says Dumouchel, "scarcity protects us from our own violence," because the exteriorizing tendency and the universalizing of rivalries that go hand in hand with it prevent violence in the modern economic arena from taking on the sacrificial form that it did in primitive societies (p. 190). In this way the "invisible hand" does the same kind of work for the modern world that sacrifice and religion did for the premodern.

Girard, on the other hand, does not agree. He is convinced both that a sacrificial crisis remains a real danger even for modern society and also that religion, though not religion of the sacrificial variety, has an essential contribution to make to its transcendence. What he has in mind is the fundamentally antisacrificial message of the Bible, which, as will be explained further in the next chapter, he believes represents a gradual revelation of the mimetic and victimizing mechanisms and culminates in the teaching that the only effective antidote to mimetism and scapegoating is the nonviolent love that became incarnate in Jesus Christ. Among the economists the one who has explained most clearly and extensively his difference from Girard in this regard is Dupuy, who describes Girard as tending sometimes to become the "prisoner" of the *système girard* (*L'Enfer,*

p. 123, n. 1). It will be worth considering his specific criticisms of Girard's approach before going on to consider more carefully the kind of radical transcendence Girard is looking for.

Dupuy says that the basic problem in Girard's thought is indicated by his statement, "Like violence, love abolishes differences" (p. 120).[11] Girard, he says, thinks that these two opposites, love and violence, are the only alternatives, that one must choose between the Kingdom of God on earth or else an apocalyptic catastrophe. He suggests that Girard has not himself noticed a fundamental ambiguity in his conception of evangelical love, which tends toward two opposing poles: "the one, which I will call the renunciation of violence, which seems to me to imply an absolute liberty; the other, which I will call fusion-love [amour-fusion], which seems to me to imply a no less absolute absence of liberty" (p. 120).

The first of these, says Dupuy, is conceived of by Girard as demanding "a radical exit from the mimetic circle," which he thinks can result from knowledge of its underlying mechanisms. Dupuy, however, argues that although the victimizing mechanism may be disarmed by knowledge in the way Girard claims, "the mimetic mechanism itself, as well as the acquisitive and conflictual mimesis that proceeds from it, is an indelible property of the human species and even of the higher mammals and is probably connected with the characteristics of their brains and their learning faculties, so that it is not possible for knowledge to bring about a complete escape from the necessities it imposes" (p. 121). A demand for radical freedom from mimesis would amount, says Dupuy, to a world-denying attempt to deny the human condition—a kind of angelism or what he calls, borrowing a term from Emmanuel Mounier, "intimism"—a tendency toward withdrawal for the sake of cultivating the soul's beauty in isolation from the social world (p. 128).[12] As such it resembles all too closely, he says, the world-denying tendency of traditional Christianity and stands in opposition to the Greek tradi-

11. Dupuy is quoting from Girard's Des choses cachées, p. 293; the quotation is found in the English translation on p. 270.

12. Referring to Mounier's Communisme, anarchie, et personnalisme (1966).

tion of humanism, which he thinks Girard unfairly dismisses as just one more expression of cultural violence.

Dupuy says that for the Greek tradition "the antithesis of violence was not love but action and speech, or rather the power people acquire when they speak and act together" (p. 125). Adam Smith's *Wealth of Nations* carried forward this tradition, he says, in its recognition that one of the most important incentives for economically productive action is "public admiration" (p. 126).[13] Human beings, suggests Dupuy, have a "need" for "prestige and greatness" that is just as basic as their biological needs, and to satisfy that need they also need "others who are really others" (p. 126). He fears that Girard's radical demand for rejection of worldly values in favor of the Gospels' ideal of love would, therefore, have a destructive effect on the best possibilities of genuinely human life. It would sap the economy's potential to generate the material wealth that can satisfy our physical needs, and it would frustrate our attempts to find a way of putting to good use our natural energies and ambitions.

It would also, he suggests, negate alterity as such, depriving us of "others who are really others."[14] This he sees as the implication of the second pole toward which he said Girard's conception of Christian love tends, that is, "fusion-love," in which one simply identifies with the other, with the result that there is no longer a possibility of conflict: "[I]f I *am* the Other, his victories will always be my victories and never my defeats" (p. 123). This extinction of the differences that make for separateness and possible rivalry might preserve a kind of peace, but at the cost of an essential element in our humanity. Dupuy acknowledges in a footnote that in subsequent conversations with Girard he found that Girard's Christian conception of love is "more nuanced" than this and that he tries to incorporate otherness into it (p. 123, n. 1), but he is not convinced that

13. Referring to *The Wealth of Nations,* book 1, ch. 10.

14. As an example of what he considers a more favorable approach to alterity, Dupuy refers to the concern of Emmanuel Levinas with the "entre-nous" (*L'Enfer,* p. 130). See also Dupuy's suggestion regarding the need for an "epistemology of the *entre-deux*" (p. 132).

Girard has succeeded in resolving the dilemma to which he thinks the *système girard* has led him.

As was seen in the last chapter, the temptations and dangers of fusion or devouring identification and the problem of how rightly to relate to interpersonal otherness have been topics of interest well beyond the bounds of the Girardian school. They have been themes of much recent French psychological thought, from Lacan on. The next chapter will consider in more detail the specifics of Girard's quest for a way to transcend conflictual mimesis while retaining a place for genuine alterity, and it will also turn outside the Girardian school proper to discuss Marie Balmary's distinctive approach to the same problem.

CHAPTER 6

Psychology and Transcendence:
Beyond the Interdividual

W E saw in the last chapter how the psychological inquiries of the Girardian school have led beyond the strictly psychological field to those of anthropology, sociology, political economy, and religion. This could hardly be surprising, since psychology, as the study of the inward lives of human beings, can be expected to reach ultimately into all the dimensions of human existence and to all possible questions about its meaning and goal, even if psychology as such cannot answer them. The inevitability of this stretching of the scope of psychology is further underscored by the fact that Marie Balmary, who cannot be classified as a member of the Girardian school, has also, in her most recent book, *Le Sacrifice interdit: Freud et la Bible* (1986), turned to the Bible as a resource for the exploration of questions having to do with the challenge of becoming a genuine individual and conducting one's interpersonal relations in a way that respects the otherness of one's children, parents, spouses, and so on. In both cases, though in their own ways, Girard and Balmary have found their psychological interests leading them not only to the study of religion as a social and historical phenomenon, but also to the exploration of properly theological issues—which in the Girardian case have also been taken up as such by the Austrian theologian Raymund Schwager.[1] Or to put it another way, both have come to believe that to understand what human being is, one must also consider questions about the nature of the relation between the human and the divine, because only in that relation does human being enter into its full dimensions. In the words with

---

1. Raymund Schwager, S.J., is professor of dogmatic theology at the University of Innsbruck and the author of *Must There Be Scapegoats?: Violence and Redemption in the Bible* (1987), a translation of *Brauchen Wir Einen Sündenbock?* (1978).

which Jean-Michel Oughourlian, in *Things Hidden,* summarized Girard's thinking on this point, "If we follow your reasoning, the real human *subject* can only come out of the rule of the Kingdom [of God]; apart from this rule, there is never anything but mimetism and the 'interdividual.' Until this happens, the only subject is the mimetic structure" (p. 199).

René Girard on True and False Transcendence

This commitment of Girard's, which he has stated again and again,[2] to what he believes is the central relevance of the Bible and particularly the Gospels to an understanding both of the modern world and of the human condition as such is one of the main reasons he is such a controversial figure in modern French thought. In a 1987 interview with Girard, Thomas F. Bertonneau asked him, "How far is your interest in religion, or indeed the religious element, responsible for the defensive attitude many people seem to take toward your theory?"[3] Girard's answer was, "I would say ninety-eight-and-a-half per cent; maybe ninety-nine-and-a-half." The problem, however, may be less one of disagreement between Girard and some of his readers than one of communication, since what Girard has in mind in his reading of the Bible is something very different from what in his "Postface" to *L'Enfer des choses* by Dumouchel and Dupuy he called "the traditional, but lazy, reading" of the evangelical texts (p. 263). What Girard had particularly in mind in that statement was the tendency of the Christian tradition to interpret the biblical predictions of apocalyptic violence as having to do with divinely inflicted vengeance rather than with the inevitable, natural consequences of strictly human violence. That particular point, however, is only one indicator of a more extensive, systematic one between Girard's conception of the revelation in Christ and that of what in *Things Hidden* he calls "historical Christianity."

The essential element in historical Christianity, according to Girard, has been its appropriation, or perhaps one should say misap-

2. See, for example, *Things Hidden,* p. 138.
3. Bertonneau, "The Logic of the Undecidable," p. 9.

propriation, of the theme of sacrifice. For Girard the essence of Christianity properly understood is the antisacrificial revelation of the workings of human violence and especially the victimizing mechanism. As Girard reads the story of Jesus, this was the central point of both his preaching and his life: Jesus had himself, on the basis of the earlier biblical tradition's progressive critique of sacrifice, come to understand the underlying mechanisms of desire, rivalry, violence, and scapegoating, and he called for their renunciation in favor of the rule of the God he believed was the source of nonviolent love. Developing Oughourlian's comment about how "the mimetic structure" is the only subjective source of human action apart from the Kingdom or rule of God,[4] Girard says that "violence, in every cultural order, is always the true *subject* of every ritual or institutional structure" (*Things Hidden*, p. 210). His special concern in his interpretation of Christianity has been to bring to light once again what he believes is its saving revelation. He believes this has the power both to free us from the mechanisms of false subjectivity and to guide us toward the development of true subjectivity, which is to be found in what he calls the "sur-transcendence of love" (p. 233) and which he believes Jesus both taught and exemplified—not the false transcendence constituted by violence.

In Girard's interpretation, the victimizing, or scapegoat, mechanism as the goal toward which all mimetic desire and rivalry ultimately tend was the secret "hidden since the foundation of the world" referred to in Matt. 13:35 and Luke 11:50–51 (and alluded to, of course, in the title of *Things Hidden since the Foundation of the World*).[5] It was hidden both because of the reluctance of people to face the reality of their own mimetic and violent motives and also, as was explained in the preceding chapter, because as the source of society, religion, and culture generally, the victimizing

---

4. It is perhaps worth mentioning that in all the places in the New Testament that speak of the "kingdom of God," the term in Greek is *basileia tou theou*, which means literally, the "rule" or "reign" of God—not a place, that is, or even a community, but a condition of being governed inwardly by the will of God.

5. See *Things Hidden*, pp. 159–60, 164.

mechanism had to be shielded from direct knowledge in order that it might carry on its needed foundational work. This is what Girard thinks the Gospels mean when they refer to Satan as the "prince of this world": the false transcendence found in victimization and negatively symbolized by the image of Satan, the victim's "adversary" or "accuser," is the foundation of the institutions, prohibitions, and differences that make up and hold together the world of our ordinary lives. As Girard put it in *The Scapegoat*, ". . . the kingdom of Satan is not one among others. The Gospels state explicitly that Satan is the principle of every kingdom" (p. 187). The Passion of Christ as a historical event and the evangelical texts that continue to present its message expose that mechanism and thereby break the power of Satan's kingdom:

> The Passion reveals the scapegoat mechanism, i.e., that which should remain invisible if these forces are to maintain themselves. By revealing that mechanism and the surrounding mimeticism, the Gospels set in motion the only textual mechanism that can put an end to humanity's imprisonment in the system of mythological representation based on the false transcendence of a victim who is made sacred because of the unanimous verdict of guilt.
>
> This transcendence is mentioned directly in the Gospels and the New Testament. It is even given many names, but the main one is Satan, who would not be considered simultaneously *murderer from the beginning, father of lies, and prince of this world* were he not identified with the false transcendence of violence. (P. 166)

Girard goes on to interpret Satan as basically a mythic image of conflictual mimetism as such, saying that it is not by chance "that, of all Satan's faults, envy and jealousy are most in evidence. Satan could be said to incarnate mimetic desire were that desire not, by definition, disincarnate. It empties all people, all things, and all texts of their substance" (p. 166). This last point tells us why the quest for subjective existence—toward becoming, in Kierkegaard's phrase, an existing individual—must lead through the question of the difference between true and false transcendence. Satan, the principle of false transcendence, is also the source of death-in-life, the incarnation not of genuine individual subjectivity but of blind, collective mechanism. Christ, on the other hand, as the incarnation of nonviolent love, is the supreme instance and universal model of actual subjective existence. The saving revelation that breaks Satan's power and opens up the possibility of true life in the Kingdom of God—that is, life governed not by mimetic desire and violence but by love—is not just taught by Jesus as the bearer of a message but is embodied in him as the beginning of the new life itself. He is a model for all humanity, the universal "external mediator" because he modeled himself with absolute fidelity on the God of nonviolent love, thereby becoming the full expression of His saving truth and His beneficent will. "For him," says Girard, "the word that comes from God, the word that enjoins us to imitate no one but God, the God who refrains from all forms of reprisal and makes his sun to shine upon the 'just' and the 'unjust' without distinction—this word remains, for him, absolutely valid. It is valid even to death, and quite clearly that is what makes him the Incarnation of that Word" (*Things Hidden*, p. 206).

It is also what made his crucifixion inevitable: he became the supreme scapegoat because the revelation embodied in his person was, and continues to be, as threatening and therefore intolerable to this world as was its verbal expression in his preaching. "[T]he Christ," says Girard, "can no longer continue to sojourn in a world in which the Word is either never mentioned, or, even worse, derided and devalued by those who take it in vain—those who claim to be faithful to it but in reality are far from being so. Jesus' destiny in the world is inseparable from that of the Word of God. That is why Christ and the Word of God are, I reaffirm, simply one and the same thing" (p. 206).

The rejection of Jesus by the people of his own time was straightforward. The subsequent de facto rejection of the Word of God by "those who claim to be faithful to it but in reality are far from being so" is a more complex matter and constitutes the essence of what has become "historical Christianity." The first led directly to Jesus' persecution and murder, the attempt to squash the revelation through direct violence. The second led by a more round-about route to a more effective covering up through distortion—specifically the distortion that interpreted Jesus' death as a propitiatory sacrifice. The early followers of Jesus may have understood his teaching—enough at least to reflect something of it in the texts that became the New Testament—but not all of them understood it very well, and their historical successors seem to have had little capacity to grasp the meaning Girard thinks is central to it. As might have been expected, they quickly assimilated the message of Jesus and the founding events of their religious community to the pattern they *were* capable of understanding, that of sacrificial religion; they interpreted the God of Jesus as the familiar God of transcendent violence, the preaching of apocalypse as a warning of the violence that would be inflicted by that God, and Jesus' death as a sacrifice required by and offered to that God.

Interpreted in this way, the Christian religion was rendered safe for the traditional culture, which required a continuing renewal of the bond of brotherhood through the exclusion of victims. Jesus, whose victimization should have exposed once and for all the irrationality of scapegoating, was interpreted as having cooperated voluntarily with his victimizers in order to offer himself as a sacrifice for the purpose of appeasing a violent God. "This conclusion," says Girard in *Things Hidden,* "was most completely formulated by the medieval theologians, and it amounted to the statement that the Father himself insisted upon the sacrifice. Efforts to explain this sacrificial pact only result in absurdities: God feels the need to revenge his honor, which has been tainted by the sins of humanity, and so on. Not only does God require a new victim, but he requires the victim who is most precious and most dear to him, his very son" (p. 182).[6]

---

6. Schwager, S.J., *Must There Be Scapegoats?* p. 232: "As soon as the idea had spread among Christians that the kingdom of God was in certain circumstances to be defended with violence or even spread with the sword, the way was clear to project, even more openly and unnoticed, one's own evil tendencies upon God. The theological idea of the appeasement of divine wrath by the Son's act of atonement constituted a compromise between what the New Testament says about God's boundless love and one's own secret projections. By the teaching that God created the fundamental

Since Girard here brings up a specifically theological point in connection with his cultural critique of the Christian tradition, it will be worth a brief excursus to place the issue he raises in a broader theological context. He does not mention any names in this passage, but the particular medieval tradition he alludes to was clearly that of Anselm of Canterbury, who presented this argument in his *Cur Deus Homo* ("Why God Became Man") in 1098: specifically, that man's sin was an offense against God's infinite honor which could be compensated only by an infinite penalty, which required an infinite suffering that in turn could be borne only by an infinite person—which meant that one of the trinitarian "persons" had to become a man in order to pay it. Although Anselm's interpretation of the crucifixion was quickly taken up by the theological tradition of the West, it remained unknown and essentially foreign to the Eastern Christian tradition, which has tended on the whole toward a point of view much closer to Girard's.[7] Generally speaking, where Latin Christianity has emphasized the idea of mankind's salvation through sacrificial atonement, the Eastern Christian tradition has interpreted the redemption of mankind as taking place through the Incarnation, with the implication that the crucifixion was not strictly necessary but was indeed a senseless murder. It is reverently commemorated because of who was killed (the God-man) and why (because of humanity's sinful rejection of him), but for the Eastern tradition what matters essentially is that in the Incarnation as such human nature was "healed" by its assumption into the divine life of the Son of God, which is offered to be "partici-

possibility for redemption by sending his Son of his own free initiative, the idea of the undeserved, prevenient love of the Father was upheld. On the other hand, under the idea of a God who demands blood satisfaction, one's own undetected projections could continue to grow uncontrollably."

7. One might consider, for example, the way the medieval Russians canonized the "holy sufferers," Saints Boris and Gleb, Vaclav, Igor Olgovich, and numerous others, simply for being the innocent victims of a murder and therefore like Christ. See George P. Fedotov, *The Russian Religious Mind: Kievan Christianity, the Tenth to the Thirteenth Centuries* (New York: Harper Torchbooks, 1960), pp. 92–110.

pated" in by all who are willing to receive it and the healing it brings.

There are also, however, some interesting differences between Girard's theological focus and that of Eastern Christianity. In particular, Girard makes the crucifixion more clearly central to the redemptive process. Like the Eastern tradition, Girard says that Jesus invited his hearers to share in the life of the Kingdom of God, which is nonviolent love, and that if they could have accepted that invitation their deliverance from violence would have been accomplished then and there, even without the crucifixion: "The events that followed the preaching of the Kingdom of God depended entirely on the response of Jesus' audience. If they had accepted the invitation unreservedly, there would have been no Apocalypse announced and no Crucifixion" (p. 202). But he also thinks that even if the crucifixion could in principle have been avoided, it was nevertheless necessary in practice, because Jesus' audience was incapable even of understanding, let alone accepting, the invitation to the life of the Kingdom. The crucifixion was not only an inevitable consequence of human violence, therefore, but also a necessary element in the process required to bring the saving truth effectively to those among Jesus' hearers who had ears to hear it at all.

The salvific efficacy of the crucifixion, as Girard sees it, lay in its dramatic exposure of the victimizing mechanism as such, primarily because in this case it was impossible to interpret the victim in the usual way as the source of evil and one who therefore deserved to be put to death. For those who knew him—his disciples—his innocence was too patent to wear the usual mask of sacred violence. Girard says that the Gospels are careful to make this clear:

> ... the sacred plays no part in the death of Jesus. If the Gospels have Jesus pronounce on the Cross those words of anguished impotence and final surrender, "Eli, Eli, lama sabachtani"—if they allow three symbolic days to elapse between death and resurrection—this is not to diminish faith in the resurrection or in the all-powerful Father. It is to make quite clear that we are dealing with something entirely differ-

ent from the sacred. Here Life does not come directly out of the violence, as in primitive religions. . . . To sum up: if Jesus' death were sacrificial, the Resurrection would be the "product" of the Crucifixion. But this is not so. Orthodox theology has always successfully resisted the temptation to transform the Passion into the process that endows Jesus with divinity. In orthodox terms, Christ's divinity—though it is obviously not external to his humanity—is not dependent on the events of his earthly life. Instead of making the Crucifixion a *cause* of his divinity . . . it is preferable to see it as a *consequence* of the latter. (Pp. 231–32, 233)

One can see from these comments that despite his criticism of "historical Christianity," Girard considers his own thought to be genuinely in line with the orthodox Christian tradition, at least as it was defined in the early councils of the Church, and in fact he says himself that "the non-sacrificial reading brings all the great canonical dogmas back into play, making them intelligible by articulating them more coherently than has been possible up to now" (p. 224). For Girard, too, Jesus was both perfect man and perfect God, and uniquely so, because he alone remains outside the vicious circle of mimetic fascinations and violence and expresses in his life the non-violent love that characterizes the true divinity. And he alone, through his example, his teaching, and his mode of existence constitutes the one avenue of redemption that can enable other humans to enter the divine life through his mediation. "Indeed, this process could only take place through him," says Girard, "since he is the only Mediator, the one bridge between the Kingdom of violence and the Kingdom of God," because, that is, he alone brings the revelation capable of freeing us from the grip of mimetic violence: "By remaining absolutely faithful to God's Word, in a world that had not received the Word, he succeeded in transmitting it all the same" (*Things Hidden*, p. 216).

What is interesting about the difference between Girard's approach to the theology of redemption and that of the Eastern Christian tradition is precisely that his psychologically grounded theory explains what that tradition has only affirmed. The Christian East also speaks, much more than the West, of salvation as coming through illumination; but when it talks about the truth communicated in this illumination, it tends to use the metaphysical language of essence, natures, and substances. The Eastern Fathers refer constantly to the principle that "God became man in order that man might become God," and they say that this implies that there had to be a true union of the divine and the human natures in Christ because, in the often-quoted words of Saint Athanasius, "what was not assumed could not be healed." But the Eastern tradition has never made much effort to explain what this "healing" must be or how it could be imparted to other human beings beside Jesus, except that, to put it in Girardian terms, their imitation of his attitudes and behavior as an external mediator would have something to do with it. The common Eastern metaphor of Christ as a sort of healing medicine represents sin as a kind of illness infecting human nature, but without much explanation of why it can be appropriately imaged that way, what the illness consists in, and how the medicine works. Girard's psychosociological analysis of Christian themes could be said, in fact, to offer an explanation that redeems such metaphors from the muteness the Christian East has allowed them to fall into.

Girard's specific criticisms, however, have been aimed primarily at the Western Christian tradition, especially as it took shape around the sacrificial theory of atonement, and they amount to the claim that this tradition fell away not only from the revelation of the mechanism of violence Girard believes is to be found in the Gospels but also from the conception of God they present.[8] For Girard, the Bible depicts a process in which, through a gradually clarified critique of the sacrificial tradition, the victim was desacralized, and along with the victim so too was the conception of God. Comparing the opening of Genesis with that of the Gospel according to John, Girard dis-

8. I should note, however, that Girard has told me in conversation that his attitude toward the "sacrificial" version of Christianity is not as negative as it might seem: he thinks it at least has had the advantage of teaching that after the "sacrifice" of Jesus no further sacrifices are either required or appropriate.

cusses the way they each deal with the theme of expulsion but from quite different viewpoints. The important difference, he says, "is that *in the story of Adam and Eve, God manipulates and expels mankind to secure the foundations of culture, whilst in the Prologue to John it is mankind who expels God*"; the writers of the Old Testatment sensed the intrinsic connection between violence and the sacred, but they came only slowly to understand it, so that Genesis "still mistakes the *real direction* in which the expulsion occurs—what it leads to, and what it signifies" (p. 275, italics in the original). The opening sentence of the Gospel according to John, on the other hand, "reverses this meaning and direction. . . . The same thing is being repeated, with just one crucial difference—the replacement [of] the God that inflicts violence with the God that only suffers violence, the Logos that is expelled" (p. 275).

As Girard sees it, that is, the Old Testament moved through a slowly developing critique of sacrifice that led away from the idea of divine violence to divine rejection of violence, and the Gospels completed this critique by their treatment of the Passion of Christ. Historical Christianity, on the other hand, recast the Father of Jesus as the old violent God who demanded sacrifices. I referred earlier to the way Girard interprets Satan as a negative symbolization of false transcendence; although Girard does not put it in exactly these terms, one might also refer to the sacralizing conception of divinity as a positive symbolization of false transcendence. Sacred violence is imaged as "God"—demanding sacrifices and wreaking vengeance—when it is not understood as false transcendence, and as "Satan" when it begins to be so understood. If the Old Testament's progressive revelation can be spoken of as a gradual unmasking of the God of false transcendence to uncover the Satanic element in the violence he represents, the course of the historical Christianity Girard criticizes, might also be described as a reversal of that process, a reexalting of the Satanic in the place of the nonviolent God of Jesus.

Girard does, in fact, say something very like this in *The Scapegoat* when he speaks of how the New Testament figure of the Paraclete, whose name means "advocate" in Greek, came to be interpreted, not as he thinks it should be—as one who testifies on behalf of martyrs before the world—but as a figure who pleads for mercy on behalf of sinners before a vengeful God. To speak of the Paraclete as an "advocate with the Father," he suggests, casts the situation in the mold of "some transcendental trial in which the Father plays the role of *Accuser*." And he goes on to add, "This sort of thinking, even with the best of intentions—hell is paved with them—constantly makes the Father into a satanic figure" (p. 209). Rather, the real struggle is between the Paraclete and Satan (whose name, as was mentioned earlier, means "accuser" or "adversary"). What is signified by the symbolism of the coming of the Paraclete, according to Girard, is the death of the martyrs, whose function is to reenact that revelatory function of the Passion: "When the Paraclete comes, Jesus says, he will bear witness to me, he will reveal the meaning of my innocent death and of every innocent death, from the beginning to the end of the world. Those who come after Christ will therefore bear witness as he did, less by their words or beliefs than by becoming martyrs and dying as Jesus died" (p. 212).

If historical Christianity has, without realizing it, recast the God of Jesus in the Satanic mold, this throws a whole new light on the opposition between modern culture and its cast-off religious tradition. For one thing, the modern critics of Christianity continue to accept uncritically the sacrificial reading of the New Testament promoted by their opponents, unwittingly submitting themselves to their authority: "Modern anti-Christianity is merely the reversal of sacrificial Christianity and as a result helps to perpetuate it. On no occasion does this anti-Christian movement return to the text in any real sense and seek to expose it to radical re-thinking. It remains piously in awe of the sacrificial reading . . . " (*Things Hidden*, p. 226). If these critics of Christianity realized that the Christian texts could be read differently, says Girard, they might also recognize that their own opposition to the Christian religion is rooted in insights originating in the New Testament itself. What they oppose is actually "historical Christianity," not the antisacrificial message of Jesus and the Gospels, and what arouses their repugnance in it, he says, is precisely the sacrificial element and all that has come from that, such as exclusivity and persecution.

Modern atheism and talk of "the death of God" are, therefore, from Girard's point of view, simultaneously correct and naïve. Atheism is correct in opposing the God of transcendent violence, but naïve in thinking that this is the genuine God of Christian faith: "What is in fact finally dying is the sacrificial concept of divinity preserved by medieval and modern theology—not the Father of Jesus, not the divinity of the Gospels, which we have been hindered—and still are hindered—from approaching, precisely by the stumbling block of sacrifice. In effect, this sacrificial concept of divinity must 'die,' and with it the whole apparatus of historical Christianity, for the Gospels to be able to rise again in our midst. . . " (pp. 235–36).

Girard also considers the demythologizing movement in modern theology to exhibit a naïveté of its own. Whereas modern anti-Christianity wants to reject Christianity as such because of the genuine stupidity and evil it accurately discovers in the historical tradition, the demythologizing movement—Girard refers to Albert Schweitzer and Rudolf Bultmann in particular—has sought to preserve the remnants of historical Christianity by excising from it those elements it finds uncomfortable, without realizing their real significance and centrality. Schweitzer and Bultmann both objected, for example, to the theme of apocalyptic violence. Schweitzer interpreted the prediction of divine violence as the central message of Jesus himself and decided that to the modern historian Jesus must seem an example of a bizarre mentality, the only real value of which was to have inspired accidentally, as a compensation for the delay of the predicted violence, a later nonapocalyptic religion that preached altruistic self-sacrifice—for which Girard has no more use than the ordinary sort of sacrifice, considering it masochistic and alien to the Gospels (p. 236). Bultmann shared Schweitzer's belief that the apocalyptic theme was a prominent element in the earliest Christian preaching, but he differed from Schweitzer over the question of its centrality to the message of the New Testament. Rather, he interpreted it as nonessential—the expression of a no longer credible, prescientific belief in the possibility of divine intervention in the course of nature. He hoped that by dismissing it modern Christianity could become free to focus on what was of real value in the New Testament, which he thought was a sort of allegorized version of Heidegger's existentialism. "Bultmann," says Girard, "simply cut out what could no longer be contained in the sacrificial interpretation and what could not yet be given a non-sacrificial reading. . . . Indeed Bultmann, like Albert Schweitzer, always saw the Apocalypse in terms of the vengeance of God. . . " (pp. 259–60), whereas Girard reads it as a lesson regarding the inevitable trajectory of human violence and consequently as genuinely central to the true Christian message. Girard also considers this apocalyptic teaching to be much more pertinent to modern man than the demythologizers could grasp, since the consequences of human violence are becoming increasingly threatening to all of us. Rather than shore up historical Christianity through selective excisions, Girard would rather see its distortions exposed and corrected by a new reading that would rediscover the original significance of the themes it twisted to fit its own misconceptions.

Even so, however, Girard has no desire to make historical Christianity into a new scapegoat. Misleading as it has been, Girard considers historical Christianity, too, to have played a needed, if ironic role in preserving the gospel of Christ. When Christianity spread in the ancient world to vast numbers of people who had no deep knowledge of the biblical tradition and its progressive critique of sacred violence, the sacrificial version of Christianity served to make it acceptable to them and thereby to preserve, like a protective envelope, the buried traces of the real message of Christ until a time would come when its true meaning could be grasped. Girard believes that with the development of modern psychological and sociological insights and the contemporary entry of lived history into apocalyptic conditions, the time for that long awaited unveiling has now come.

What will be specifically unveiled, he believes, besides the mimetic and victimizing mechanisms, is the real meaning of the invitation to life that Jesus delivered. This is above all an invitation to share fully in the life that Jesus shared with the Father, a life of nonviolent love:

> ... the gospel text contains an explicit revelation of the foundation of all religions in victimage, and this revelation takes place thanks to a non-violent deity—the Father of Jesus—for this revelation appears in the close association between Father and Son, in their common nature, and in the idea, repeated several times in John, that Jesus is the only way to the Father, that he is himself the same thing as the Father, that he is not only the Way, but also the Truth and the Life. Indeed, this is why those who have seen Jesus have seen the Father himself. (P. 184).

This is what Girard considers the true meaning of the orthodox doctrine of the Incarnation, but he thinks it can only be properly understood if one shifts from historical Christianity's metaphysically oriented idea that the Incarnation was an exclusive relation between Jesus and the Father to the realization, grounded in the insights of interdividual psychology, that the Incarnation revealed a mode of existence capable of being shared by all mankind:

> The theology of the Incarnation is not just a fantastic and irrelevant invention of the theologians; it adheres rigorously to the logic implicit in the text. But it only succeeds in becoming intelligible if we read the text in non-sacrificial rather than sacrificial terms. This is, in effect, the only time that this notion of a fullness of humanity that is also a fullness of divinity makes sense in a context that is as "humanist" as it is "religious". . . . The non-sacrificial reading allows us to understand that the Son alone is united with the Father in the fullness of humanity and divinity. But it does not imply that this union is an exclusive one, or prevent us from envisaging the possibility of mankind becoming like God through the Son's mediation. (P. 216)

Historical Christianity, by recasting Jesus as divine in the old mold, and exclusively so, has made his invitation to share his life seem just another instance of the double bind, a command to imitate what was by its very nature inimitable, since no one could really be what that tradition supposes him to have been: a uniquely divine being. It has, in effect, represented Jesus himself as a *skandalon,* or "stumbling block," standing as an impediment to our entry into the Kingdom.

The theme of the *skandalon* is one of the major themes of the New Testament, but it has been almost entirely ignored by the historical tradition as well as by modern commentators. Girard considers it nevertheless one of the key symbols in the New Testament's elucidation of the psychology of desire. "Derived from *skadzein,* which means to limp," he says in *The Scapegoat,* "*skandalon* designates the obstacle that both attracts and repels at the same time" (p. 132). He goes on to say that through this combination of attraction and repulsion, the "stumbling block" becomes "so fascinating that one must always return to it" and that with each return its power of fascination is augmented.

The *skandalon,* even when it wears the mask of God, is a kind of Satanic incarnation, whose power is a demonic force working to enslave those who fall under its thrall. In psychological terms, it is the most intense form in which mimetic desire takes hold of its prey, playing on what Girard, referring to Oughourlian's discussion of possession, says is "the strongest desire of all, the desire to be possessed" (p. 141). "Disoriented by this desire," he says, "the subject tries to become a part of the orbit of the sun that dazzles him, and he literally becomes a 'satellite.' " There is no more powerful form of that desire than that of the double bind, in which the model and the obstacle become one and the same, with the result that, as was explained in the preceding chapter, the model's opposition as obstacle makes whatever, as model, he possesses or desires seem all the more desirable and makes him seem himself all the more fascinating.

Jesus' insight into the psychological structure of the stumbling block as a function of the entanglements of mimetism seems to have been something his hearers had particular difficulty understanding. One might speak of it as a kind of psychological demythologizing for which his audience was not yet ready. "A careful reading of the Gospels," says Girard, "shows us that Jesus prefers the language of *skandalon* to that of the demonic" while the opposite is true for the disciples and the editors of the Gospels (p. 194). "Only Jesus can master the language of *skandalon*," he goes on to say, "the most important passages clearly reveal that the two languages are applied to the same objects, and they show us Jesus translating the demonic *logos* in terms of mimetic scandal. This is achieved in the famous admonition to Peter: 'Get behind me, Satan! you are a scandal to me [an obstacle] because the way you think is not God's way but man's' " (p. 194). In the passage in question (Mark 8:27–33 and Matt. 16:21–23), in which Peter objects to Jesus' saying his mission is going to end in crucifixion rather than in the triumph of a traditionally conceived messiah, we see Jesus experiencing, but resisting, the temptation to be the kind of messiah Peter wanted: "by exposing Jesus to the contagious temptation of his own worldly desire, Peter transforms the divine mission into a worldly undertaking that must inevitably come up against rival ambitions which it arouses or by which it is aroused, Peter's own for example. In this context Peter plays the role of Satan's substitute, *suppositus*, the model-obstacle of mimetic desire" (p. 194; see also p. 157).[9] (Viewed in this light, it must seem one of the great ironies of the tradition of historical Christianity that so much of it has involved struggles over rival claims to represent the authority of Peter.)

It is important to remember in this context the principle Jean-Michel Oughourlian referred to in the passage cited at the beginning of this chapter: "If we follow your reasoning, the real human *subject* can only come out of the rule of the Kingdom; apart from this rule, there is never anything but mimetism and the 'interdividual.' Until this happens, the only subject is the mimetic structure" (*Things Hidden*, p. 199). Peter was in the grip of a desire he had "caught" from the surrounding religious culture, with its dreams of a restored worldly kingdom under the rule of a Davidic messiah who would be the incarnation of violence. Each human being is called, like Jesus

---

9. This was, of course, the very temptation Jesus was represented (in Matt. 4:1–10 and Luke 4:3–12) as experiencing at the hands of Satan himself before he began his preaching.

himself, to choose between two kingdoms—that of violence and that of love, the kingdom of Satan and the Kingdom of God—but in the case of every human being other than the Jesus depicted in the Gospels, a choice has already taken shape unwittingly, so that one has already made a home in the kingdom ruled by the prince of this world. To cross the abyss that separates this from the Kingdom of God requires that one become capable, for the first time, of functioning as a genuine person, an individual subject, free from the trammels of mimetism. "Mankind can cross this abyss," says Girard, "but to do so all men together should adopt the single rule of the Kingdom of God. The decision to do so must come from each individual *separately*, however; for once, others are not involved" (p. 199).

To do this—to echo Kierkegaard once more—is to come into subjective existence, to be reborn as an existing individual. Although neither Girard nor his theological commentator, Raymund Schwager, ever refer to Kierkegaard, it seems at least a significant accident that both evoke echoes of his thought, since more than any other modern Christian thinker he emphasized both the challenge and the imperative of becoming a genuine subject and described it as a transition from nonbeing to being, to a radically new life requiring a "New Birth" into filiation to God.[10] To make this transition, one must undergo, as Kierkegaard's Johannes Climacus puts it in the *Philosophical Fragments,* the paradoxical realization "that he does not exist."[11] Father Schwager puts it in very similar words when he says that to enter into the new life revealed in Christ's love, the disciples "have to arrive at the most profound insight and experience: that of themselves they are nothing."[12] Only in that life does one truly live as a conscious, free person—a "subject" in the sense in which Kierkegaard used the word. So also in Girard's thought, in the kingdom of Satan there is no genuinely subjective existence—

10. See, for example, Kierkegaard's *Philosophical Fragments,* 1962 translation, pp. 23, 27, 90–93; 1985 translation, pp. 18–19, 22, 73–75. For a discussion of this point in Kierkegaard's thought, see Webb, *Philosophers of Consciousness,* pp. 255–58.

11. 1985 translation, p. 22.

12. *Must There Be Scapegoats?* p. 179.

that is to say, no free, intelligent, responsible existence—but only the automatism of violence: ". . . violence, in every cultural order, is always the true *subject* of every ritual or institutional structure. From the moment when the sacrificial order begins to come apart, this subject can no longer be anything but the *adversary par excellence,* which combats the installation of the Kingdom of God. This is the devil known to us from tradition—Satan himself, of whom some theologians tell us that he is both subject and not subject at once" (*Things Hidden,* p. 210).

The opposite is the love exemplified in Christ, a love which is above all intelligent—which is, in fact, the only foundation and source, as both Girard and Oughourlian see it, of genuine intelligence among people whose consciousness is dimmed and clouded by mimetic desire, rivalry, and the fascination of the *skandalon.* In *Things Hidden,* toward the end of their discussion of the Judaeo-Christian scriptures, Oughourlian says, "Love is the true demystifying power because it gives the victims back their humanity" (p. 276), to which Girard replies:

> . . . love is certainly not a renunciation of any form of rationality or an abandonment to the forces of ignorance. Love is at one and the same time the divine being and the basis of any real knowledge. . . . Love is the only true revelatory power because it escapes from, and strictly limits, the spirit of revenge and recrimination that still characterizes the revelation in our own world. . . . Only Christ's perfect love can achieve without violence the perfect revelation toward which we have been progressing—in spite of everything—by way of the dissensions and divisions that were predicted in the Gospels. (P. 277)

This contrasts, of course, with the Enlightenment ideal of a "pure rationality," which Girard thinks is impossible in practice, since apart from a conversion of the heart that conditions a corresponding clarification of the mind, no thinking ever really takes place free from the vicious circles of desire and violence: "There is no purely 'intellectual' process that can arrive at true knowledge because the very detachment of the person who contemplates the warring brothers from the heights of his wisdom is an illusion" (p. 277).

More needs to be done, as I will suggest at greater length in the next chapter, to flesh out and develop this idea of a rationality grounded in love. The critique of mimetism in the Girardian school goes very deep, but its discussion of the alternative to it remains rather abstract and sketchy. One major contribution toward giving this a more concrete psychological content is to be found in the recent work of Marie Balmary, who although not exactly a Girardian, has read Girard appreciatively and has also pursued in her own way the avenue he opened up through his exploration of biblical themes.

Marie Balmary and the Knife of Differentiation

Balmary tells us in *Le Sacrifice interdit* ('Sacrifice Prohibited," 1986) that the reason she took up the study of the Bible was to broaden the scope of the kind of psychology in which she had become interested. As was indicated in the second chapter above in the discussion of her earlier book, *Psychoanalyzing Psychoanalysis,* Balmary had become persuaded that psychological disturbances cannot be understood except as disturbances in personal relationships, the most important of which are usually family relationships, and that they cannot be healed except by changing the pattern of those relationships—which may in turn require adopting a critical attitude toward the culture that gives rise to them. She also found, as she tells us in *Le Sacrifice interdit,* that this idea turned out to be not very welcome among the members of the psychoanalytic establishment in Paris: "My concern for social change was discouraged and even sometimes attacked by my teaching analysts, both at the university and in Lacan's group. To take an interest, as I was naïvely beginning to do, in questions of conscience and the social group was to engage in philosophical, sociological, or historical research. A psychoanalyst was not supposed to be concerned with anything except the unconscious, desire, castration, and the Oedipal" (p. 183). Her actual practice of psychotherapy during the years that followed convinced her, however, that this dimension had to be included in her research, and she found that the Bible offered her a rich field of data and insight for the type of exploration she wanted to undertake. "Biblical research," she says, "came to seem to me the best way I could think of to proceed in a labor of soul and memory without being snared by the current divisions of the human sciences or by the various conflicting ideologies that control them" (p. 183). What interested her particularly in the Bible were the stories of tangled family relationships and the processes by which they either led to constriction of human possibilities or to healing. She tells us (p. 184) that she has been deeply impressed by Girard's anti-sacrificial interpretation of the New Testament in particular, and much of her discussion of Jesus builds on his foundation; but her own focus in *Le Sacrifice interdit* is primarily the book of Genesis and the stories of the patriarchal families, and she tries to find in them and other Old Testament stories a basis for a more positive understanding of sacrifice that can stand alongside and supplement Girard's negative critique.[13]

As fits her Lacanian training, Balmary takes a special interest in the problem of relationships of devouring identification. She sees sacrifice in the Bible as an ambiguous theme, sometimes leading toward such identification and sometimes working to counter it. Stated briefly, her idea is that people are constantly tempted to retreat from genuinely individual existence, with respect for the individuality and alterity of others, into relationships of "fusion," in which one either tries to devour the other or to yield oneself to being devoured.[14] Either way, where there had been two, or at least the possibility of two, the result is that there remains only one—a situation nicely symbolized, she suggests, in the repeated phrase in the story of Abraham's intended sacrifice of Isaac (traditionally known in the Jewish tradition as the "binding" of Isaac) that can be literally translated from the Hebrew as "they two oned" (p. 201). Duality of this sort, she says, "is fusional; it tends always toward the single; to be made one in this manner is solitude" (pp. 201–2).

13. Mme. Balmary told me in conversation in Paris in June 1989 that she is currently working on a new book on the Gospels.

14. It should be noted that Balmary's use of the word "fusion" is more general than that of Lacan, in which, as was explained above, the term "fusion" applies only to the pre-imaginary and "identification" to the imaginary stages of development.

Even before the "binding" on the mountain of sacrifice, Abraham had already "bound" Isaac to him within the field of language, says Balmary, by the possessive pronouns that made him "his." The divine command to make an offering of "*your* son, *your* only" was deeply ambiguous in a way that reveals the ambiguity of the theme of sacrifice as such. Abraham interpreted it to mean a sacrifice in the traditional sense, the killing of a victim and the offering of his flesh to the god; but a closer reading, she suggests, shows that the important factor here is that this is not represented as God's explicit intention but Abraham's interpretation, in which he is projecting onto the divine, in a manner like that of psychological transference with an analyst, his own habitual pattern of thinking. The biblical narrative, read literally, contains no actual command to sacrifice or make a burnt offering of Isaac, although all the usual translations also interpret the command that way and interpolate that reading into the translated text. (The only exception Balmary found was in the interpretation of the medieval Jewish commentator, Rashi, who said that God did not ask for Isaac's immolation but only that he be offered to Him, after which he would be allowed to go on living; *Sacrifice*, p. 197). In the very literal French translation by André Chouraqui that Balmary draws on,[15] Gen. 22:1–2 reads:

> Elohim put Abraham to the test. He said to him: "Abraham!" He said, "Here I am."
> He said: "Take, then, your son, your only, he whom you love, Isaac, go for you [*va pour toi*] into the land of Moriah, there raise him up on high [*monte-le en montée*] on one of the mountains that I will tell you.

The passage is loaded with rarely noticed ambiguities that Balmary thinks are highly significant, of which the most important is perhaps the phrase, "raise him up on high." This phrase is often used to refer to sacrifice, but Balmary insists that its "polysemiousness" should be preserved: ". . . burning the victim is not the only way to make him rise toward God. The original text is more ambiguous and therefore genuinely symbolic; like a door pivoting on its

---

15. Paris: Desclées de Brouwer, 1974.

hinges, the phrase 'raise up' can point either toward the idea of immolation or toward that of 'raising toward the Other' . . ." (p. 216).

Another important ambiguity is found in the word for "God." The word used here is Elohim. This is the name used in the text, she says, whenever there is a divine demand for sacrifices, whereas the name YHWH is used when God prohibits sacrifice. Elohim means literally "the gods" in Hebrew and was used both to signify gods generally and to refer to the particular god of the ancient Israelites. The difference between the two names is usually explained by biblical scholars primarily as stemming from different textual sources combined by the Priestly group of editors in Jerusalem in the fifth to fourth centuries B.C. Balmary, however, thinks the use of the two different names has thematic significance, and it is true that in the story of the binding of Isaac, the command for the offering comes from Elohim while the name YHWH is used for the source of the message that a ram is to be subsituted for the boy. Balmary interprets the initial command as having been cast in accord with Abraham's perspective, so that the god-image is fundamentally the same as that of the typical ancient Near Eastern gods ("elohim") who demanded sacrifices—gods as possessive and devouring in their way as Abraham was in his.

It seems significant in this respect that the Hebrew word for the sacrificial knife also means "the eater" (p. 277)—an image that suggests the drive toward fusion that shapes Abraham's imagination and leads him to cast his God in his own image, as one who devours. The narrative, she suggests, amounts to "the unveiling of the 'imaginary' [*imaginaire*] of Abraham" (p. 197), using the Lacanian term for the systematic pattern of imagining that structures the personal unconscious and sets it in conflict with the "symbolic," which for Lacan is the voice of the true unconscious, which is structured as the language of the Other. God lets himself be taken for an idol in the familiar pagan way as "the gods," then later reveals himself as the radically "other," YHWH, who does not want Isaac killed. "Abraham," she says, "has given in accord with what he could understand about the gift. The divine, that great therapist, has allowed the attitudes of Abraham to be ascribed to him, because it is only by starting from them that a real transformation becomes possible" (p.203).

The transformation in question involves both liberation and self-discovery—with the first a prerequisite of the second. To become free himself—free, above all, to be or become himself—Abraham must accept the freedom, which is to say the alterity of the other who is his son. "Setting free his son," says Balmary, "he also becomes free himself from an imaginary God, that is, from an idol" (p. 212, again using the "imaginary" as a reference to Lacan's *imaginaire*). The devouring idol-God of Abraham's initial belief stood for the negation of alterity and therefore of the possibility of individuation. The God who is finally revealed as commanding Abraham not to sacrifice his son, on the other hand, is the fountain-head of otherness and therefore of individual selfhood as such. As Balmary puts it, "The divine himself is alterity, and alterity is his image . . ." (p. 270).

The possibility of self-discovery for Abraham is indicated by the phrase "go for you" (*lekh lekha* in Hebrew), which can also be translated literally as "go toward you" (p. 123). This phrase is almost always left out in translations, presumably because in most readings it does not seem to have any particular meaning. To Balmary, on the other hand, the phrase suggests what God has called Abraham to and is trying to educate him for:

To go toward himself, toward his name, toward the new life . . . that this new name opens for him. "Only son" does not fit with "father of a multitude." Something has to happen; after the departure of Ishmael, Abraham is in contradiction with his name. He is the father of a single son only, and when the divine commands him to 'raise him up,' Abraham proceeds along the same trajectory as before: life is diminishing—from two sons, to one, and finally to none. Sarah demanded the first son as a sacrifice so that one alone would inherit. She did not understand the calling implied by Abraham's name any more than he did. This time it is the turn of the second son, who is now the only son, to disappear. (P. 199)

To Balmary "go toward you" means, in one aspect, to go toward the generativity to which God calls Abraham as symbolized by the new name God has given him. It also means something else equally significant: to move toward becoming a genuine "Thou," an instance of what, in the sort of more philosophical and theological language she does not herself use, might be called an instance of incarnate subjectivity. The same phrase, *lekh lekha,* also appeared in the command of YHWH in Gen. 12:1 that "Abram" should leave Mesopotamia and go to the new land of promise—in Chouraqui's translation: "Go for you, from your land, of your childhood, from the house of your father, toward the land that I will show you." Rashi interpreted the *lekh lekha* as meaning to go "for your good, for your happiness," that is, from a state of deficiency to one of fulfillment (quoted, p. 123). Balmary, following his lead, interprets it as pointing toward a growth that is both psychological and spiritual at once: "Not 'toward you' in the sense of introspection, but in the sense of a search for the speaking subject" (p. 123). She says that "YHWH is he who calls man toward man" (p. 124), and she notes the parallel to Nietzsche's famous "Become who you are" and Freud's "Wo Es war, soll Ich werden," translated in the *Standard Edition* as "Where id was, there shall ego be," but literally, "Where 'It' was, there should become 'I.' "[16] The Promised Land, therefore, is the "land of I and Thou," "the land that 'I' will show to 'thou,' " which a person can see only when he becomes "a genuine 'Thou' " (p. 131).

To do this, however, Abraham must also learn to respect the "Thou," the free person in the other, in this case the other who is his son. This is what Balmary thinks the ending of the episode indicates is taking place. In Gen. 22:11–12 it says that at the mo-

16. Cf. Bruno Bettelheim on the general tendency in the the standard translation to shift Freud's vocabulary from ordinary language to something with a more "scientific" and, technical sound. *Freud and Man's Soul,* pp. 49–64, especially pp. 61–62. The Nietzsche maxim is an allusion to the subtitle of *Ecce Homo,* translated by Walter Kaufmann as "How One Becomes What One Is" (in German: "Wie man wird was man ist"). The source for the Freud quotation was given in chapter 1, note 35.

ment when Isaac lies bound on the altar and Abraham has raised his hand with the knife, "the messenger of YHWH" calls out to Abraham from the heavens and tells him, in Chouraqui's translation, "Do not cast your hand toward the boy. Yes, now I know that you, you fear Elohim! For me you have not spared your son, your only." The last sentence, which Balmary says can be rendered still more literally as "You have not kept back from me your son, your only," she interprets as meaning, "You have not kept him back from me [*moi*], held him back from "I," deprived him of The One who speaks in the first person. You have not prevented him from Speech, held him back from the Word, deprived him of the divine" (p. 202).[17] To fear Elohim means in this context, she suggests, "to respect the Creator who separates his creatures and who maintains the gap [*leur écart*] between them" (p. 203).

This, then, is the realization toward which Abraham had to be led in order to become genuinely "the father of a multitude." Abraham's basic inclination has been to devour his son, drawing him into fusion with his own person, as Balmary says his own father had done both to him and to Sarah. This attitude carried over into Abraham's response to the sacrifice he heard himself called to, but which according to the intentions of God as subsequently revealed was to be not a destruction of life but rather an offering of life to the source of the 'I,' the ground of genuinely human subjectivity in each person. This is why Balmary says that, despite the strong influence Girard's antisacrificial reading of the Bible has had on her, she has not been led by it "to reject the word 'sacrifice' or even the need for sacrifice" altogether (p. 215). There is a true and important sense, she thinks, in which a kind of sacrifice, though a nonbloody one, really was demanded of Abraham, but it had to be fulfilled despite the best intentions he was capable of at the beginning. "Abraham thinks of cutting into the 'son,' " she says, "but discovers that the knife passes through the 'my'—*there* is the handiwork of the Therapist, the God of Israel" (p. 216). Or as she also puts the same idea in

17. It should be remembered that "moi" is the standard French term for Freud's "*ich*," which in English has been translated as "ego."

another place: " 'I love you because you are mine' differs from 'I love you because you are you' only by the thickness of a knifeblade" (p. 96).

Balmary believes, therefore, that the biblical treatment of the theme of sacrifice must be appreciated precisely for the depth of its ambiguity. She agrees that the Bible moves, as Girard claims, toward a rejection of sacrifice, but she also thinks that even in its early, bloody form the idea of sacrifice was the ambiguous bearer of a lesson essential to the human-divine calling: ". . . the movement that impels humans to make sacrifices can be seen as one in which they are looking for a way to cut the ties that bind them; the biblical tradition . . . reveals where it is that the knife must pass in order that identity and alterity may each have a place. The prohibition of sacrifice takes up sacrificial violence and enables it to attain its true goal: differentiation in the field of the Word" (p. 278). By this she means that the Word of God becomes incarnate in the "I" spoken from the true center of each person's being, which is that point at which he or she emerges as a genuine subject by way of the creative presence of the God whose proper name is "I am." She also links this notion with Lacan's discussion of language as the system of symbolic differentiation that makes individuality and alterity both recognizable and possible, referring particularly to the way Lacan said of the Decalogue given on Sinai that "on these tablets, nothing is written, for one who knows how to read them, except the laws of Speech itself."[18]

The same idea is the basis for her interpretation both of the teachings of Jesus and of his person and work as the Word of God. In her discussion of Genesis she interprets the story of the Tower of Babel as having to do with the "confusion of tongues" that merges people into an undifferentiated mass, symbolized by the new way in which the people who build the tower say "we"—in such a way, that is, that "language no longer serves as a light to illuminate differences and the 'we' is no longer an alliance between 'I's, each speaking his own

18. "Remarque sur le rapport de Daniel Lagache," *Ecrits*, p. 684; quoted in *Sacrifice*, pp. 97 and 274.

word" (p. 81). Jesus, as she interprets his story, speaks on behalf of the divine effort to correct that false movement, which had resulted not in a genuine unanimity of individuals in harmony but rather in the deathly uniformity of fusional identification. He called his hearers to a new level of differentiation that would require the breakdown, indeed the sacrifice, of such identifications.

This is what she thinks is meant in the passage from Luke (12:49–53) in which Jesus speaks of how he has come to bring not peace but division, so that where there are five in a house they will be divided, three against two or two against three, father against son and son against father, and so on, and in the passage from Matthew (10:34–36) where, evoking the same image of divisions in a family, he says, "I come not to bring peace, but a sword." The word here that is usually translated "sword," she points out, is *machaira* in the Greek, the actual primary meaning of which is "knife, and especially the large knife used for sacrifices" (p. 94).[19]

Balmary points out also that the term usually translated as "setting against" (*dikazo . . . kata*), in "I have come to set a man against his father, a daughter against her mother . . ." (Matt. 10:35), can also be translated as to divide or separate, to "make two," which she interprets as referring to the possibility of changing a fusional "one" into two genuine "I"s. This is also what she thinks is meant when Jesus says that he who loves father or mother, son or daughter, "more than 'I' " is "not worthy of 'I' "—not worthy, that is, of the 'I,'" the first person singular (pp. 95–96). These passages dealing with family divisions, therefore, point, according to her reading, to the same meaning as the story of the sacrifice of Isaac: that the ties binding the members of a family together in a state of fusion must be sundered if they are to be able to accede to the true "I" that seeks to be born in each and to speak in each.

Balmary interprets Jesus himself as representing the supreme ful-

---

19. *Machaira* is also the term used in the Septuagint for the "sword" Solomon calls for in the story (1 Kings 3:16–28) of the dispute between two harlots over a baby. A comparison between Balmary's and Girard's discussions of this story will be taken up in the next chapter.

fillment of that divinely engendered process. This is what she thinks it means to speak of Jesus as the "Son of God" or the "Speech of God," two titles that, in her interpretation, are closely coordinated in meaning.[20] To interpret Jesus as divine in a mythic, exclusivistic way, on the other hand, would amount to idolatry and would negate the possibility of joining him, as he intended us to, in his life of divine sonship. The ecclesiastical declarations of the uniqueness of Jesus have tended to make us forget, she says, that in Luke's genealogy of Jesus "our father Adam" is also described as "the son of God," with the result that "the celebration of Jesus seems paradoxically to have led more often to an occultation, rather than a revelation, of man's divine filiation" (p. 231).

Balmary's interpretation of the symbolism of the Eucharist is closely connected with this issue. The tradition of what Girard calls "historical Christianity" has tended, despite the dogmas that affirm the genuine union of both the human and the divine in Christ, to emphasize his divinity in such a way that it often tended to imply for the imagination of Christians generally an ontological gulf separating Jesus from other human beings—if indeed he could be considered genuinely human at all. From a Girardian point of view, it would therefore seem no accident that the same tradition has also strongly emphasized an interpretation of the Eucharist as a sacrifice. According to Girard's theory of the origins of religion, the sacrificial victim has to be seen as unique if the victimizing mechanism is to work; it is polarization of violence against a single figure that produces unanimity among the warring brothers and grounds the victim's sacred status as simultaneously the most abased and the most exalted of beings. Sacrificial religion and the uniqueness of the

20. The phrase in French for the latter title (*Logos tou theou* in the Greek, commonly rendered in English as "Word of God") is *Parole de Dieu*. Madame Balmary suggested in converstion in Paris, in June 1989, that its meaning for her would be rendered more clearly in English as "Speech of God," especially since the term *parole* is central to the Lacanian tradition and is always translated as "speech." The Lacanian idea is that *parole* is speech in which a self-disclosing openness to the "Other" (*Autre*) is attempted but often fails. The "Speech of God," therefore, would be *parole* that attains genuine openness—even, of course, if it falls on deaf ears.

victim therefore go hand in hand, and it is not surprising that the Eucharist would be drawn into the same complex of meaning and be interpreted as a symbol of fusion rather than of differentiation— of fusion, that is, into the idolatrous collective following of a single figure whose identity engulfs all others because he alone is thought of as possessing a legitimate identity of his own. Balmary interprets this historical tendency of sacramental thinking as a fundamental misinterpretation of the Eucharistic symbolism, which she thinks points neither toward an exclusivistic claim on the part of Jesus to divinity nor toward sacrifice, but rather toward the potential of all human beings to share fully in the true "I" of which Jesus was the revelation and incarnation.

She opens her discussion of the Eucharistic symbolism by pointing out its seeming kinship to rituals in which eating represents fusion: "Is it not to eat together of the same bread and drink of the same cup so as to become a single body, the body of some other particular person? Is not the Eucharist precisely the opposite of differentiation?" (p. 275). The answer, she suggests, can be found by paying careful attention to the symbolism itself, especially the fact that it has to do not simply with bread and wine, but with the "breaking" of the bread, followed by its presentation as "my body" (p. 276). The traditional emphasis on the collective "sharing" of the bread is misplaced, she thinks. Rather what Jesus gives is "a rupture, a breaking of bread. A breaking preceded by a blessing. Each is invited to eat, and that act, which usually undoes difference, will in this case bear—most paradoxically—on a thing marked by an act of differentiation. The one loaf is broken in order to nourish each one with separateness, the condition of alliance" (p. 276).

When Jesus said "This is my body," what he meant, according to her interpretation, is not that it was his material body, which was still physically present that evening, but rather "the body of Speech . . . the body of 'I,' revealed as present in the bread broken into pieces" (pp. 276–77). Her description of the combined effect of the symbolism of the broken bread and that of the wine poured out to be drunk by all is particularly difficult to translate with all its connotations intact. What she says in French is "Après le pain brisé, pour délier, le vin versé pour allier ('vin d'alliance') sans relier" (p. 277), which implies multiple plays on the word *lier*, meaning to "tie" or "bind." Roughly rendered, the meaning would be something like: "After the bread, which is broken in order to unbind, the wine is poured out in order to bring together ('wine of togetherness') without 'binding' again." "The Eucharist, in this reading," she goes on to say, "becomes a meal that separates those whom it assembles. It becomes this thanks . . . to the fact that the fusional body [*le corps fusionnel*] is broken, freeing human beings in order to ally them in a body of speech [*un corps de Parole*] that could not exist without separation [literally without "*coupure*" or "cutting"]" (p. 277).[21]

The "fusional body," if left as that and not broken, would be the body of an idol and a lure into idolatry, which would have the effect of negating freedom and separateness and therefore of undermining individuation. In Balmary's reading, Jesus seems to have sensed the danger of this among his disciples and to have tried to counteract it by the symbolism of his words and gestures at the last supper. Balmary thinks the historical Christian tradition has generally failed to understand what Jesus himself had in mind, and has tended, with its emphasis on the exclusivity of his sonship, to make him into precisely the sort of idol he tried not to be. "The question of idolatry," she says, "poses itself in every cure, and the idolizing of Jesus is no exception to the rule: it makes for madness just as much as any other" (p. 231). She also says that psychoanalysts who have been suspicious of religion have been right to criticize the idolatry of Jesus, because "like all idolatry, it destroys life" (pp. 95–96). Here,

---

21. Although Balmary does not note this, her interpretation of the Eucharist comes close to that of the Eastern Christian tradition, which has emphasized "deification" through "participation" in Christ's incarnation more than the theme of sacrificial atonement. In the Liturgy of Saint John Chrysostom, for example, at the breaking of the bread (with the use of a symbolic sacrificial knife) just before the communion, the deacon says, "Divide, Master, the Holy Bread," to which the priest responds, "Divided and distributed is the Lamb of God: who is divided, yet not disunited; who is ever eaten, yet never consumed; but sanctifying those who partake thereof."

of course, Balmary is fully in accord with Girard and in opposition to the kind of mythological thinking he thought worked against heeding the actual message of Jesus as a call to join him in the life he proclaimed, embodied, and exemplified.

What Balmary thinks is new in the message of Jesus is not its essential meaning, which she finds pervading the Old Testament, but its location. The "good news" of the New Testament is not that a divine figure in the mythic sense has descended to earth, but that the ancient message of the possibility of life, the divine call to the new life of a genuine "I" in relation to other genuine "Thous," is now being spoken by a person who is able to live and embody that message. It is found "in the precise place from which he speaks, from within his own body, in the very place where he speaks as an individual being" (p. 97). This means that "the fact that he is simultaneously called the only Son and the first among brothers is no longer a contradiction: if he has indeed succeeded in saying 'I' without any admixture, without confusion with his parents, or his friends, or his enemies, or strangers, or even with God, then he is truly 'one' and single," perhaps the first human being to speak as a genuine individual from the heart of "his own 'I' " (p. 97). In this sense, she says, Jesus can be interpreted as rejoining "the place of the name of God, the first person singular and the verb 'to be'—the place from which Speech [la Parole] issues and to which each of us in turn seeks to find our way."[22]

This raises, however, the question of what it is we discover when we arrive at that place. As Balmary discusses it, the essential thing one discovers is one's own desire—one's own, that is, as compared with that of the others in one's life with whom one's self has become more or less confused. Rather than reproaching man for desiring, she says, Jesus calls him to greater desire, to discover his "own" desire, and she suggests that a number of the healing stories in the

22. Cf. Raymond E. Brown, S.S., *The Gospel According to John (I–XII)* (Anchor Bible, 29:537), on the idea that in John "I am" ("*ego eimi*") is "the divine name that has been given to Jesus and that he glorifies through his death, resurrection, and ascension."

Gospels have to do with the liberation of a child from the imprison-
ment imposed by the desires of others, especially parental desires
(pp. 36–37). What made Jesus a unique person and indeed perhaps
the only fully realized subject in history was precisely that his "I"
was without any admixture or confusion with his parents, his
friends, his enemies, and so on. What makes human beings in general, on the other hand, something less than fully developed subjects
is that in them the "I" is alloyed with the identities of others.
Commenting on the passage from Matt. 10 referred to earlier, in
which Jesus says, in Balmary's interpretation, that he who is unwill-
ing to separate from father or mother, son or daugher, for the sake
of the "I" is "not worthy of me," she compares such dependency for
a sense of personal existence with the problem of the collective
"we" in Genesis 11: "The 'We' of the people of Babel was empty: it
pretended to reunite instances of the first person that had in fact
disappeared. In this case, it is the opposite danger that is represented: an 'I' that comprises more than one person" (p. 96). Both
dangers, of course, lead to the same loss and the same result: the
engulfing of the individual in the collective; and both involve, from
her point of view, a difficulty in distinguishing between genuine and
false desires—one's own, that is, and those of others with whom
one has become bound in fusional blurrings of identity.

On this point Balmary sees an underlying parallel between the
Bible and the main thrust of psychoanalytic thought. What psychoanalysis calls the *prise de conscience* or coming to consciousness,
she suggests, amounts to a scientific formulation of the biblical "Go
toward you": in a successful analysis the patient learns to hear
clearly the true inner voice that he has not heard previously except
by way of the symptom; and this voice, she says, is recognized by
both Freud and Lacan as "that of desire, that of the subject" (p.
129).[23] This voice, when heeded, teaches one about the envelopes
that contain and possess one and that have to be broken out of if
one is to become a free and responsible person able to stand alone

23. On the psychoanalytic concept of the *prise de conscience,* see Laplanche and
Pontalis, *The Language of Psychoanalysis,* p. 87.

and act for oneself—or as she puts it somewhat later, "The work of becoming conscious in analysis enables one to pass from the third person to the first" (p. 212). This means, first of all, to grasp the difference between the desire felt by the true "I" and the desire of some "he" or "she" or "they" that one feels confusedly present within one.

Here there is an especially important comparison to be made between Balmary and Girard, but unfortunately it is only half-developed in the thought of either. I mentioned earlier that Girard makes a key distinction between "appetites and needs" on the one hand and "desires" on the other. The first are natural and spontaneous, the second artificial and imitative. Girard uses the term "desire" consistently in the latter, negative sense in order to distinguish it from the first, whereas Balmary uses the same word to cover both meanings. The question remains, however, of exactly what the difference is—what it is that one can discover is the "appetite" or desire of the true "I" when one becomes capable of speaking that word in a way that realizes its full possibility of intention. At the very end of *Le Sacrifice interdit,* Balmary suggests that psychoanalysis has need of *une érotique nouvelle,* a new theory of desire; but it is not altogether clear what that must be, other than that it must have its center in the possibility of genuine self-discovery. Nor does it appear that psychology and psychoanalysis, even if their contributions to such a theory might be essential, can develop it entirely out of their own resources. It seems no accident that as both Girard and Balmary begin to press toward the transcendence of the self between, and toward the possibility of a self that could stand alone and think for itself, as well as love with a love that is completely genuine, they have found it both necessary and natural to gravitate toward the languages of philosophy and theology, seeking the ground of genuine human love in a love that transcends the world. What it means to speak in this way, however, can become clearer only if the context of discourse is broadened still further.

CHAPTER 7

From Psychology
to Philosophy of Consciousness

AT the end of this overview of the new social psychology that has been developing in France, several themes stand out as characteristic and related. Found in both the Lacanian and Girardian schools is the theme of the inherent mutual involvement between the individual and either other individuals or the culture and society as a whole—the relation with either the little "other" or the great "Other," as we saw Jean-Michel Oughourlian phrase it. All the figures here discussed, whatever their divergences, share a common rejection of any psychology oriented toward radical individualism, just as they also reject what they refer to as "subject psychology"— that is, a quasi-Cartesian conception of the person as characterized by a consciousness intrinsically rational and self-transparent as well as monadically unitary. The rejection of Cartesian psychological conceptions was closely tied up, both as cause and as result, with the widespread espousal of Freudianism that took place so widely in the 1960s and early 1970s. As was discussed earlier, however, the Freudianism that finally won a broad French audience after a long period of early disinterest was a distinctly French adaptation that replaced the more individualistic thrust of the original Freudian movement with a social and cultural emphasis, primarily by way of structural linguistics as interpreted by Jacques Lacan.

The thinkers of the later 1970s and 1980s on whom the present study has focused have tended to be more critical of Freud and Freudianism than were their immediate predecessors. One theme, however, that they have all brought forward from the Lacanian-Freudian heritage is that of the deeply rooted human tendency toward "fusion" or extreme "identification" with the other, whether that is another person or one's own self-image as developed initially in the Lacanian mirror stage. This is true whether they speak of it in psychoanalytic language (Roustang, Borch-Jacobsen, and Balmary) or in the language of "mediation," "metaphysical desire," or "possession" (the Girardians). As we saw in the second chapter, the insidiousness of the temptation to merge with another in a way that would undermine individuation was the central preoccupation of François Roustang in his criticisms of both Freudian and Lacanian practice: he believed that their commitment to the responsible freedom of the analysand as the ultimate goal of analysis was undermined by their own behavior in trying to foster a virtually slavish discipleship. Roustang also raised doubts as to whether the process of analysis did not set up a kind of double bind that worked against its own supposed goal.

We also saw in the same chapter how Marie Balmary turned the techniques of psychoanalytic inquiry back on Freud himself to probe both his personal weaknesses as a man and a thinker and also the theoretical weaknesses these led to in his development of the Oedipal theory—weaknesses partly explained by the fact that he was the victim, even if a rather willing one, of the strategies, of dominance and prevarication practiced on him by his own parents. We further saw how Mikkel Borch-Jacobsen, partly on the basis of René Girard's theory of mimesis but with a more Lacanian orientation, echoed and rendered still sharper Roustang's suggestion of a tragic dilemma at the heart not only of the psychoanalytic enterprise but of the human enterprise as well.

To anyone familiar with French literature and cinema in the first decades after the Second World War, such a sense of being inescapably closed in might seem characteristically Gallic, but neither Balmary nor the Girardians fit that mold at all. The strong sense of concern that they share for the victims of those who seek to dominate points not toward a savoring of the pathos of a world with "no exit" but toward hope and the need to work for a world of greater openness, tolerance, and independence for both the individual and society. In this respect they seem expressions, if not of a new France, then at least of a rather different one. The Girardians in particular, extending their reach into politics and economics as well as psychiatry, literary criticism, and theology, bring a sense of moral urgency regarding the mechanism of victimization and also confidence that a new understanding of the psychological mechanisms growing out of the innate human tendency toward mimesis of the attitudes and especially the desires of others can win increased effective freedom on every level—personal, social, and cultural.

Girardian thought has its center in the theory of psychological mimesis. Both Girard's theory regarding the scapegoat phenomenon as the origin of society and hominization generally and his theory of metaphysical desire as the ultimate root of rivalry, masochism, sadism, fascination with doubles, and other psychological disturbances are grounded in the basic principles of mimetic psychology. The first of these has on the whole given rise to more controversy than the second. Those who attack Girard's thought usually take the scapegoat mechanism and his theory of origins as their point of departure, and unfortunately many seem to have difficulty seeing beyond them to the larger scheme of mimetic analysis of which they are only one aspect. Although this is an aspect Girard believes is true and important, he also recognizes that it is not fundamental and that others can find profit in his analysis of mimetic psychology, and even accept the idea that the mechanisms of mimesis tend to produce conflicts that can and often do result in the victimization of a scapegoat, without being committed to the idea that specifically human consciousness, language as such, religion, and society are all the result of actual historical instances of scapegoating. As Girard himself wrote in 1987, "Violence does not play a primordial role in my perspective; only mimesis does."[1]

In my own previous discussion of this issue in *Philosophers of Consciousness,* I pointed out the possibility of other approaches to the question of the historical evolution of societies, citing in particular Eli Sagan's pertinent hypothesis, in his *At the Dawn of Tyranny: The Origins of Individualism, Political Oppression, and the State* (1985), about the relatively late point at which violence began to play a major role in the formation of actual societies, at least on the basis of the historical evidence regarding the only large-scale primi-

1. *Violent Origins* (1987), ed. Hammerton-Kelly, p. 123.

tive societies for which such evidence is available.[2] On the other hand, I also concluded there that Girard's point need not ultimately depend on the historical claim that a "founding murder" has actually taken place at the origin of a given society or at the origin of *Homo sapiens* as we know him. Even if mimetic rivalry among early hominids may not have proceeded unchecked so that it had to culminate in a collective murder followed by peace and social harmony, the *tendency* to rivalry based on mimesis of desire is an undeniable feature of human life, and it can be a powerful force in society even if it does not proceed unchecked and culminate in a collective victimization. Anyone who knows the history of Nazi Germany or Khmer Rouge Cambodia, among other historical episodes of the present century, has to appreciate the way in which collective persecutions are often made use of, sometimes very effectively, in the establishment of a sense of communal cohesion. Indeed in some sense, even if not in a strictly diachronic one, it may play an essential role in all. W. H. Auden said before Girard, in the "Vespers" of his "Horae Canonicae," that it is always on the immolation of some victim, even a mythic one, "call him Abel, Remus, whom you will," that "arcadias, utopias, our dear old bag of a democracy, are alike founded: For without a cement of blood (it must be human, it must be innocent) no secular wall will safely stand."[3]

Girard, therefore, has a point when he says that conflicts of desire can lead to dangerous levels of the kind of rivalry that often results in collective violence and the murder of some victim. Not all, on the other hand, even among the Girardians, as we have seen, espouse his particular theory regarding collective violence as the inevitable result of mimetic mechanisms and the only possible foundation for society. There are many thinkers like them in the fields of economics, politics, anthropology, and law in France today who have read Girard with great interest and have participated in several conferences devoted to his ideas and their implications, but who have been

2. Webb, *Philosophers of Consciousness*, pp. 197–99.
3. Auden, *The Shield of Achilles*, p. 80.

concerned primarily with trying to understand ways that order can grow out of disorder other than by collective victimization.[4]

Another probable barrier to wide acceptance of Girard's theory of origins is the fact that one of the striking features of the intellectual history of the present century has been a shift in the conception of scientific or scholarly understanding away from what had once been a virtually universal interest in questions of origination and of the first, presumably primordial and pristine, form of a phenomenon. Whereas it was common a few generations ago to assume that knowing the origins of a phenomenon was of fundamental importance for really understanding it, now it is generally held that what matters is a grasp of systematic relations between elements in some present structure. Chemists no longer look for an *Urstoffe,* for example, as they did in the eighteenth and nineteenth centuries, and historians of religion no longer think, as many still did in the early twentieth century, that determining the earliest form of religion would enable one to know what religion was in its most essential form and therefore what it is in *essence.*[5] Rather chemists now investigate the structures of molecules and the ways they link together, and historians of religion try to understand the way rituals, myths (including myths of origin), dietary practices, magic, sacred geography, and conceptions of kinship, for example, may be connected in a given tradition. As E. E. Evans-Pritchard summarized this shift in paradigm in the field of the history of religions, it is now generally held that: (1) the search for the origins of religion was fundamentally unsound, since they cannot be directly investigated due to lack of historical records; (2) it is not possible to identify a common primitive mentality which could serve as a clue to that of the first originators of religion; and (3) not only is it impossible to determine the origins of religion, but there would be little value in

4. Examples can be found in several volumes of conference proceedings, such as *Disorder and Order: Proceedings of the Stanford International Symposium* (September 14–16, 1981), ed. Paisley Livingston, and *Violence et vérité: Autour de René Girard* (1985), ed. Paul Dumouchel.

5. Cf. Mircea Eliade, "The Quest for the Origins of Religion," in his *The Quest: History and Meaning in Religion,* pp. 37–53.

doing so, since modern scientific thought does not look for origins and essences but rather seeks to discover constant relations, such as those between ancestor cults and kinship systems, the role of ritual in defining social status, and so on.[6]

For this and perhaps a variety of reasons, it is not to be expected that, whatever its possible merits as a historical-psychological hypothesis, Girard's theory of origins will win wide acceptance in the English-speaking world. But as was noted above, he himself has said that it is not the historical claim that is fundamental in his thinking but rather his theory of psychological mimesis: Thus there is good reason to think not only that the latter deserves a careful hearing but also that it should prove widely useful for psychologists in providing an explanatory framework for the sorts of systematic relationship that many are currently investigating. I mentioned in chapter two, for example, in regard to Balmary's discussion of the connections Freud had sketched between various family members who were involved in a pattern of seductions, that her own theory of the transmission of faults from one generation within a family to another seems itself in need of a theory to explain it, and that Girard's seems made to order for the task. With respect to the case in question, one in which a male patient who had been seduced by his uncle subsequently seduced the uncle's eldest son and two of his own sisters, not only does Girard's discussion of mimesis suggest that a pattern of behavior, such as seduction, might be repeated through imitation based on modeling, but it also explains why the force of the model in a case of this sort would be especially strong: The seducer is perceived as a figure of power and therefore can be expected to excite in the seduced a sense of deficiency that can precipitate what Girard calls metaphysical desire—the feeling that if the seduced could play the same dominant role in relation to another person, he or she would take on similar power and therefore enjoy a similar plenitude of being. Hence the seduced young man in the case mentioned became a new seducer of his sister and cousins. Or, as Girard analyzes another possible variation on this

6. Evans-Pritchard, *Theories of Primitive Religion*, pp. 100–112.

theme, a seduction might, depending on the case, precipitate a masochistic version of metaphysical desire, in which the seduced would so identify with the seducer that he or she might seek to participate again and again in the seducer's power, not by emulating it actively, but by submitting to it passively in further seductions.

Whether the kind of Girardian psychological analysis represented in this book by Girard's own thought and that of Jean-Michel Oughourlian will be taken up and made use of by English-speaking investigators in the fields of psychology and psychotherapy remains to be seen, but there are numerous indications in psychological research currently being published in English that mimetic phenomena are attracting attention, even if they are being regarded from another point of view than that of a particular interest in mimesis. Reference was made in chapter four to Oughourlian's citation of a paper published in 1977 by Andrew N. Meltzoff and M. Keith Moore having to do with infant learning as evidenced by the capacity for imitation. Meltzoff and Moore were interested specifically in learning, and in disproving some of Jean Piaget's claims about its late development, rather than in imitation as such. Imitation was for them simply a means of testing preverbal learning. But in the process of making their own claim by showing how early the capacity for imitation shows itself, they were indirectly providing support for Oughourlian's further claim that a tendency to imitate is so basic to human beings that it enters into every aspect of their psychological lives and plays a role in personal relations similar to that which gravitation did in Newton's physics. Since Oughourlian wrote his book, Meltzoff has been continuing his study of infant learning in ways that similarly support the mimetic hypothesis. In 1988 he published three articles on the way children as young as fourteen months were able to learn to manipulate, disassemble, and reassemble a toy they had never seen before by watching a demonstration on videotape and then repeating the action, either immediately or after an interval of up to a week.[7] Infants in the control

7. "Infant Imitation and Memory: Nine-Month-Olds in Immediate and Deferred Tests," *Child Development* 59: 217–25; "Imitation of Televised Models by Infants,"

groups who were not given a model to imitate learned much more slowly. Other experimentalists have recently been turning up similar results that also point indirectly toward a theory of universal mimesis. Mabel Rice and Linda Woodsmall, for example, reported that children learned new words more easily when they saw them being used by others on television.[8]

One area of experimental research that seems especially pertinent to some of the questions raised by the French thinkers discussed in the present book is that of empathy. As we saw, a major theme linking the Lacanian and Girardian schools is the problem of how to understand and achieve a healthy relationship with the "other," and one of the principal ways psychologists generally have gone about conceiving of this issue is in terms of the capacity to enter empathetically into the mood-states and feelings of other people. The mimetic hypothesis seems especially well suited to explaining both the presence and absence of empathy. If Girard and Oughourlian are correct that mimesis is a virtually instinctive tendency that underlies all human behavior and consciousness, and extends to the imitation not only of outward behavior but also of attitudes and feelings, then one would expect empathy to be as nearly universal among human beings as it in fact is. Why, however, would it sometimes be absent or attenuated, as in the case of autism or psychopathy? Although he does not himself explore this point, Oughourlian suggests that underlying the mimetic effects on the level of the psychological phenonema he focuses on there must also be "neurological or neurophysiological systems . . . indispensable to its operation" (*Puppet of Desire*, p. 9). The answer to the question of why empathy is sometimes lacking is probably, at least in many cases, to be found on that level, although failures in the learning process may also play a role.

Experimental research into empathy has been reaching in both

Child Development 59: 1221–29; and "Infant Imitation after a 1-Week Delay," *Developmental Psychology* 24: 470–76.

8. Rice and Woodsmall, "Lessons from Television: Children's Word Learning When Viewing," *Child Development* 59: 420–29.

directions in a way that parallels Meltzoff's research into the role of imitation in infant learning. As was mentioned in chapter four above, Meltzoff has been trying in part to correct Jean Piaget by showing that imitation of facial gestures, which Jean Piaget and others had thought could take place only after about eight to twelve months, can and do take place within weeks or even days. Piaget also thought that the capacity for empathy could not develop until children had achieved cognitive abilities allowing them to perform the complex mental operations necessary to reconstruct and represent to themselves another person's point of view, abilities he thought did not develop until seven or eight years of age. Various researchers have been finding recently that a virtually automatic inward imitation of the feelings of others occurs long before a child acquires the sense of existing apart from other people at all. Leslie Brothers of the California Institute of Technology, for example, says, "Studies of human and non-human primate infants reveal the presence of innate and early responses to facial expressions."[9] Brothers has been especially interested in identifying the brain circuits and neurons essential to these emotional responses and has shown in the process that monkeys, too, are evidently capable of empathy, since particular neurons in their brains are triggered by their seeing facial expressions. Others, such as Richard Davidson of the University of Wisconsin and Nathan Fox of the University of Maryland, have studied human infants by measuring the brain waves of ten-month-olds watching videotapes depicting an actress acting out the expression of various emotions by laughing, crying, and so on.[10] The children's brain waves show that as they watch, they experience inwardly the emotions they see enacted. As was the case with Meltzoff and Moore, Davidson and Fox's purpose in their study was simply to find a way to see if children so young could learn something from watching television, but what they found was also

9. Brothers, "A Biological Perspective on Empathy," *American Journal of Psychiatry* 146, no. 1 (January 1989): 17.

10. Fox and Davidson, "Patterns of Brain Electrical Activity during Facial Signs of Emotion in 10-Month-Old Infants," *Developmental Psychology* 24 (1988): 230–36.

that babies had emotional reactions that mimicked those they watched.

The American experimental research into this subject has so far taken place mainly within the framework of developmental psychology and neurology, but it should be only a matter of time before psychiatrists and psychotherapists become interested in the implications of such studies for understanding the psychology of adults. When they do, they should find the French Girardian contributions pertinent. In fact, although the two sides seem to be completely unaware of each other, there are already some indications of virtual convergence, most notably in Daniel N. Stern's studies of the psychology of interpersonal relations. His recent book, *The Interpersonal World of the Infant: A View from Psychoanalysis and Developmental Psychology* (1985), starts off with the study of early experience but goes on to argue against the Freudian assumption that there is a crucial early period that determines personality throughout life. Rather, he says, in a way that accords well with Girard and Oughourlian's interdividual psychology, that personality development is a lifelong process shaped continuously by the sort of interpersonal, empathetic relationship of which the infant's relation with his mother is its first but far from its last experience. That this type of approach to an understanding of personality has the potential to be of broad interest for psychotherapy is indicated by the fact that a special issue of *Contemporary Psychoanalysis* was devoted to a symposium on Stern's book.[11]

The question of the psychotherapeutic implications of all of this experimental research and the possible challenges it can present for traditional Freudian doctrine suggests an important point of general comparison between the Girardian and Freudian school of psychological thought. It has often been remarked that Freudianism has an ambiguous status as science because it does not connect significantly with the results of any other branch of scien-

---

11. *Contemporary Psychoanalysis* 23, no. 1 (January 1987). For an opposing view that defends traditional Freudian psychoanalysis, see the contribution by Louise Kaplan, pp. 27–44.

tific inquiry. Daniel N. Robinson stated the problem clearly in his *Systems of Modern Psychology:*

> There is no psychoanalytic *theory;* there are formulations of personality based upon psychoanalytic hypotheses. The *theory* continues to evolve. But it does not evolve in the way that, for example, evolutionary theory did. In the later case, advances in genetics and molecular biology made it possible to fill gaps unavoidably present in Darwin's original formulations. The accomplishments of science made it possible to replace Lamarckian with Mendelian modes of hereditary transmission.... One test of the scientific status of a theory ... is the extent to which it is accessible to the enriching and modifying effects of discoveries in science at large. Evolutionary theory passes this test; Freudian theory fails it. (P. 225)

It is too soon to tell exactly how successfully interdividual psychology will pass the same test, but it seems a good sign, at least, that experimentalists working in complete independence of its concepts have been turning up exactly the sort of findings that the hypothesis of universal subjective mimesis would be expected to predict. Such results certainly suggest that Girard, Oughourlian, and their colleagues are on solid ground in claiming that mimesis is fundamental to human psychology both within the individual and in social relations, and that it contributes to all psychological processes on every level of development. A great deal more development will clearly be needed, however, in the way of case studies and the testing of specific therapeutic procedures before the school of interdividual psychology will realize its full potential and be fully testable as an alternative to current methods of psychotherapy.

Another question that will require considerably more thought than the Girardians have yet given it, moreover, is that of how to understand the relative transcendence of more or less mechanical mimetism that can and sometimes does take place on the higher levels of human development. A small child's mimetic responses are, as was mentioned, virtually automatic and therefore involuntary; but the voluntary and nonmimetic, too, must be understood somehow, and this will call for an extension of the inquiry beyond psychology alone into the territory of philosophy—toward a philosophical anthropology capable of embracing the ethical, spiritual, and ontological dimensions of human being as well as the strictly psychological.

Most important, it seems to me, is the question of how one is to understand the mental functioning of a person who has won a relatively high degree of freedom from mimetism. Even if universal mimesis can be expected to add its coloration to all psychological processes, even on the hightest levels of development, the kind of mimetism that draws us into an unwitting, unintelligent, and frequently conflictual imitation of the desires of others must play a decreasing role as maturation takes place and the capacity for rational and responsible freedom is actualized.

This is not to suggest, of course, that such freedom could ever be absolute. In fact, an absolute freedom from the tendency to mimesis would not be a human good, even if it were attainable. With their strong innate tendency to imitate, children learn language, for example, virtually automatically, just as they normally learn to sense and share the feelings of others. As the experimental studies referred to above indicate, learning and empathy, communication and community, would be impossible without mimesis. To recall Oughourlian's Newtonian analogy, a human world without mimesis would be like an astrophysical universe without a force of gravitation, a world that would simply fly apart into isolated elements. Or to put in in psychological terms, the lack of any tendency to imitate inwardly the attitudes and feelings of others would lead to something like universal autism, a world of virtual psychopaths utterly lacking in empathy—like the inhabitants of the wasteland W. H. Auden described in "The Shield of Achilles": "That girls are raped, that two boys knife a third" would be axiomatic to one who had never heard of a world "where promises were kept / Or one could weep because another wept."[12]

In fact, as was suggested above, it may be that psychopathy will eventually be found to be precisely the result of a deficiency, per-

12. Auden, *The Shield of Achilles*, p. 37.

haps neurological at base, in the innate mimetic drive shared by normal, nonpsychopathic human beings. The transcendence of mimetism, therefore, should not be understood as the opposite of mimesis, but rather as a complement to it. Mimesis itself is not the problem; rather the problem is the way it can malfunction when it is not understood. To transcend mimetism is to win freedom not *from* mimesis but *within* the common life it makes possible.

This is not to say that Girard and his colleagues do not take the voluntary as well as the possible positive role of mimesis into account. Girard's discussion of "external mediation" and Oughourlian's of "adorcism" relate to these matters directly insofar as they have to do with deliberate efforts to seek out and imitate good models; and Girard's concern, as was discussed in chapter six, with the possibility of winning radical freedom from the tendency to mimetic rivalry and violence also pertains to it. But it is also significant that the language we saw Girard using to discuss this theme tended to be more a language of biblical imagery than a conceptual one. This does not mean that religious language of that sort may not be adequate in its own way to that purpose. As Eric Voegelin once said, commenting on the Enlightenment aspiration to replace all "mythic" language with something more rational and modern, religious language "was, at the time of its original employment, the precise instrument for expressing the irruption of transcendental reality, its incarnation and its operation in man," and it became "mythic" in the pejorative sense only when thinkers who had lost a sense of what those symbols had meant in their own traditions came to see them "in a 'literal,' disenchanted opaqueness from the outside."[13] Still, it must be acknowledged that even for a person attuned to its special symbolic language, there are pertinent issues the biblical tradition never articulated with the kind of explicitness that is called for in contemporary reflection. One of these is the question of what precisely, besides Girardian nonviolence, is to be looked for in the kind of figure one would seek out as a good model. What does it mean to be an exemplary instance of human being? Or to

13. Voegelin, *From Enlightenment to Revolution*, p. 21.

put it in terms that connect the question more clearly with influential currents in the tradition of recent continental philosophy, what are the characteristics of authentic human existence?

As a first approach to exploring this question, it may be helpful to go over a few points of comparison between Girard's thought and that of one of the most influential of contemporary philosophical thinkers on this subject, Martin Heidegger. Perhaps a good point to begin will be where Heidegger connects with the Girardian theme of imitation. Imitation comes up in Heidegger's thought in two ways. It comes up implicitly in connection with the temptation to self-loss in collectivity—the theme of what Heidegger calls "the 'they' " ("*das Man*"). Heidegger's "they" corresponds, at least in part, in his system of thought with the role of mimetic others as models of "desire" in Girard's, but he does not really say much to explain the force of the attraction such collectivity exerts. Heidegger's emphasis is on the negative effect, the power of repulsion, of the prospect of one's future death, so that the attraction to "the 'they' " is conceived of less as a positive pull than as simply a virtually reflex movement of escapist flight.

The reason Heidegger gives for the impulse to flight from authentic existence—which for him is "anticipatory resoluteness" in the face of "Being towards death," that is, of one's own fundamental mortality—is, as is well known, the anxiety (*Angst*) growing out of one of the fundamental human characteristics: care. In Heidegger's anthropology, the specifically human mode of being, or "Dasein," is marked by care because it is aware of itself as a contingent process taking place between two poles of nonbeing: its beginning in "thrownness" or radical contingency, and its end in death. As he summed it up at one point in *Being and Time,* "Thrownness and that Being towards death in which one either flees it or anticipates it, form a unity; and in this unity birth and death are 'connected' in a manner characteristic of Dasein. As care, Dasein *is* the 'between' " (pp. 426–27). Conscious of its inherent precariousness, Dasein is constantly tempted to flee from that consciousness toward futile attempts either to deny itself through self-loss in "the 'they' " or to bolster its ontological position through the acquisition of objects that may be useful to it in the attempt to fight off its doom, or at least its anxiety about it. Either way, it flees from authentic subjectivity (honest awareness of its real situation) toward inauthentic objectivity—either toward identification with a crowd of others lost in objectivistic concern or toward the instrumental use of objects in the world to make for oneself an illusory status as an objectified entity.

Girard's system is actually quite compatible with Heidegger's regarding these temptations to inauthenticity, although he might reasonably claim that Heidegger's discussion cries out for completion by his own theory of mimetic and especially "metaphysical" desire, which would offer a deeper phenomenology of both modes of flight and a more comprehensive explanation of what motivates them.

The other, and more explicit, place that the theme of imitation comes up in Heidegger is in his discussion of "repetition" in human "historicality"—the possibility of imitating examples of authentic existence. In Girardian language this would be the search for a model as an "external mediator." In Heidegger this takes the form of appropriating in one's own temporal life the pattern set by a historical example, "the authentic repetition of a possibility of existence that has been—the possibility that Dasein may choose its hero" (p. 437). What Heidegger especially emphasizes is the way "choice" and "resolve" figure in this: "The more authentically Dasein resolves—and this means that in anticipating death it understands itself unambiguously in terms of its ownmost distinctive possibility [that is, of its own death]—the more unequivocally does it choose and find the possibility of its existence, and the less does it do so by accident" (p. 435). It is only such resoluteness that makes it possible even for one to have a "heritage" at all, since heritage as such, in what Heidegger considers the authentic sense, is constituted by the search for authenticity in relation to one's mortality:

> In one's coming back resolutely to one's thrownness, there is hidden a *handing down* to oneself of the possibilities that have come down to one.... Once one has grasped the finitude of one's existence, it

snatches one back from the endless multiplicity of possibilities which offer themselves as closest to one—those of comfortableness, shirking, and taking things lightly—brings Dasein into the simplicity of its *fate.* . . . This is how we designate Dasein's primordial historizing [that is, its appropriation of its temporality], which lies in authentic resoluteness and in which Dasein *hands* itself *down* to itself, free for death, in a possibility which it has inherited and yet has chosen. (P. 435)

This sounds bracing, and one can understand the appeal it has had—not least among French intellectuals especially in the period after the Second World War. One may well wonder, however, whether there might not be more to existential fullness than just resoluteness in the face of death, whether there might not be some more positive plenitude intrinsically worth seeking. The notion of heroism here also seems rather limited. These issues have to do ultimately with matters of value, a topic that—despite what seem value-charged connotations to such terms as "authentic" and "inauthentic," "resoluteness" and "hero"—Heidegger explicitly sets aside in favor of what he intends as a purely descriptive, nonevaluative phenomenology of Dasein. One may well ask, however—and many have been asking it, especially with reference to Heidegger's membership in the Nazi party—whether there is not some deep evasiveness, perhaps even "inauthenticity," involved in the attempt to formulate a conception of existential heroism without addressing the question of the good.

One voice that has raised that question in a pertinent way recently is Jean-François Lyotard in *Heidegger et "les juifs"* ("Heidegger and 'the Jews,' " 1988). Lyotard uses the term "the Jews" to stand not for just any people of Jewish descent but specifically for those who are committed to the Jewish sense of a divine calling to take seriously questions of right and wrong. He says that whereas Heidegger spoke of a "forgetfulness of being" in the Western philosophical tradition descending from the Greeks, there has also existed alongside it all the while the alien tradition of the Jews, a non-Western people in the midst of the West, that has served to remind us of our forgetfulness not of Being but of "the Law." That, he says, is the really significant point of the question about Heidegger's association with the Nazis: "that Nazism tried to make us forget once and for all the idea of something owed, of the difference between good and evil. To try to free the soul from obligation, to tear up the note of debt. To unbind it definitively from owing anything at all" (p. 135). "That unbinding," says Lyotard, "is evil itself."

Clearly one of the important differences between Heidegger and Girard in this respect is that whereas Heidegger's way of thinking essentially set aside any questions about, and virtually blinded him to, the victimization perpetrated by the "heroes" he had "chosen" in his own "existential" situation,[14] one of the prominent features of Girard's own thought has been that it not only analyzes the roots of interpersonal violence in mimesis and "metaphysical desire," but it also returns explicitly to the heritage of both Jews and Christians in opposing all victimization and unmasking the processes by which the victim has traditionally been deprived of his humanity. This raises, moreover, another related point that penetrates still deeper into the problematic character of Heidegger's thought: the ambiguous status of the "other" as such. Heidegger talks at length of the "call" of conscience, but what that is a call to is strictly a relation to oneself—that is, to authentic consciousness of one's "ownmost" possibility, which is simply the possiblity of choosing to face with open eyes one's own mortality. Not only is there no real place in Heidegger's thought for the alterity of a genuinely "other" person, but when he does speak of others it is either as potential sources of temptation to inauthenticity ("the 'they' ") or else as examples to be used as instruments in one's own quest for authenticity. Even when he speaks explicitly of otherness, it has nothing to do with the possibility of a relation to a personal other, a "thou"; it is only that which he says one can discover when "an experience of Being as

14. "Existentiell" is a special term Heidegger coined to refer to the concrete possibilities of existence open to a particular individual in a particular situation (as compared with "existential" possibilities, which are universal to Dasein as such).

sometimes 'other' than everything that 'is' comes to us in dread, provided we do not, from dread of dread, i.e. in sheer timidity, shut our ears to the soundless voice which attunes us to the horrors of the abyss."[15]

One might say that, like the whole heritage of German idealistic philosophy it grows out of, even while he denounces it for its "forgetfulness of Being," Heidegger's philosophy remains haunted by the spirit of solipsism. As Thomas Langan said long before the recent revival of questions about Heidegger and the Jews, "Heidegger's political critics are perhaps troubled on more philosophical grounds than just an accusation of failure to intervene at a critical moment."[16] Even if one may feel that there is something rather hollow in the rhetoric of a thinker whose writings solemnly intone an invocation to heed the call of conscience to the heroism of authentic existence by facing death resolutely in a spirit of "sacrifice,"[17] while their author sets aside questions of right and wrong and enjoys the privileges of academic eminence in the Nazi state while ignoring the cries of the victims around him, one cannot really accuse him of philosophical inconsistency. Heidegger's is a philosophy with an "I" and an "it" but no real "thou," either human or divine, and no place for a theory of obligation that would be tied up with a relation to a personal other.

The "other" as a center of value is central, on the other hand, to the thought of both Girard and Balmary, as should be clear from the discussion in the previous chapter, but one must also acknowledge that in the absence of a fully developed philosophical anthropology, its centrality seems to depend more on the personal good instincts of the thinker than on a well-developed theoretical foundation. Heidegger at least tried to work out the basis for a theory of human existence, and if he were not so committed personally to a phenome-

---

15. "What Is Metaphysics," trans. R. F. C. Hull and Alan Crick, in *Existence and Being*, p. 354.

16. Langan, *The Meaning of Heidegger: A Critical Study of an Existentialist Philosopher*, p. 224.

17. For Heidegger on "sacrifice," see *Existence and Being*, pp. 358–59.

nological bracketing with respect to questions of value, perhaps he might have extended his exploration of this topic to a point at which the limitations of the approach he did take might have been transcended. That he did not do so was his choice, as well as perhaps his failure, but to explain why this constituted a failure would require the development of a theoretical framework with less narrow limits than his.

Balmary pointed to this very problem, even if it was psychoanalysis she had in mind rather than Heideggerian philosophy, when she said in *Psychoanalyzing Psychoanalysis* that science without conscience is the soul's ruin and lamented, "We are in the habit of distinguishing psychological consciousness and moral conscience" (p. 159). She called there for "a new theory of consciousness/ conscience" (p. 159). Although she made no explicit connection herself between this idea and her later statement, mentioned in the preceding chapter, that we need *une érotique nouvelle*, a new theory of desire, the two ideas must be intrinsically linked, I believe, since without a theory that can ground the ideas of good and evil in a conception of what constitutes the best possibilities of human love, and also human anger, the conception of value as such must remain an abstraction.

The need for such a theory seems also to have been felt, at least implicitly, by many other recent thinkers in France insofar as they have discussed human existence as rendered problematic by desires that can never be satisfied—as when Sartre, in his famous phrase, speaks of man as "a futile passion," or Jacques Lacan speaks of desire as an aberration growing out of an essential disproportion between appetite and our unlimited demand to be loved,[18] or Maurice Blanchot and George Bataille speak of the essential absurdity of a human existence that will never be able to attain satisfaction, not even after the "end of history" that Kojève announced.[19] None of these approaches, however, seem likely to be especially helpful for the purpose Balmary has in mind, since they are less theories of

18. *Ecrits* (French), p. 691.
19. Descombes, *Modern French Philosophy*, pp. 112–14.

desire than theories of inevitable frustration. If human desires can never ultimately escape frustration, one could hardly hope to find in a theory of desire a foundation for a conception of genuine value. Nor have the efforts to construct one on such foundations, like Bataille's idea of sacrifice as a noble cult of glorious expenditure through pure waste and destruction, ever had much persuasive power. The only possible foundation for a theory of value adequate to the needs of a psychology concerned with helping people to discover and attain a true human good would be one that enabled them realistically to commit themselves in "basic trust," as Erik Erikson put it, to the possibilities of genuine happiness in their own lives and those of others, and on that basis to develop through "autonomy" and "initiative," and the various other stages he describes, toward the self-transcending love that constitutes "generativity" as compared with "stagnation" and enables one to crown one's life with "ego integrity" instead of "despair."[20] Even if there is, as I think, a profound truth in the idea that some human desires are inherently unsatisfiable, a theory of desire adequate to our needs would also have to take full account of the satisfactions that are nevertheless possible and that go beyond sensual pleasure alone.

Since the question of satisfiable versus unsatisfiable desire is clearly an issue here, and since this is also a topic that we saw come up in connection with the thought of Girard and Oughourlian, perhaps a good way to begin thinking about what such a theory would have to involve would be to consider further the distinction they make between appetite and need on the one hand and desire, in their sense of that term, on the other. As will be remembered, desire, in their conception, is specifically mimetic. Girard defines man as the being who does not know what to desire but must learn it from others, and he defines desire itself as an artificial craving learned by imitation of the desires, or supposed desires, of others, who are assumed to desire some object because they know that it will create or augment in them the sufficiency of being and power that the apprentice desirer feels himself to be lacking. We also saw that

20. Erikson, *Childhood and Society*, pp. 247–71.

Girard analyzes all desire as for this reason ultimately both meta-physical and nihilistic in orientation. It is ultimately metaphysical because, whatever its ostensible object, its goal is always the being of the other. It is also nihilistic because, as Girard analyzes it, this goal is fraught with contradictions that make it inherently impossi-ble to attain and that drive the desirer to increasingly violent levels of conflict as he tries to find a mediator who will be unconquerable and therefore really valid in his eyes as a mediator. This is why Girard says, "[T]he truth of metaphysical desire is death."

The logic of Girard's analysis of metaphysical desire is powerful, and in its own context irrefutable, since he conceives of desire *by definition* as inherently oriented toward objects and indeed preemi-nently toward those objects that are demonstrated to be desirable by the fact that they are defended with invincible force. Still, there is more in this issue than Girard's analysis brings to light. There is no necessary reason why mediated aspirations must be bound to the pursuit of objects. Nor is there any reason why an aspiration ori-ented toward the ontological possibilities believed to be disclosed by a model could not be directed toward some actually imitable aspect of the model's mode of being. That is, instead of attempting an impossible grab for the model's subjectivity by way of some object mistakenly identified with it, an apprentice who was not deceived about the power of objects to confer subjectivity might seek instead to exist well himself by learning from the model how it is done. In such a case an aspiration bearing on the "being" of the other might lead not to death but to life. Or at least it might if it is understood as bearing not properly on objects but on subjectivity as such.

Of course, this would not then be "metaphysical desire" in the strict sense, and so a new term will be needed to avoid confusion, but even within Girard's own context some way of speaking of such aspirations is clearly called for. With his introduction of the theme of "Christ's perfect love" as an alternative to violence, Girard him-self invokes the possibility of a mimesis of subjectivity that would not become "tripped up" or "scandalized" by a confusion between that love, as subjectivity, and any mundane object that might seem to be associated with it, such as an anti-Roman messianic state in Palestine of the sort Peter and some of the other disciples expected. Since the idea of a beneficent motivation bearing directly on subjectivity is, therefore, one that Girard's own analysis of desire seems to call for, and since a term for it is needed, I will suggest borrowing Kierkegaard's word "existential." Or another term that could be used, and one that is also equivalent to this in Kierkegaard's thought, would be "spiritual."

The term "existential" is, of course, familiar also from Heidegger and Sartre, both of whom derived it from Kierkegaard. The connection with Sartre seems especially pertinent to the theme of metaphysical desire as conceived by Girard, since one of Sartre's own central themes was the tendency of people to flee from subjective "existence" toward objective "being." Girard speaks with appreciation of this side of Sartre, and there is a definite link between his critique of the "metaphysical" element in mimetic desire and Sartre's discussion of the temptation to fuse the *pour-soi* with the *en-soi*, as well as between his and Sartre's analyses of sadism and masochism as expressions of that same tendency. It may be that French thought in general has not yet fully absorbed the implications of the existentialism Sartre brought into it from Kierkegaard and Heidegger before he turned aside from that toward Marxism. Now that their Marxist interlude is clearly over, Girard's thought may prove to be a means by which the French will continue that process of assimilation.

Still, even if terms such as "existential" and "spiritual" may be useful in speaking of an aspiration focusing not on the mediator's objects but on his mode of existence, within the strict framework of Girard's terminology it would be contradictory to speak of existential or spiritual "desire," since in that context desire is conceived of as always aiming at objects. Even when Girard says that the ultimate goal of metaphysical desire is death, he means that that is the indirect goal lying beyond the direct one, which for the victim of metaphysical desire is always the object either possessed or sought by the envied other. It would be suitable in the present context, therefore, to speak of an "existential" or "spiritual" appetite—

especially since "appetite" is a word Girard himself uses to refer to natural inclination in contrast with the artificiality of desire as he conceives it. Thus one could speak of an "existential appetite" that seeks to enjoy a mode of existence, and this would contrast both with the strictly animal appetites for food, drink, sexual pleasure, physical exercise, sleep, and so on, and with mimetic "desires" for objects that function socially as symbols of power or sufficiency.

Girard himself, as we saw in chapter three, tends to limit his own use of the term "appetite" to the biological level, as in the reference quoted there to Sancho Panza's appetite for a piece of cheese or a goatskin of wine. Oughourlian does the same in his treatment of "instincts and needs" as the nonmimetic counterpole to mimetic desire (*Puppet*, p. 21). Nevertheless, it makes good sense to think of the possibility of appetites that are not oriented toward strictly sensual satisfactions but aim rather at spiritual ones. This is what Balmary points to when she speaks of Jesus as calling not for the renunciation of desires but for greater desire and the discovery of one's own desire. She does not try to define or specify the nature of this desire. She only says that to discover it as one's own would be a key element in a process of self-discovery that she leaves basically undefined, referring to it rather in the theological language of mystery, as in the closing lines of *Le Sacrifice interdit*, where she says, "He who comes to a psychoanalyst is one unknown approaching another unknown. When he leaves, he is a mystery" (p. 287).

Once again this marks a point at which psychology as it is usually conceived reaches its limits as the questions that drive it open out into a new territory both Balmary and Girard seem to feel the need of a religious language to explore. Although there is no indication that Balmary has read the work of the Girardian theologian, Raymund Schwager, there is a notable parallel between her way of talking about the importance of respect for the divinely grounded difference that manifests itself in alterity and Schwager's interpretation of the mystery of Pentecost:

> . . . peace as the fruit of the Spirit is clearly distinct from the unity that the scapegoat mechanism creates. The latter is nothing but a unifor-

mity necessitated by the image of the common enemy. The Holy Spirit, on the contrary, gathers the people by respecting in each individually his or her singularity and freedom, and by unifying all, not *against* but *for* someone, *for* the Lord.

In its account of the feast of Pentecost, the Acts of the Apostles stresses that the tongues of fire separated and descended on *each of the gathered persons* (Acts 2:3). In the same way it does not say that the miracle of tongues made all understand one language, but that the apostles began to speak in *foreign* tongues and that all in Jerusalem were amazed because everyone heard them speak in *his or her own mother tongue* (Acts 2:4–8). The Spirit produced a unified understanding while conserving full respect for existing differences.[21]

The key idea in both cases is that the essential, and indeed sacred, calling of each human being is to become, as Kierkegaard phrased it, an "existing individual." Balmary's own conception of how this process can take place involves the idea that a crucial step in it is the inner disentanglement of one's own genuine appetites from the desires of others that have somehow come to possess one. This was a theme she announced at the start of her first book when she spoke of how "Lacan's decisive innovation that one's desire is always the desire of the Other" leads to the question "Who made you ill?" (*Psychoanalyzing Psychoanalysis,* p. 1). In her conception of it, the main task of psychoanalysis is to help the patient to answer that question so that he or she will become able to ask and answer the still deeper question, "What were your desires?" and thereby begin the process of self-discovery that is our response to the divine calling to think and live as a free person—a "subject" in Kierkegaard's sense of that word.

Both the Lacanian and the Girardian schools agree, therefore, on the importance of individuation, to use the term we saw Roustang using for it. And yet this poses the question alluded to earlier: if, as

---

21. Schwager, *Must There Be Scapegoats?* pp. 220–21. Italics in original. There is a significant parallel to this interpretation of Pentecost in W. H. Auden's poem, "Whitsunday in Kirchstetten," in *About the House,* p. 83.

Balmary puts it, one is called to pass from the third person to the first by learning to desire with one's own desires rather than with those of others, what kind of desire or appetite is being referred to? It also poses the closely related question of what one means by "a subject." This is a concept that is generally approached with suspicion among French thinkers who have absorbed the various critiques of the notion of a subject on the part of thinkers ranging from the later, Marxist Sartre to Lévi-Strauss and Foucault. Girard, too, even though he assented, as we saw in the preceding chapter, to Oughourlian's statement contrasting "the real human subject" who "can only come out of the rule of the Kingdom" with the false subject constituted by "the mimetic structure" itself, indicates his wariness of becoming associated in any way with a notion of the subject he identifies as tied up with a naïve individualism. "I avoid saying 'desiring subject.' " he says, "so as not to give the impression of relapsing into a psychology of the subject" (*Things Hidden*, p. 303).

The "subject" of which Girard and others in the French tradition are so wary is not, however, the existential subject conceived by Kierkegaard but rather the Cartesian *res cogitans* described above. On the other hand, it is not clear exactly what Girard thinks a "real human subject" could be understood to be. Even his positive references to the concept of a subject tend to be cast more in negative than positive terms, as when he explains the Christian doctrine of the divinity of Christ by saying that he is the only agent (*"sujet"* in the French) who is free from the controlling power of violence and therefore capable of radically nonviolent action.[22] Nor do any of the other thinkers discussed in this book have anything more concrete to provide in the way of a positive characterization.

It will be worthwhile, therefore, to take a few steps beyond their particular realm of discourse to consider how one might understand in positive terms the type of "subject" who could be conceived of with Girard and Oughourlian as emerging from "the rule of the Kingdom" or the "I" that Balmary describes as emerging within a

22. *Things Hidden*, p. 219; *Des choses cachées* (*Livre de poche* edition), p. 318.

human personality by way of the creative presence of the God whose proper name is "I am." First, however, we must consider what it would not be: it would not be a kind of preexisting "true self within" that needs only to be located. That would indeed be a return to a subject psychology of the sort none of the thinkers we have been studying would advocate. Rather, it seems to me, the inner agent or "I" of which they are speaking must be conceived in functional rather than metaphysical terms, just as the interdividual "self of desire" analyzed by Oughourlian is conceived of as a matter of relationship and functioning rather than ontology.[23] Self-discovery of the sort these thinkers are concerned with is not the discovery of something that was already there; it is the discovery of a self or center of subjectivity that comes into existence in its functioning, and that never exists at all except in the mode of coming into existence, that is, as a function of its operations.

What sort of functioning and consciousness, then, would be involved in the constitution of such an existential subject? To address this question fully would mean not only to go beyond the psychological explorations considered in the present book but to commence a whole new one. As it is, however, this was the focus of my previous book, *Philosophers of Consciousness,* so I will limit myself to summarizing briefly some of the ideas on this topic discussed there in connection with the thought of Michael Polanyi, Eric Voegelin, Paul Ricoeur, Kierkegaard, and particularly Bernard Lonergan, whose schematization of successive and cumulative mental operations is helpfully concise.

Even to take up the topic of such operations is, of course, to step outside the framework of analytical psychology, even as broadly conceived as it is among the thinkers studied in the present book. Freudian psychoanalysis came into being as an attempt to understand and correct mental malfunctioning due to the exclusion of

---

23. Cf. *Puppet,* pp. 198–99: "Consciousness, like the self, is a function of the relation to otherness. The self as such is a mythic notion. To the extent that there is such an entity, it is in a permanent process of becoming, modified at every moment by its relation to the other, that is, by the pull of the other's desire."

painful memories from consciousness and the consequent misinter-
pretations of the patient's world and relationships that then developed on the basis of both the continuing repressed pain and the
truncated memories remaining available. Oughourlian's shift from
the standard psychoanalytic idea of the unconscious to his own idea
that, as we saw him put it, "The unconscious is the other," radical as
it is, still leaves him within the general framework of psychopathology, since as a therapist his main attention is given to the ways
the interdividual relation becomes distorted and enslaving when its
reality is denied and its workings are left in darkness. To consider the
mental operations of a well-functioning human subject, on the other
hand, is to consider not the pathological and truncated but the normal and whole. These consist of the full range and sequence of operations that can take place naturally when the innate dynamism—or
"existential appetite"—that normally gives rise to them is not
thwarted or deflected by some impediment, such as the exclusion of
some important area of experience from attention.

Fortunately it is simpler to describe what can go right in the well-
functioning consciousness than what can go wrong in its malfunctioning. Tolstoy said at the beginning of *Anna Karenina* that happy
families are all alike, while every unhappy family is unhappy in its
own way. The same could be said of psychologically sound consciousness compared with the twists and turns of the abnormal.

Briefly summed up, the normal operations of consciousness consist of the following: attention to experience; construing of the
elements of experience in some intelligible pattern; critical reflection and judgment regarding the adequacy of such interpretations
to actual experience; deliberation and decision regarding possible
courses of action within the reality known by way of these operations; and action proceeding from such deliberation and decision.
These operations, when they are well executed, relate to one another cumulatively according to the order listed: what one interprets is what one has succeeded in noticing, what one knows is what
one can verify that one has understood correctly, and so on. They
therefore build on one another, and unless each is carried out well
on the level where it is called for, the higher levels of operation will

be subverted. Acts of understanding will be limited and possibly distorted if important aspects of the experiential field are left out of account because of a failure to attend carefully to everything that might be relevant. Judgments of truth will be inadequate if the operations on the levels of experiencing and understanding that they are founded on have not been performed well. So also, deliberation will be truncated and the resulting decisions inappropriate if they refer not to the real world in which the action decided upon will have to be carried out and its consequences dealt with, but rather to some imaginary world constructed on the basis of inadequate attention to evidence, sloppy or self-serving interpretations, uncritical judgment, and so on. As Saul Bellow's Henderson the rain king put it, "So what if reality is terrible—it's better than what we've got!"

To list what can go wrong in this way, when the normal operations are carried out poorly or even willfully suppressed, begins to sound more like psychopathology than philosophy, and indeed Eric Voegelin, drawing on the terminology of the Stoics, used the word "psychopathology" in exactly that way in his essay, "Reason: The Classic Experience" (*Anamnesis*, p. 97). In fact, one of the ways philosophy and psychology can be distinguished is to say, with Lonergan, that philosophy is a systematic reflection on the operations of intentional consciousness and the kinds of object they imply and, with Voegelin, that pathological psychology has to do, on its most fundamental level and prior to any particular psychological symptoms or complexes, with flight from consciousness and what he calls "the eclipse of reality."[24]

This implies, of course, that even if the study of psychology needs to be complemented by an adequate philosophy of consciousness, it is equally true that philosophy needs to be balanced by attention to the sort of psychological problems taken up by the figures studied in this volume. If philosophy is to carry out its task of clarification of the possibilities of attentive, intelligent, reasonable thinking and

---

24. See, for example, Lonergan, *Method in Theology*, pp. 94–95, and Voegelin, "The Eclipse of Reality," in *What Is History? and Other Late Unpublished Writings*.

living, then it also needs to be aware of the forces that can subvert it, lest it be deflected from its goal by irrational factors working in its own shadows. It would be too much, of course, to try to sketch out in detail the ways in which philosophical thinking could become subject to such distortion. Even Tolstoy limited himself to the Oblonsky family. An example, however, might be useful, and there is one that seems particularly pertinent to the theme of how powerful can be the effects of unnoticed mimeticism: the thought of John Henry Newman.

In his *An Essay in Aid of A Grammar of Assent* (1870), Newman made a distinction between what he called "real" and "notional" apprehension. Real apprehension was the fruit of a concrete judgment founded on one's own genuine experience, understanding, and critical reflection; and notional apprehension was merely an abstract sort of knowledge founded on the experience, understanding, and reflection of others. Both may be forms of knowledge, but they differ fundamentally in their mode and in the concreteness of their contents. As an example he pointed to the difference between two ways one could apprehend the truth of the proposition that Great Britain is an island: one might have learned it from a book or lesson, in which case one would be grasping it abstractly and at second hand; or one might actually have sailed around Britain and found it concretely to be surrounded by water, in which case the proposition would be filled with experiential content and one's knowledge of its truth would be the more confident for not having to rely on a chain of testimonies and inferences. His word for this sort of cognitive confidence was "certitude," which he defined as a specific sense of intellectual satisfaction and repose that comes when one really understands something and knows how one knows it. On the basis of this analysis Newman argued for a cognitional theory that emphasized the importance of performing concretely for oneself as an individual the operations of critical reflection and judgment. As he stated the issue, "certitude is not a passive impression made upon the mind from without, by argumentative compulsion . . . it is an active recognition of propositions as true such as it is the duty of each individual himself to exercise at the bidding of reason, and, when reason forbids, to withhold" (p. 262). Everyone who wishes to arrive at certitude, that is, must perform for himself the operations that produce it. To ask another's opinion in order to find encouragement for your own judgments, he says, is like asking someone else to tell you whether or not you have eaten or drunk to your satisfaction.

All of this fits well into the analysis of sound intentional operations sketched in the paragraphs above. Newman is also known, however, for his extensive and eloquent defense of one particular judgment—that involved in his conversion, and in that case an analysis in terms of mimetic psychology seems even more pertinent than one based on cognitional theory—setting aside any question about the objective adequacy of the decision he reached. Newman seems to have spent much of his life before the conversion trying either to find or to assemble about him a body of fellow believers who could help to counter the effects of the general erosion of confident belief that his contemporary, Matthew Arnold, referred to in "Dover Beach":

> The Sea of Faith
> Was once, too, at the full, and round earth's shore
> Lay like the folds of a bright girdle furled.
> But now I only hear
> Its melancholy, long, withdrawing roar,
> Retreating, to the breath
> Of the night wind, down the vast edges drear
> And naked shingles of the world.

A major motive in Newman's eventual conversion seems to have been that the much larger Roman Catholic Church was able to provide a better shelter than his own comparatively small English Church against the mass of unbelief that was spreading in the Victorian world. The reasons it was able to offer this to him were not, however, entirely a matter of rational evidence.

As Newman describes it in his *Apologia Pro Vita Sua* (1864), one of the major turning points in his consideration of the claims of Rome to supreme ecclesiastical authority came when, in studying the Donatist controversy of the fifth century, he realized that the fact that the Donatists were relatively few in number compared with the vast church for which Augustine of Hippo was the spokesman made them comparable with the Anglicans of his own time. What particularly affected him was Augustine's statement that the Donatists must have been wrong because, as he put it, "Securus judicat orbis terrarum" ("The judgment of the world is firm"). This amounts to saying that the mass of the vast number of Christians under the leadership of Rome in comparison with the smaller mass of the Donatists is what gives certitude to the judgment against them—a point that has a special meaning when one considers that for Newman one of the hallmarks of certitude is the feeling of satisfaction and repose that accompanies it.

Newman was undoubtedly correct in saying that those feelings can follow naturally from the concrete performance of the relevant intentional operations, but it is equally true as a psychological fact that it is always going to be easier to come comfortably to rest in a way of thinking when the psychological mass of those whose opinion one shares is greater than that of those who hold another view, and this may in the actual case have little or nothing to do with carefulness of one's own or anyone else's process of critical reflection and judgement. As Oughourlian points out, the effects of group psychology become easy to understand when one considers the relative disproportion between the psychological mass of the group and that of the individual, and crowds are not notable for the judiciousness of their acts of assent.

Even if a specific sense of intellectual satisfaction and repose is one mark of a well-considered judgment, therefore, the mere fact that one feels comfortably secure in an opinion does not necessarily guarantee that it will be true or even that one's judgment concerning the matter has been well considered. Newman's contribution to cognitional theory was genuine, but it seems clear that, whether or not his conversion may ultimately have been justified, the pull of the mimetic undertow coming from the largest single body in the religious world of his era also played an unnoticed and unanalyzed role in the concrete processes of his own thinking.

The obvious conclusion to be drawn is that however well-developed one's theory of the philosophical life may be, its practice will always require a sufficient awareness of the psychological forces that can influence or subvert it to enable one to be on guard against them. To the extent, moreover, that that practice must involve acts of judgment that are measured according to the degree of satisfaction they lead to, the possible effects of interdividual mimesis need always to be taken into account, since these can offer a fairly credible surrogate for the real satisfaction of the appetite for understanding and knowledge. They can anesthetize it, one might say, while deflecting it from its real goal. The specific task of philosophy is to understand what that appetite actually is and how it can find genuine fulfillment while avoiding the various traps or distractions that might prevent it from doing so—of which the undertow of mimeticism is at least one.

Eric Voegelin approached this problem by interpreting both philosophy and pathological psychology as two possible expressions of a single underlying energy or appetite. In the essay referred to above, he speaks of how the Stoics considered "mental disease" to be "a disturbance of noetically ordered existence" and went on to say, "The disease affects both the passions and reason, but it [is] caused neither by one nor the other; it originates in the questioning unrest . . . and in man's freedom to actualize the meaning of humanity potentially contained in the unrest or to botch the meaning" (*Anamnesis,* p. 101). Another term Voegelin used for this "unrest" was "existential tension." Polanyi and Kierkegaard used the word "passion" for it, and Ricoeur used both "tension" and "passion," while Lonergan spoke of "transcendental notions" as the movements of energy driving us in the performance of intentional operations. It is precisely a "questioning unrest" because questioning, the appetite for understanding and knowledge, is the fundamental form in which this energy manifests itself in human consciousness. Even the slightest experience can give rise to wonder, triggering such questions as "What is that?" and "What does it mean?" and leading, by "the force of the further question" (to use Lonergan's phrase), to "Is it really that?" "What should I do about it?" and so on. Any thwarting of that energy in an attempt to close off from questioning some area of experience, some possible interpretation, some grasp of reality or sense of what is worthy of love, can be expected to result in various forms of psychological and spiritual disturbance as the fundamental unrest continues to struggle to fulfill itself in the operations that, unimpeded, it would normally generate.

It is illuminating to consider the Freudian, Lacanian, and Girardian approaches to psychopathology in the light of this type of philosophical analysis. All of these share the belief that the refusal to admit into consciousness certain elements of experience can be a source of psychological disturbance. Each school, on the other hand, has its own emphasis regarding what in particular is repressed. It is possible, in fact, that each may be correct with regard to what pertains to its own emphasis, but if so, that must be because the inherent drive of consciousness toward its own multileveled unfolding is what is really basic.[25] It is not, that is, only sexual material or only the influence of the other that needs to be integrated into consciousness, but rather that everything in experience that is relevant both to self-understanding and to knowledge of reality needs to be recognized and adequately understood if we are to bring to genuine fulfillment the fundamental drive of our being.

One common way to trace the birth of psychoanalysis is to describe it as originating in the "talking cure" invented by Breuer's famous patient, Anna O., who decided to discuss with him the painful memories associated with her symptoms. Breuer interpreted as "purgative" the beneficial effect she found in talking to him about these experiences, and that is why he chose the term "catharsis" for it. That interpretation and term were subsequently adopted also by

---

25. The idea of psychological development as such a multileveled unfolding that progresses through a variety of stages has become a central theme of much of recent American psychological thought, as exemplified by Lawrence Kohlberg, Erik Erikson, Robert Kegan, and others. It is an implicit theme among some French thinkers (for example, Balmary is centrally concerned with the demands of what Kegan calls the "interindividual" level, which he considers the highest of all), and French psychological thought generally could probably profit by giving it more explicit attention.

Freud, who assumed that the repressed force needing evacuation in this way was specifically sexual. Another way to interpret the effect of the talking cure, however, would be to trace the benefit directly to the process of articulating and bringing to intelligibility experiences that were previously neither discussed nor thought about; that is, to interpret it as offering satisfaction to a previously thwarted "existential appetite" for experience, understanding, knowing, deliberation, and action that is fundamental to consciousness as such—an appetite to perform fully and carefully the intentional operations that constitute fully developed human life. Triangular desire, desire for fusion with one's own image or with the Other, the attempt to possess and dominate one's children, or to supplant one's father—all of these can be understood as ways in which we try to flee from the demands of our real existential appetite toward some illusory goal that only frustrates and exacerbates it.

The shift in focus that such an approach entails—from the imagery of pathology and trauma to that of appetite and fulfillment—can therefore help to explain the pertinence of Lacan's emphasis on language and speech in the psychoanalytic process and also to make clear how profoundly correct he was in insisting that one should not speak of a "cure" in psychoanalysis. The medical metaphors of "trauma" and "disease" carry the implication that once a trauma is uncovered and taken care of, the result should in fact be a cure, a movement from the pain of an abnormal condition to a pain-free normality. To reconceive the entire issue, on the other hand, as a matter not of disease grounded in trauma but of appetite grounded in "existential tension" is to replace that implication with one much more in keeping with human experience. The tension of existence is not a wound in human life—it is the energy of that life itself. It is not an unhealthy abnormality of which we need to be cured—it is our very normality. Even without seductions, the hidden fault of the father, mimetic rivalry, or sexual frustrations, we would still feel a pressing and sometimes disturbing need to come to an understanding of our experience. And that experience, by its very nature as a "questioning unrest" confronting the mystery of our source and goal, must include a sense of perpetual and radical incompleteness.

This is the profound truth in the idea that there are human appetites (and not only "desires" in the strict Girardian sense) that can never find satisfaction in our life in the world. Our problem is not one of escaping into a tension-free existence but of living creatively and joyfully with the tension that is the animating principle of our lives. The tensional unrest is experienced as painful when one lives in a way that is in conflict with its dynamic, trying to close oneself against it by fleeing from reality and the questions that drive us inwardly toward reasonable and responsible existence. But when one cooperates with the pull of that tension and thereby allows it to lead into fullness of life, it can be experienced as love and joy.

And yet even at its most open, even when the existential appetite to perform the operations that constitute human existence attains maximum fulfillment, human existence remains contingent and incomplete, precisely because it is constituted essentially of those operations. Considered both philosophically and psychologically, a person is never an ontologically solid substance, a finished "thing." There is no self other than that which is continuously coming into being through the creative energy of its existential appetites. Nor is there any self other than the "self-between." But its betweenness must be understood not only as that of the interdividual relation, the constitution of a self of desire through the interaction of self-holon and other-holon, nor only, as in Heidegger, that of Dasein between two abysses of nothingness, but also as the intermediateness of a being who exists only as a dynamism of operations, a continuing movement of existence that is never final—between a possible nonexistence and an impossible absolute existence.

To understand this is to understand the deeper truth in Lacan's critique of illusory self-objectification when he described the mirror-stage, as was mentioned in chapter one, as the beginning of a lifelong pursuit of one's own image as an idealized object. It also helps to make clear what is true but only partly articulated in Borch-Jacobsen's development of this notion of Lacan's when he speaks of "the ineradicable megalomania of desire—which is, finally, nothing other than a will-to-be-a-subject." The misguided intent of which he speaks is not, in fact, a willingness to be an existential subject of the sort referred to above—a subject enjoying, and suffering, the kind of fleeting, mysterious existence we experience in the careful performance of the operations that constitute our actual subjectivity. It is, rather, the will to be an objective subject-entity, not really to exist subjectively at all but to be an object.

It is the misguided will to be such an object-subject, that lures us to seek psychological fusion with figures of power, individual and collective, to try to find in the desires of rivals the secret of ontological self-sufficiency. It is what leads us to seek to be seen and admired by others: so that we can believe in our own substantial reality. It is also what leads us, in an extension of that effort, to try through relationships of domination and victimization to turn ourselves into gods.

To awaken from these dreams requires psychological insight of the sort each of the thinkers discussed here contributes, but it also requires something more. It requires understanding of what genuine subjective life can be and of the difference between that and the various forms of false objectivity to which the "megalomania of desire" holds us in thrall. It also requires courage—the courage to endure the tension of genuinely human existence and to accept our inherently contingent lives precisely as the gift of that tension. Above all, it requires radically self-transcending love—love of the unrealized possibilities of subjective actuality both in oneself and in others, the love that makes one willing not only to exist subjectively oneself but also to bless and let go of every other so that he or she may do so as well. It is here that philosophy and psychology both find their ultimate work: in the elucidation of that love, by rendering it self-aware and intelligent and liberating it from the illusory desires that otherwise mask it and lead it astray.

Oughourlian's analysis of "the 'I' or 'self' in psychology" as "an unstable, constantly changing, and ultimately evanescent structure" (*Puppet*, p. 11) and Girard's exposure of the ultimately nihilistic thrust of "metaphysical desire" can serve as a valuable propaedeutic to the radical self-transcendence just referred to, but the movement beyond such selfhood requires what Kierkegaard (and of course many others) called "conversion," "repentance," and "rebirth." Psychological insight of this kind may prepare one for this by helping one to deal with the problem Kierkegaard was speaking of when he said, "It would be unreasonable to require a person to find out all by himself that he does not exist. But this transition is precisely the transition of the rebirth from not existing to existing" (*Philosophical Fragments*, p. 22). But such spiritual transformation has always been understood as requiring a "dying to self" that psychology alone cannot speak of.

One of the principal ways this has been spoken of historically has been in the language of sacrifice. This is why, I think, even many of Girard's appreciative readers have felt a lingering sense of incompleteness about at least one central aspect of his thought: his critique of sacrifice. This also suggests one further interesting point of comparison between his thought and that of Kierkegaard. Girard's conception of sacrifice is as restricted in its own way as is Heidegger's of existential authenticity. Heidegger centered the latter in resoluteness in the face of death. Girard centered the concept of sacrifice in victimization—the expulsion and possible slaughter of a person chosen as a scapegoat in order that peace may be established or restored in some exclusionary group. It is true that sacrifice has often taken this form historically, and Girard makes a cogent case for the idea that much of the imagery of sacrifice in the Bible constitutes a cumulative exposé of the victimizing mechanism. But the fact remains that the idea of sacrifice, even in the Bible and throughout the history of theology, has always included another major dimension as well: that of consecration—the dedication not of a victim but of one's own life to the calling of self-transcendence. Perhaps it was something he drew from his reading of Kierkegaard—even if he denied the particular possibilities of self-transcendence that Kierkegaard, as a Christian, believed in—that led Heidegger to draw on the language of sacrifice to express his own sense of consecration when he said, for example, that "in sacrifice there is expressed that hidden *thanking* which alone does homage to the grace wherewith Being has endowed the nature of man, in order that he may take over in his relationship to Being the guardianship of Being" (*Existence and Being*, p. 358). Heidegger also spoke of the way the notion of sacrifice could fall from this to a debased form that would make it deserve something like a Girardian critique: "Sacrifice is rooted in the nature of the event through which Being claims man for the truth of Being. Therefore it is that sacrifice brooks no calculation, for calculation always miscalculates sacrifice in terms of the expedient and the inexpedient, no matter whether the aims are set high or low. Such calculation distorts the nature of sacrifice" (p. 359). But in his positive conception of sacrifice there is something that suggests that in some manner his imagination was reaching toward a further meaning that deserves to be taken seriously.

Girard is correct to point out, in *Things Hidden*, that "self-sacrifice" may become a masochistic notion (p. 236) and to say that although in the Gospels "Christ agrees to die so that mankind will live," nevertheless "we must beware of calling his action sacrificial, even if we then have no words or categories to convey its meaning" (pp. 241–42), but this does not necessarily imply that there cannot be a meaning having to do with self-transcendence for which the language of self-sacrifice might indeed be appropriate. Christ himself said that unless a seed falls into the ground and dies it cannot bring forth life, and it would be reductionistic to interpret that idea as an expression merely of masochism.

Perhaps a final comparison between Girard and Balmary may indicate that there is a deeper level in the notion of sacrifice than Girard has yet fully accounted for. Both he and she comment on the well-known biblical story of the judgment of Solomon (1 Kings 3:16–28) in which two harlots both claim the same child and the king tests their love for it by offering to cut it in half so each can have a share (*Things Hidden*, pp. 237–43; *Sacrifice interdit*, pp. 97–99).

Girard, as one would expect, emphasizes the mimetic symmetries in the story, especially the way the two mothers, rivals in their desire for the same child, are represented as outwardly indistinguishable doubles of one another. His main point, in keeping with his general critique of sacrifice, is that the good mother's renunciation of the child should not be interpreted as an act of self-sacrifice. He says (p. 240) that the good mother "demonstrates the possession of maternal feelings and rejects the sacrificial solution with horror," and he goes on to add immediately that "we cannot interpret the good mother's renunciation in terms of 'self-sacrifice' " either, because she makes it not for the sake of the loss she will suffer but for the sake of the child.

Now this is true as far as it goes, but I think Balmary's reading of the story brings out something in the symbolism of sacrifice that shows there is more to the issue than Girard takes into account. She concurs with his analysis of the symmetries, and she agrees also that the good mother's act is not self-sacrificial in a masochistic sense, but she thinks nevertheless that the story does present a type of sacrifice: she likens the good mother's willingness to give up her claim to her child to the sacrifice every parent is called to make to allow his or her child to become a genuinely separate person. Commenting on the symbolism of the sacrificial knife that Solomon calls for to cut the child in two, she says that it differentiates and separates the doubles as it cuts through the ties with which the false mother had tried to bind the child to her. A true mother, she says, is one "who loves her child more than what ties the child to her. . . . the word of truth comes from the mother who agrees to let the knife pass between her child and herself" (p. 98), just as Abraham attains to true fatherhood when he is able to make a sacrifice of his intended sacrifice of Isaac and thereby also becomes a true "I" in relation to a true "thou."

Whether such self-transcendence and sacrifice lead to death or to life, to the end of possibilities or to an opening toward unlimited possibilities, however, is not a question for psychology or finally even for philosophy. This is a question that calls not for an opinion but for a commitment—for dedication and a willingness to risk the meaning of one's life for the sake of something unknown. It is a question that leads beyond all abstraction and all theory into what Erikson called "basic trust" and Kierkegaard "faith."

Now to end on such a note a book on recent French psychological thought may seem surprising—a wandering off the main path onto a detour that leads nowhere. From the point of view of much contemporary French thought, on the other hand, it would not seem such a surprise. Just as the aftermath of the unrest of 1968 led in France to a great interest in psychology, so the same movement, fed by the further streams of disappointment with French socialism in the early to mid-eighties and then the collapse of communism in Eastern Europe in the late eighties and early nineties, has led to increasing interest in religion on the part of many French intellectuals. Sartre's communist phase is well known in the English-speaking world, for example, but few know that he spent the last years of his life absorbed in the study of the Old Testament.[26] Julia Kristeva has become known in this country as a leading French feminist, but relatively few realize that she is also a convert to Catholicism whose writings on the problem of our relation to alterity also express a strong interest in the theological dimension of that theme.[27] Then, to mention just one other prominent name, there is also Kristeva's husband, Phillipe Sollers, who was editor of the left-wing avant-garde periodical, *Tel quel,* and after his own religious conversion closed it down and established in its place a new periodical, *L'Infini,* with a major focus on religious themes.

These developments, moreover, have had deeper roots than might at first seem apparent. Jacques Lacan, for example, whose influence on the various currents of thought discussed in this book has been enormous, is still rather narrowly understood in the English-speaking world, since most of his work remains untranslated and since the commentaries on his thought that have appeared in English have tended not to focus on the really quite important religious dimension of his thought. There are basically two ways of reading Lacan. One is an aestheticizing way that tends to assimilate him to figures like Georges Bataille and interprets his interest in the Kojèvian-Heideggerian themes of struggle, death, and "nothing" as pointing toward something close to nihilism. Another is one that

26. See Benny Lévy, *L'Espoir maintenant* (1991).
27. See, for example, Kristeva's *Etrangers à nous-même* (1988), a work on the spiritual as well as political implications of the modern French "melting pot" and one that, like Marie Balmary's *Le Sacrifice interdit,* recalls Martin Buber's famous *I and Thou.*

reads the same themes as expressions of an ethical monotheism and a critique of idolatry, emphasizing the way the "object *a*" for Lacan becomes an idol standing in the way of a fundamental thrust of radical transcendence that alone is able to deliver us from the solipsistic prison of our "*imaginaire*" into a mode of being in which genuine dialogue between a true "I" and a true "thou" becomes possible.[28]

This is precisely the point at which all the thinkers here discussed find a common ground, and for many of them, at least, it is a point at which questions extending beyond the strictly psychological into the philosophical and theological open up. What all this will lead to in the future of French thought remains to be seen, but to point out the importance of these questions both in themselves and in relation to some important currents of contemporary French thought can hardly be considered a detour. The next chapter, of course, will be written by history—but history, too, may turn out to have a beyond.

---

28. See, for example, Bernard Sichère, *Le Moment lacanien* (1983). Also pertinent, even if it is not specifically about Lacan, is another recent work, by the philosopher Jean-Luc Marion, *La Croisée du visible et de l'invisible* (1991), which discusses the difference between an "idol" and an "icon" in terms that have Lacanian echoes: an "idol" absorbs your "look" (*le regard*) into itself, putting an end to the interplay between the visible and the invisible (i.e., the "objective" and the "subjective," conceived in the Kierkegaardian manner), whereas an "icon," by a kind of sacrificial kenoticism, not only elicits the viewer's "look" but effaces itself in order to lead that look toward an invisibility beyond itself. Or as Marion puts it in one place (p. 107), the difference between an icon and a profane image is that in the latter, one only sees (unseen) an object, whereas before an icon one experiences oneself also as "seen." One can see here an obvious kinship to Lacan's idea, cited in the first chapter above (at note 25), that "[t]he subject . . . begins the analysis by speaking about himself without speaking to you, or by speaking to you without speaking about himself" and that when he can break out of this monologue into genuine dialogue with the analyst, the analysis will be finished.

Bibliography

Aglietta, Michel, and André Orléan. *La Violence de la monnaie*. Paris: Presses Universitaires de France, 1982.

Anzieu, Didier. *L'Auto-analyse de Freud*. 2 vols. Paris: Presses Universitaires de France, 1975.

Arendt, Hannah. "Reflections of Violence." *Journal of International Affairs* 23 (1969): 1–35.

Auden, Wystan Hugh. *About the House*. New York: Random House, 1965.

———. *The Shield of Achilles*. New York: Random House, 1955.

Balmary, Marie. *Le Sacrifice interdit: Freud et la Bible*. Paris: Grasset, 1986.

———. *Psychoanalyzing Psychoanalysis: Freud and the Hidden Fault of the Father*. Translated by Ned Lukacher. Baltimore and London: Johns Hopkins University Press, 1982. Originally published in French as *L'Homme aux statues: Freud et la faute cachée du père*. Paris: Grasset, 1979.

Benvenuto, Bice, and Roger Kennedy. *The Works of Jacques Lacan: An Introduction*. New York: St. Martin's Press, 1986.

Bernheim, Hippolyte. *De la suggestion et de ses applications à la thérapeutique*. Paris: Octave Doin, 1886.

Bertonneau, Thomas F. "The Logic of the Undecidable: An Interview with René Girard." *Paroles gelées, UCLA French Studies* 5 (1987): 1–24.

Bettelheim, Bruno. *Freud and Man's Soul*. New York: Knopf, 1983.

Borch-Jacobsen, Mikkel. *The Freudian Subject*. Translated by Catherine Porter. Foreword by François Roustang. Stanford: Stanford University Press, 1988. Originally published in French as *Le Sujet freudien*. Paris: Flammarion, 1982.

———. "L'Hypnose dans la psychanalyse." In Léon Chertok, ed., *Hypnose et psychanalyse: Réponses à Mikkel Borch-Jacobsen*, pp. 29–54. Paris: Dunod, 1987. Translated as "Hypnosis in Psychoanalysis," *Representations* 27 (Summer 1989): 92–110.

———. "L'Inconscient malgré tout." *Les Etudes Philosophiques* (January–March 1988), pp. 1–36.

———. *Lacan: The Absolute Master.* Translated by Douglas Brick. Stanford: Stanford University Press, 1991. Translation of *Lacan: Le mâitre absolu.* Paris: Flammarion, 1990.

———. "Talking Cure." *Psychanalyse à L'Université* 55 (1989): 3–27.

Borkenau, Franz. *End and Beginning: On the Generations of Cultures and the Origins of the West.* Edited with an introduction by Richard Lowenthal. New York: Columbia University Press, 1981.

Brothers, Leslie. "A Biological Perspective on Empathy." *American Journal of Psychiatry* 146, no. 1 (January 1989): 10–19.

Brown, Raymond E., S.S. *The Gospel According to John (I–XII).* Anchor Bible, vol. 29. Garden City, N.Y.: Doubleday, 1966.

Chertok, Léon, ed. *Hypnose et psychanalyse: Réponses à Mikkel Borch-Jacobsen.* Paris: Dunod, 1987.

———. *Résurgence de l'hypnose: Une bataille de deux cents ans.* Paris: Desclée de Brouwer, 1984.

Darnton, Robert, *Mesmerism and the End of the Enlightenment in France.* Cambridge: Harvard University Press, 1968.

Deguy, Michel, and Jean-Pierre Dupuy, eds. *René Girard et le Problème du mal.* Paris: Grasset, 1982.

Descombes, Vincent. *Modern French Philosophy.* Cambridge: Cambridge University Press, 1980.

Dumouchel, Paul. "Différences et paradoxes: Réflexions sur l'amour et la violence dans l'oeuvre de Girard." In Michel Deguy and Jean-Pierre Dupuy, eds., *René Girard et le Problème du mal,* pp. 215–24. Paris: Grasset, 1982.

———, ed. *Violence et vérité: Autour de René Girard.* Paris: Grasset, 1985.

Dumouchel, Paul, and Jean-Pierre Dupuy. *L'Enfer des choses: René Girard et la logique de l'économie.* Paris: Seuil, 1979.

Dupuy, Jean-Pierre. "Mimésis et morphogénèse." In Michel Deguy and Jean-Pierre Dupuy, eds. *René Girard et le Problème de mal,* pp. 225–78. Paris: Grasset, 1982.

———. *Ordres et désordres: Enquêtes sur un nouveau paradigme.* Paris: Seuil, 1982.

———. "Shaking the Invisible Hand." In Paisley Livingston, ed., *Disorder and Order,* pp. 129–44. Saratoga, Calif: ANMA Libri, 1984.

Dussault, J. C. "René Girard: La révélation évangélique et le bouddhisme." *Studies in Religion/Sciences Religieuses* 10 (1981): 59–66.

Eissler, Kurt R. *Talent and Genius: The Fictitious Case of Tausk contra Freud.* New York: Quadrangle Books, 1971.

Eliade, Mircea. *The Quest: History and Meaning in Religion.* Chicago: University of Chicago Press, 1969.

Erickson, Milton H. *My Voice Will Go With You: The Teaching Tales of Milton H. Erickson, M.D.* Edited with commentary by Sidney Rosen. Foreword by Lynn Hoffman. New York: Norton, 1982.

Erikson, Erik. *Childhood and Society.* Second edition. New York: Norton, 1963.

Evans-Pritchard, Edward Evan. *Theories of Primitive Religion.* Oxford: Clarendon Press, 1965.

Ey, Henri. *La Conscience.* Paris: Presses Universitaires de France, 1963.

Fedotov, George P. *The Russian Religious Mind: Kievan Christianity, the Tenth to the Thirteenth Centuries.* New York: Harper Torchbooks, 1960.

Foucault, Michel. *Power/Knowledge: Selected Interviews and Other Writings, 1972–1977.* Edited by Colin Gordon. Translated by Colin Gordon and others. New York: Pantheon, 1980.

Fowler, James W. *Stages of Faith: The Psychology of Human Development and the Quest for Meaning.* San Francisco: Harper and Row, 1981.

Fox, Nathan A., and Richard J. Davidson. "Patterns of Brain Electrical Activity during Facial Signs of Emotion in 10-Month-Old-Infants." *Developmental Psychology* 24 (1988): 230–36.

Freud, Sigmund. *Gesammelte Werke.* 18 vols. Edited by Anna Freud with the collaboration of Marie Bonaparte and others. Vols. 1–17, London: Imago Publishing Co., 1940–52; vol. 18, Frankfurt am Main: S. Fischer, 1968.

———. *Moses and Monotheism: Three Essays.* In *Standard Edition,* 23: 3–137.

———. *The Origins of Psychoanalysis: Letters to Wilhelm Fliess.* Edited by Marie Bonaparte, Anna Freud, and Ernst Kris. Translated by Eric Mosbacher and James Strachey. New York: Basic Books, 1977.

———. *The Standard Edition of the Complete Psychological Works of Sigmund Freud.* 24 vols. Edited and translated by James Strachey in collaboration with Anna Freud. Assisted by Alix Strachey and Alan

Tyson. London: Hogarth Press and The Institute of Psychoanalysis, 1953–74.

——. *Totem and Taboo*. In *Standard Edition*, 13:1–161.

Freud, Sigmund, and Karl Abraham. *A Psychoanalytic Dialogue: The Letters of Sigmund Freud and Karl Abraham, 1907–1926*. Edited by Hilda C. Abraham and Ernst L. Freud. Translated by Bernard Marsh and Hilda C. Abraham. New York: Basic Books, 1965.

Galvin, John P. "Jesus as Scapegoat? *Violence and the Sacred* in the Theology of Raymund Schwager." *The Thomist* 46, no. 2 (April 1982): 173–94.

Gans, Eric. "Scandal to the Jews, Folly to the Pagans." *Diacritics* 9, no. 3 (Fall 1979): 43–55.

Girard, René. *Critiques dans un souterrain*. Paris: Grasset, 1976.

——. *Deceit, Desire, and the Novel: Self and Other in Literary Structure*. Translated by Yvonne Freccero. Baltimore: Johns Hopkins University Press, 1965.

——. "Disorder and Order in Mythology." In Paisley Livingston, ed., *Disorder and Order*, pp. 80–99. Saratoga, Calif.: ANMA Libri, 1984.

——. *"To Double Business Bound": Essays on Literature, Mimesis, and Anthropology*. Baltimore: Johns Hopkins University Press, 1978.

——. "Generative Scapegoating." In *Violent Origins: Walter Burkert, René Girard, and Jonathan Z. Smith on Ritual Killing and Cultural Formation*. Edited by Robert G. Hammerton-Kelly. Introduction by Burton Mack. Commentary by Renato Rosaldo. Stanford: Stanford University Press, 1987.

——. *Job: The Victim of His People*. Translated by Yvonne Freccero. Stanford: Stanford University Press, 1987. Translation of *La Route antique des hommes pervers*. Paris: Grasset, 1985.

——. "Le Meurtre fondateur dans la pensée de Nietzsche." In Paul Dumouchel, ed., *Violence et vérité: Autour de René Girard*, pp. 597–613. Paris: Grasset, 1985.

Girard, René, and others. "Séminaire de recherche sur l'oeuvre de René Girard tenu au RIER (Regroupement Interuniversitaire pour l'Étude de la Religion), Montréal, 15 février 1980." *Studies in Religion / Sciences Religieuses* 10 (1981): 67–107.

Girard, René, with Jean-Michel Oughourlian and Guy Lefort. *Things Hidden since the Foundation of the World*. Translated by Stephen Bann and Michael Metteer. Stanford: Stanford University Press, 1987.

Translation of *Des choses cachées depuis la foundation du monde.* Paris: Grasset, 1978.

Goleman, Daniel. "Infants under 2 Seem to Learn from TV." *New York Times,* November 22, 1988, national edition, pp. 13ff.

———. "The Roots of Empathy Are Traced to Infancy." *New York Times,* March 28, 1989, national edition, pp. 13ff.

———. *Vital Lies, Simple Truths: The Psychology of Self-Deception,* New York: Simon and Schuster, 1985.

Graf, Max. "Reminiscences of Professor Sigmund Freud." *Psychoanalytic Quarterly* 11 (1942): 465–76.

Granoff, Wladimir. *Filiation: L'Avenir du complexe d'Oedipe.* Paris: Editions de Minuit, 1975.

Grimal, Pierre. *Dictionnaire de la mythologie grecque et romaine.* Paris: Presses Universitaires de France, 1969.

Groddeck, George. *The Meaning of Illness: Selected Psychoanalytic Writings.* Edited by Lore Schacht. Translated by Gertrud Mander. London: Hogarth Press, 1977.

Haley, Jay. "The Contribution of Milton H. Erickson, M.D." *Ericksonian Approaches to Hypnosis and Psychotherapy.* Edited by Jeffrey K. Zeig. New York: Brunner/Mazel, 1982.

———. *Uncommon Therapy: The Psychiatric Techniques of Milton H. Erickson, M.D.* New York: Ballantine Books, 1973.

Hammerton-Kelly, Robert G., ed. *Violent Origins: Walter Burkert, René Girard, and Jonathan Z. Smith on Ritual Killing and Cultural Formation.* Introduction by Burton Mack. Commentary by Renato Rosaldo. Stanford: Stanford University Press, 1987.

Handwerk, Gary. *Irony and Ethics in Narrative: From Schlegel to Lacan.* New Haven and London: Yale University Press, 1985.

Hegel, Georg Wilhelm Friedrich. *Phenomenology of Spirit.* Translated by A. V. Miller. Oxford: Oxford University Press, 1977.

Heidegger, Martin. *Being and Time.* Translated by John Macquarrie and Edward Robinson. New York: Harper and Row, 1962.

———. *Existence and Being.* Introduction and analysis by Werner Brock. Chicago: Regnery, 1949.

Henry, Michel. *La Barbarie.* Paris: Grasset, 1987.

———. *Généalogie de la psychanalyse.* Paris: Presses Universitaires de France, 1985.

Hollier, Denis, ed. *The College of Sociology, 1937–39.* Translated by Betsy

Wing. Theory and History of Literature, vol. 41. Minneapolis: University of Minnesota Press, 1988.

Horkheimer, Max, and Theodor W. Adorno. *Dialectic of Enlightenment.* Translated by John Cumming. New York: Continuum, 1987.

Janet, Pierre. *L'Automatisme psychologique.* Paris: Société Pierre Janet et Laboratoire du Centre National de la Recherche Scientifique, 1973.

Hughes, H. Stuart, *Between Commitment and Disillusion: The Obstructed Path and The Sea Change, 1930–1965.* Middletown, Conn.: Wesleyan University Press, 1987.

Jensen, A. E. *Myth and Cult Among Primitive Peoples.* Translated by Marianna Tax Choldin and Wolfgang Weissleder. Chicago: University of Chicago Press, 1963. Originally published as *Mythos und Kult bei Naturvölkern: Religionswissenschaftliche Betrachtungen.* Wiesbaden, 1953.

Jones, Ernest. *The Life and Work of Sigmund Freud.* 3 vols. New York: Basic Books; London: Hogarth Press, 1953–57.

Kaplan, Louise. "The Interpersonal World of the Infant: A Symposium." *Contemporary Psychoanalysis* 23, no. 1 (January 1987): 27–44.

Kegan, Robert. *The Evolving Self: Problem and Process in Human Development.* Cambridge, Mass.: Harvard University Press, 1982.

Kierkegaard, Søren. *Philosophical Fragments or A Fragment of Philosophy and Johannes Climacus or De omnibus dubitandum est.* Edited and translated by Howard V. Hong and Edna H. Hong. Princeton: Princeton University Press, 1985.

Koestler, Arthur. *The Ghost in the Machine.* New York: Macmillan, 1968.

———. *Janus.* London: Hutchinson, 1978.

Kohlberg, Lawrence. *Essays on Moral Development.* 2 vols. San Francisco: Harper and Row, 1981 and 1984.

Kojève, Alexandre. *Introduction to the Reading of Hegel: Lectures on the Phenomenology of Spirit.* Assembled by Raymond Queneau. Edited by Allan Bloom. Translated by James H. Nichols, Jr. Ithaca and London: Cornell University Press, 1969.

Krafft-Ebing, Richard von. *Psychopathia Sexualis, with Especial Reference to Antipathic Sexual Instinct: A Medico-Forensic Study.* Translated from the 10th [1898] German edition by F. J. Rebman. London: Rebman, 1899. Originally published in German, 1886.

Kristeva, Julia. *Etrangers à nous-même.* Paris: Fayard, 1988.

Kugler, Paul K. "Jacques Lacan: Postmodern Depth Psychology and the

Birth of the Self-Reflexive Subject." In Polly Young-Eisendrath and James A. Hall, eds., *The Book of the Self,* pp. 173–84. New York: New York University Press, 1987.

Lacan, Jacques. *Les Complexes familiaux dans la formation de l'individu.* Paris: Navarin, 1984.

———. *Ecrits: A Selection.* Translated by Alan Sheridan. New York: Norton, 1977. A partial translation of *Ecrits.* Paris: Seuil, 1966.

———. *Ecrits.* Paris: Seuil, 1966.

———. *Le Séminaire, 1: Les écrits techniques de Freud.* Paris: Seuil, 1975.

———. *Le Séminaire, 7: "L'éthique de la psychanalyse."* Paris: Seuil, 1986.

———. *Speech and Language in Psychoanalysis.* Translated, with notes and commentary, by Anthony Wilden. Baltimore and London: Johns Hopkins University Press, 1968.

———. *The Four Fundamental concepts of Psycho-Analysis.* Edited by Jacques-Alain Miller. Translated by Alan Sheridan. New York: Norton, 1981. French original: *Le Séminaire, 11: "Les quatre concepts fondamentaux de la psychanalyse."* Paris: Seuil, 1973.

Lacan, Jacques and the école freudienne. *Feminine Sexuality.* Edited by Juliet Mitchell and Jacqueline Rose. Translated by Jacqueline Rose. New York: Norton, 1985.

Langan, Thomas. *The Meaning of Heidegger: A Critical Study of an Existentialist Philosopher.* New York: Columbia University Press, 1959.

Laplanche, J., and J.-B. Pontalis. *The Language of Psychoanalysis.* Translated by Donald Nicholson-Smith. New York: Norton, 1973.

Le Bon, Gustave. *La Psychologie des foules.* New edition, edited by Otto Klineberg. Paris: Presses Universitaires de France, 1963.

Lefort, Guy, with René Girard and Jean-Michel Oughourlian. *Des choses cachées depuis la fondation du monde.* Paris: Grasset, 1978.

Legué, Gabriel, and Gilles de La Tourette. *Soeur Jeanne des Anges, supérieure des ursulines de Loudun.* Preface by J.-M. Charcot. Paris: Bibliothèque diabolique, A. Delahaye and Lecroisnier, 1886.

Lemaire, Anika. *Jacques Lacan.* Translated by David Macey. London: Routledge and Kegan Paul, 1977.

Lévy, Benny. *L'Espoir maintenant.* Paris: Verdier, 1991.

Liébault, Auguste-Ambroise. *Du sommeil et des états analogues, considérés surtout au point de vue de l'action du moral sur le physique.* Paris: V. Masson et fils; Nancy: N. Grosjean, 1866.

Lifton, Robert Jay. *The Life of the Self: Toward a New Psychology.* New York: Simon and Schuster, 1976.

——. *Thought Reform and the Psychology of Totalism: A Study of "Brainwashing" in China.* New York: Norton, 1961.

Livingston, Paisley. "Girard and Literary Knowledge." *To Honor René Girard,* pp. 221–35. Saratoga, Calif.: ANMA Libri, 1986.

——, ed. *Disorder and Order: Proceedings of the Stanford International Symposium* (September 14–16, 1981). Stanford Literature Studies, vol. 1. Saratoga, Calif.: ANMA Libri, 1984.

Lonergan, Bernard J. F., S. J. *Method in Theology.* New York: Herder and Herder, 1972.

Lyotard, Jean-François. *Heidegger et "les juifs."* Paris: Galilée, 1988.

Marion, Jean-Luc. *La Croisée du visible et de l'invisible.* Paris: La Différance, 1991.

Masson, Jeffrey Moussaieff. *The Assault on Truth: Freud's Suppression of the Seduction Theory.* New York: Farrar, Straus, and Giroux, 1984.

McDougall, William, *The Group Mind.* Cambridge: Cambridge University Press, 1920.

McKenna, Andrew J., ed. *René Girard and Biblical Studies.* Vol. 33 of *Semeia: An Experimental Journal for Biblical Criticism* (1985).

Medawar, Peter. "Victims of Psychiatry." Review of *The Victim Is Always the Same,* by I. S. Cooper. *New York Review of Books,* January 23, 1975, p. 17.

Meltzoff, Andrew N. "Imitation of Televised Models by Infants." *Child Development* 59 (1988): 1221–29.

——. "Infant Imitation after a 1-Week Delay." *Developmental Psychology* 24 (1988): 470–76.

——. "Infant Imitation and Memory: Nine-Month-Olds in Immediate and Deferred Tests." *Child Development* 59 (1988): 217–25.

Meltzoff, Andrew N., and M. K. Moore. "Imitation of Facial and Manual Gestures by Human Neonates." *Science* 198 (October 7, 1977): 75–78.

——. "The Origins of Imitation in Infancy: Paradigm, Phenomena, and Theories." In L. P. Lippit, ed., *Advances in Infancy Research,* 2: 265–301. Norwood, N.J.: Ablex, 1983.

Melville, Stephen W. *Philosophy Beside Itself: On Deconstruction and Modernism.* Theory and History of Literature, vol. 27. Minneapolis: University of Minnesota Press, 1986.

Mounier, Emmanuel. *Communisme, anarchie, et personnalisme.* Paris: Seuil, 1966.

Nemoianu, Virgil. "René Girard and the Dialectics of Imperfection." In *To Honor René Girard,* pp. 1–16. Saratoga, Calif.: ANMA Libri, 1986.

Newman, John Henry. *Apologia Pro Vita Sua.* Oxford: Clarendon Press, 1967.

———. *As Essay in Aid of A Grammar of Assent.* Edited by Charles Frederick Harrold. New York: Longmans, Green, 1947.

North, Robert, S.J. "Violence and the Bible: The Girard Connection." *Catholic Biblical Quarterly* 47 (1985): 1–27.

Orléan, André. "La Théorie mimétique face aux phénomènes économiques." In *To Honor René Girard,* pp. 121–33. Saratoga, Calif.: ANMA Libri, 1986.

Oughourlian, Jean-Michel. "L'Hypnose, révélation du rapport interdividuel." In Leon Chertok, ed., *Résurgence de l'hypnose: Une bataille de deux cents ans.* Paris: Desclée de Brouwer, 1984.

———. "Mimetic Desire as a Key to Psychotic and Neurotic Structure." In Paisley Livingston, ed., *Disorder and Order,* pp. 72–77. Saratoga, Calif.: ANMA Libri, 1984.

———. *La Personne du toxicomane: Psychosociologie des toxicomanies actuelles dans la jeunesse occidentale.* Toulouse: Edouard Privat, 1978.

———. *The Puppet of Desire: The Psychology of Hysteria, Possession, and Hypnosis.* Translated by Eugene Webb. Stanford: Stanford University Press, 1991. Translation of *Un Mime nommé désir; Hystérie, transe, possession, adorcisme.* Paris: Grasset, 1982.

Oughourlian, Jean-Michel, with René Girard and Guy Lefort. *Des choses cachées depuis la fondation du monde.* Paris: Grasset, 1978.

Proust, Marcel. *L'Indifférent.* With a preface by Philip Kolb. Paris: Gallimard, 1978.

Ragland-Sullivan, Ellie. *Jacques Lacan and the Philosophy of Psychoanalysis.* Urbana and Chicago: University of Illinois Press, 1986.

Rice, Mabel L., and Linda Woodsmall. "Lessons from Television: Children's Word Learning When Viewing." *Child Development* 59 (1988): 420–29.

Ricoeur, Paul. *Freud and Philosophy: An Essay on Interpretation.* Translated by Denis Savage. New Haven and London: Yale University Press, 1970. Originally published in French, 1965.

Robinson, Daniel N. *Systems of Modern Psychology: A Critical Sketch.* New York: Columbia University Press, 1979.

Roudinesco, Elisabeth. *La Bataille de cent ans: Histoire de la psychanalyse en France.* Vol. 2 (1925–1985). Paris: Seuil, 1986.

Roustang, François. *Dire Mastery: Discipleship from Freud to Lacan.* Translated by Ned Lukacher. Baltimore and London: Johns Hopkins University Press, 1982. Originally published in French as *Un Destin si funeste.* Paris: Editions de Minuit, 1976.

———. "L'Esquive de la rivalité." In *Violence et vérité: Autour de René Girard,* pp. 349–58. Paris: Grasset, 1985.

———. *Lacan: De l'équivoque à l'impasse.* Paris: Editions de Minuit, 1986.

———. *Psychoanalysis Never Lets Go.* Translated by Ned Lukacher. Baltimore and London: Johns Hopkins University Press, 1983. Originally published in French as *. . . elle ne le lâche plus.* Paris: Editions de Minuit, 1980.

Sagan, Eli. *At the Dawn of Tyranny: The Origins of Individualism, Political Oppression, and the State.* New York: Knopf, 1985.

Sahlins, Marshall. *Stone Age Economics.* Chicago: Aldine Press, 1972.

Sajner, Josef. "Sigmund Freuds Beziehungen zu seinem Geburtsort Freiberg (Pribor) und zu Mähren." *Clio Medica* 3 (1968): 167–80.

Schorske, Carl E. *Fin-de-Siècle Vienna: Politics and Culture.* New York: Knopf, 1980.

Schur, Max. *Freud: Living and Dying.* New York: International Universities Press, 1972.

Schwager, Raymund, S.J. *Must There Be Scapegoats?: Violence and Redemption in the Bible.* Translated by Maria L. Assad. Foreword by Robert J. Daly, S.J. San Francisco: Harper and Row, 1987. Translation of *Brauchen Wir Einen Sündenbock?* Munich: Kösel, 1978.

Scubla, Lucien. "Le Christianisme de René Girard et la nature de la religion." In Paul Dumouchel, ed., *Violence et vérité: Autour de René Girard,* pp. 243–57. Paris: Grasset, 1985.

———. "Théorie du sacrifice et théorie du désir chez René Girard." In Paul Dumouchel, ed., *Violence et vérité: Autour de René Girard* pp. 359–74. Paris: Grasset, 1985.

Serres, Michel. *Génèse.* Paris: Grasset, 1982.

Sichère, Bernard. *Le Moment lacanien.* Paris: Grasset, 1983.

Simon, J. "A Conversation with Michel Foucault." *Partisan Review* 2 (1971): 192–201.

Stern, Daniel N. *First Relationship: Mother and Infant.* Cambridge, Mass.: Harvard University Press, 1977.

————. *The Interpersonal World of the Infant: A View from Psychoanalysis and Developmental Psychology.* New York: Basic Books, 1985.

Sulloway, Frank J. *Freud, Biologist of the Mind: Beyond the Psychoanalytic Legend.* New York: Basic Books, 1979.

Tarde, Gabriel. *The Laws of Imitation.* Translated by Elsie Clews Parsons. Introduction by Franklin H. Giddings. New York: Henry Holt, 1903.

————. *L'Opposition universelle: Essai d'une théorie des contraires.* Paris: Felix Alcan, 1895.

————. *Social Laws: An Outline of Sociology.* Translated by Howard C. Warren. Preface by James Mark Baldwin. New York: Macmillan, 1899.

To Honor René Girard. Stanford French and Italian Studies, vol. 34. Saratoga, Calif.: ANMA Libri, 1986.

Trilling, Lionel. *The Liberal Imagination,* New York: Viking Press, 1950.

Turkle, Sherry. *Psychoanalytic Politics: Freud's Revolution.* New York: Basic Books, 1978.

Vitz, Paul C. *Sigmund Freud's Christian Unconscious.* New York and London: Guilford Press. 1988.

Voegelin, Eric. *Anamnesis.* Translated and edited by Gerhart Niemeyer. Notre Dame and London: University of Notre Dame Press, 1978.

————. "The Eclipse of Reality." In Maurice Natanson, ed., *Phenomenology and Social Reality,* pp. 185–94. The Hague: Martinus Nijhoff, 1970.

————. *From Enlightenment to Revolution.* Edited by John H. Hallowell. Durham, N.C.: Duke University Press, 1975.

————. *What is History? and Other Late Unpublished Writings.* Edited with an introduction by Thomas A. Hollweck and Paul Caringella. Baton Rouge: Louisiana State University Press, 1990.

Webb, Eugene. *Philosophers of Consciousness: Polanyi, Lonergan, Voegelin, Ricoeur, Girard, Kierkegaard.* Seattle and London: University of Washington Press, 1988.

Whyte, Lancelot Law. *The Unconscious before Freud.* New York: Basic Books, 1960; London: Tavistock Publications, 1962.

Williams, James G. *The Bible, Violence, and the Sacred: Liberation from the Myth of Sanctioned Violence.* Foreword by René Girard. San Francisco: Harper, 1991.

————. "The Innocent Victim: René Girard on Violence, Sacrifice, and the Sacred." *Religious Studies Review* 14 (1988): 320–26.

Young-Eisendrath, Polly, and James A. Hall, eds. *The Book of the Self: Person, Pretext, and Process.* New York: New York University Press, 1987.

Index

8/07